# 3rd Workshop on Discourse in Machine Translation (DiscoMT 2017)

Copenhagen, Denmark
8 September 2017

ISBN: 978-1-5108-4752-1

DiscoMT 2017

**Discourse in
Machine Translation**

**Proceedings of the Workshop**

September 8, 2017
Copenhagen, Denmark

# Preface

It is well-known that texts have properties that go beyond those of their individual sentences and that reveal themselves in the frequency and distribution of words, word senses, referential forms and syntactic structures, including:

- document-wide properties, such as style, register, reading level and genre;

- patterns of topical or functional sub-structure;

- patterns of discourse coherence, as realized through explicit and/or implicit relations between sentences, clauses or referring forms;

- anaphoric and elliptic expressions, in which speakers exploit the previous discourse context to convey subsequent information very succinctly.

By the end of the 1990s, these properties had stimulated considerable research in Machine Translation, aimed at endowing machine-translated texts with similar document and discourse properties as their source texts. A period of ten years then elapsed before interest resumed in these topics, now from the perspectives of Statistical and/or Hybrid Machine Translation. This led in 2013 to the *First Workshop on Discourse in Machine Translation (DiscoMT)*, held in Sofia, Bulgaria, in conjunction to the annual ACL conference.

The evolution of Statistical MT, in ways that reflected more interest in and provided more access to needed linguistic knowledge was charted in the *Second Workshop on Discourse in Machine Translation (DiscoMT 2015)*, held in Lisbon, Portugal, in conjunction to EMNLP. Part of this evolution has been the growth of interest in one particular problem: the translation of pronouns whose form in the target language may be constrained in challenging ways by their context. This shared interest has created an environment in which a shared task on pronoun translation or prediction from English-to-French was able to stimulate responses from several research groups.

The shared task in pronoun prediction has been continued as one of the shared tasks of the First Conference on Machine Translation (WMT 2016), and then again at this year's *Third Workshop on Discourse in Machine Translation (DiscoMT 2017)*, held in Copenhagen, Denmark, in conjunction to EMNLP. As observed with systems presented at previous shared tasks, and confirmed by several papers at DiscoMT 2017, the neural turn in MT has started having a significant impact on discourse-level or document-level translation, with neural networks being adapted to consider wider contexts when generating translations.

We hope that workshops such as this one will continue to stimulate work on Discourse and Machine Translation, in a wide range of discourse phenomena and MT architectures.

We would like to thank all the authors who submitted papers to the workshop, as well as all the members of the Program Committee who reviewed the submissions and delivered thoughtful, informative reviews.

The Chairs
July 21, 2017

**Chairs**

Bonnie Webber, University of Edinburgh, UK
Andrei Popescu-Belis, Idiap Research Institute, Martigny, Switzerland
Jörg Tiedemann, University of Helsinki, Finland

**Program Committee**

Mauro Cettolo, Fondazione Bruno Kessler, Trento, Italy
Filip Ginter, University of Turku, Finland
Liane Guillou, Brainnwave, Edinburgh, UK
Christian Hardmeier, Uppsala University, Sweden
Shafiq Joty, Qatar Computing Research Institute, Doha, Qatar
Lori Levin, Carnegie Mellon University, Pittsburgh, PA, USA
Ekaterina Lapshinova-Koltunski, Saarland University, Germany
Ngoc-Quang Luong, Nuance Communications, Belgium
Thomas Meyer, Google, Zurich, Switzerland
Preslav Nakov, Qatar Computing Research Institute, Doha, Qatar
Michal Novak, Charles University, Prague, Czech Republic
Maja Popovic, DFKI, Berlin, Germany
Annette Rios, University of Zurich, Switzerland
Rico Sennrich, University of Edinburgh, UK
Lucia Specia, University of Sheffield, UK
Sara Stymne, Uppsala University, Sweden
Yannick Versley, LangTec, Hamburg, Germany
Martin Volk, University of Zurich, Switzerland
Min Zhang, Soochow University, Suzhou, China
Sandrine Zufferey, University of Bern, Switzerland

**Shared Task Organizers**

Sharid Loáiciga Sánchez, Uppsala University, Sweden, *coordinator*
Christian Hardmeier, Uppsala University, Sweden
Preslav Nakov, Qatar Computing Research Institute, Doha, Qatar
Sara Stymne, Uppsala University, Sweden
Jörg Tiedemann, University of Helsinki, Finland
Yannick Versley, LangTec, Hamburg, Germany

# Table of Contents

# Conference Program

**11:00–12:30    Session 2b: Shared Task Posters**

*A BiLSTM-based System for Cross-lingual Pronoun Prediction*
Sara Stymne, Sharid Loáiciga and Fabienne Cap

*Neural Machine Translation for Cross-Lingual Pronoun Prediction*
Sébastien Jean, Stanislas Lauly, Orhan Firat and Kyunghyun Cho

*Predicting Pronouns with a Convolutional Network and an N-gram Model*
Christian Hardmeier

*Cross-Lingual Pronoun Prediction with Deep Recurrent Neural Networks v2.0*
Juhani Luotolahti, Jenna Kanerva and Filip Ginter


**11:00–12:30    Session 2c: Posters Related to Oral Presentations**

*Combining the output of two coreference resolution systems for two source languages to improve annotation projection*
Yulia Grishina

*Discovery of Discourse-Related Language Contrasts through Alignment Discrepancies in English-German Translation*
Ekaterina Lapshinova-Koltunski and Christian Hardmeier

*Findings of the 2017 DiscoMT Shared Task on Cross-lingual Pronoun Prediction*
Sharid Loáiciga, Sara Stymne, Preslav Nakov, Christian Hardmeier, Jörg Tiedemann, Mauro Cettolo and Yannick Versley

*Neural Machine Translation with Extended Context*
Jörg Tiedemann and Yves Scherrer

*Translating Implicit Discourse Connectives Based on Cross-lingual Annotation and Alignment*
Hongzheng Li, Philippe Langlais and Yaohong Jin

*Validation of an Automatic Metric for the Accuracy of Pronoun Translation (APT)*
Lesly Miculicich Werlen and Andrei Popescu-Belis


**12:30–14:00    *Lunch Break***

# Findings of the 2017 DiscoMT Shared Task
## on Cross-lingual Pronoun Prediction


**Sharid Loáiciga**
Uppsala University
Dept. of Linguistics & Philology
Uppsala, Sweden
sharid.loaiciga@lingfil.uu.se

**Sara Stymne**
Uppsala University
Dept. of Linguistics & Philology
Uppsala, Sweden
sara.stymne@lingfil.uu.se

**Preslav Nakov**
Qatar Computing Research Institute
ALT group, HBKU
Doha, Qatar
pnakov@hbku.edu.qa

**Christian Hardmeier**
Uppsala University
Dept. of Linguistics & Philology
Uppsala, Sweden
christian.hardmeier@lingfil.uu.se

**Jörg Tiedemann**
University of Helsinki
Dept. of Modern Languages
Helsinki, Finland
jorg.tiedemann@helsinki.fi

**Mauro Cettolo**
Fondazione Bruno Kessler
Trento, Italy
cettolo@fbk.eu

**Yannick Versley**
LinkedIn
Dublin, Ireland
yversley@gmail.com


## Abstract


We describe the design, the setup, and the evaluation results of the DiscoMT 2017 shared task on cross-lingual pronoun prediction. The task asked participants to predict a target-language pronoun given a source-language pronoun in the context of a sentence. We further provided a lemmatized target-language human-authored translation of the source sentence, and automatic word alignments between the source sentence words and the target-language lemmata. The aim of the task was to predict, for each target-language pronoun placeholder, the word that should replace it from a small, closed set of classes, using any type of information that can be extracted from the entire document.

We offered four subtasks, each for a different language pair and translation direction: English-to-French, English-to-German, German-to-English, and Spanish-to-English. Five teams participated in the shared task, making submissions for all language pairs. The evaluation results show that all participating teams outperformed two strong $n$-gram-based language model-based baseline systems by a sizable margin.


## 1 Introduction

Pronoun translation poses a problem for machine translation (MT) as pronoun systems do not map well across languages, e.g., due to differences in gender, number, case, formality, or humanness, as well as because of language-specific restrictions about where pronouns may be used. For example, when translating the English *it* into French an MT system needs to choose between *il*, *elle*, and *cela*, while translating the same pronoun into German would require a choice between *er*, *sie*, and *es*. This is hard as selecting the correct pronoun may need discourse analysis as well as linguistic and world knowledge. Null subjects in pro-drop languages pose additional challenges as they express person and number within the verb's morphology, rendering a subject pronoun or noun phrase redundant. Thus, translating from such languages requires generating a pronoun in the target language for which there is no pronoun in the source.

Pronoun translation is known to be challenging not only for MT in general, but also for Statistical Machine Translation (SMT) in particular (Le Nagard and Koehn, 2010; Hardmeier and Federico, 2010; Novák, 2011; Guillou, 2012; Hardmeier, 2014). Phrase-based SMT (Koehn et al., 2013) was state of the art until recently, but it is gradually being replaced by Neural Machine Translation, or NMT, (Cho et al., 2014; Sutskever et al., 2014; Bahdanau et al., 2015; Luong et al., 2015).

1


*Proceedings of the Third Workshop on Discourse in Machine Translation*, pages 1–16,
Copenhagen, Denmark, September 8, 2017. ©2017 Association for Computational Linguistics.

NMT yields generally higher-quality translation, but is harder to analyze, and thus little is known about how well it handles pronoun translation. Yet, it is clear that it has access to larger context compared to phrase-based SMT models, potentially spanning multiple sentences, which can improve pronoun translation (Jean et al., 2017a).

Motivated by these challenges, the DiscoMT 2017 workshop on Discourse in Machine Translation offered a shared task on cross-lingual pronoun prediction. This was a classification task, asking the participants to make predictions about which pronoun should replace a placeholder in the target-language text. The task required no MT expertise and was designed to be interesting as a machine learning task on its own right, e.g., for researchers working on co-reference resolution.

| | |
|---|---|
| Source | *me ayudan a ser escuchada* |
| | *lit.* "me help$_{3.Pers.Pl}$ to be heard" |
| Target | **REPLACE** help me to be heard |
| POS tags | PRON VERB PRON PART AUX VERB |
| Reference | They help me to be heard |

Figure 1: Spanish-English example.

The shared task targets subject pronouns, and this year this also includes null subjects, e.g., as shown in Figure 1. In linguistics, this characteristic is known as *pro-drop*, since an invisible pronoun *pro* is assumed to occupy the subject position. Whenever a null subject is used, the grammatical person features are inferred from the verb (Neeleman and Szendői, 2005). In pro-drop languages, an explicit pronoun is used mostly for stressing the subject, since mentioning the pronoun in every subject position results in an output that is perceived as less fluent (Clemens, 2001). However, in impersonal sentences, using a subject pronoun is not an option; it is ungrammatical.

We further target the problem of *functional ambiguity*, whereby pronouns with the same surface form may perform multiple functions (Guillou, 2016). For example, the English pronoun *it* may function as an anaphoric, pleonastic, or event reference pronoun. An *anaphoric* pronoun corefers with a noun phrase (NP). A *pleonastic* pronoun does not refer to anything, but it is required by syntax to fill the subject position. An *event reference* pronoun may refer to a verb phrase (VP), a clause, an entire sentence, or a longer passage of text. These different functions may entail different translations in another language.

Previous studies have focused on the translation of anaphoric pronouns. In this case, a well-known constraint of languages with grammatical gender is that agreement must hold between an anaphoric pronoun and the NP with which it corefers, called its *antecedent*. The pronoun and its antecedent may occur in the same sentence (*intra-sentential anaphora*) or in different sentences (*inter-sentential anaphora*). Most MT systems translate sentences in isolation, and thus inter-sentential anaphoric pronouns will be translated without knowledge of their antecedent, and thus pronoun-antecedent agreement cannot be guaranteed.

The above constraints start playing a role in pronoun translation in situations where several translation options are possible for a given source-language pronoun, a large number of options being likely to affect negatively the translation quality. In other words, pronoun types that exhibit significant *translation divergence* are more likely to be wrongly translated by an MT system that is not aware of the above constraints. For example, when translating the English pronoun *she* into French, there is one main option, *elle*; yet, there are some exceptions, e.g., in references to ships. However, several options exist for the translation of anaphoric *it*: *il* (for an antecedent that is masculine in French) or *elle* (for a feminine antecedent), but also *cela*, *ça* or sometimes *ce* (non-gendered demonstratives).

The challenges that pronouns pose for machine translation have gradually raised interest in the research community for a shared task that would allow to compare various competing proposals and to quantify the extent to which they improve the translation of different pronouns for different language pairs and different translation directions. However, evaluating pronoun translation comes with its own challenges, as reference-based evaluation, which is standard for machine translation in general, cannot easily take into account legitimate variations of translated pronouns or their placement in the sentence. Thus, building upon experience from DiscoMT 2015 (Hardmeier et al., 2015) and WMT 2016 (Guillou et al., 2016), this year's cross-lingual pronoun prediction shared task has been designed to test the capacity of the participating systems for translating pronouns correctly, in a framework that allows for objective evaluation, as we will explain below.

| ce OTHER | ce\|PRON qui\|PRON | It 's an idiotic debate . It has to stop . | REPLACE_0 |

être\|VER un\|DET débat\|NOM idiot\|ADJ REPLACE_6 devoir\|VER stopper\|VER .\|. 0-0 1-1 2-2 3-4 4-3 6-5 7-6 8-6 9-7 10-8

Figure 2: English→French example from the development dataset. First come the gold class labels, followed by the pronouns (these are given for training, hidden for test), then the English input, the French lemmatized and PoS-tagged output with REPLACE placeholders, and finally word alignments. Here is a French reference translation (not given to the participants): *C'est un débat idiot qui doit stopper.*

| Subtask | Year | Source Pronouns | Target Pronouns |
|---|---|---|---|
| EN-FR | 2015 | it, they | ce, elle, elles, il, ils, cela, ça, on, OTHER |
| FR-EN | 2016 | elle, elles, il, ils | he, she, it, they, this, these, there, OTHER |
| EN-FR | 2016,2017 | it, they | ce, elle, elles, il, ils, cela/ça, on, OTHER |
| EN-DE | 2016,2017 | it, they | er, sie, es, man, OTHER |
| DE-EN | 2016,2017 | er, sie, es | he, she, it, you, they, this, these, there, OTHER |
| ES-EN | 2017 | 3rd person null subjects | he, she, it, you, they, there OTHER |

Table 1: Source and target pronouns defined for the 2015, 2016 & 2017 shared tasks on cross-lingual pronoun prediction. The OTHER class is a catch-all category for translations such as lexical noun phrases, paraphrases or nothing at all (when the pronoun is not translated).

## 2 Task Description

Similarly to the setup of the WMT 2016 shared task (Guillou et al., 2016), the participants had to predict a target-language pronoun given a source-language pronoun in the context of a sentence, which in turn was given in the context of a full document. We further provided a lemmatized and part-of-speech (POS) tagged target-language human-authored translation of the source sentence, as well as automatic token-level alignments between the source-sentence words and the target-language lemmata.

In the translation, we substituted the words aligned to a subset of the source-language third-person subject pronouns by placeholders. The aim of the task was to predict, for each such placeholder, the pronoun class (we group some pronouns in an equivalence class, e.g., cela/ça, and we further have a catch-all OTHER class for translations such as lexical noun phrases, paraphrases or nothing at all, when the pronoun is not translated) that should replace it from a small, closed set, using any type of information that can be extracted from the text of the entire document. Thus, the evaluation can be performed in a fully automatic way, by comparing whether the class predicted by the system is identical to the reference one, assuming that the constraints of the lemmatized target text allow only one correct class.

Figure 2 shows an English→French example sentence from the development dataset. It contains two pronouns to be predicted, which are indicated by REPLACE placeholders in the target sentence. The first *it* corresponds to *ce*, while the second *it* corresponds to *qui* (which can be translated in English as *which*), which belongs to the OTHER class, i.e., does not need to be predicted as a word but rather as the OTHER class. This example illustrates some of the difficulties of the task: the two source sentences are merged into one target sentence, the second *it* is translated as a relative pronoun instead of a subject one, and the second French verb has a rare intransitive usage.

Table 1 shows the set of source-language pronouns and the target-language classes to be predicted for each of the subtasks in all editions of the task. Note that the subtasks are asymmetric in terms of the source-language pronouns and the prediction classes. The selection of the source-language pronouns and their target-language prediction classes for each subtask is based on the variation that is to be expected when translating a given source-language pronoun. For example, when translating the English pronoun *it* into French, a decision needs to be made as to the gender of the French pronoun, with *il* and *elle* both providing valid options. Alternatively, a non-gendered pronoun such as *cela* may also be used.

3

Compared to the WMT 2016 version of the task, this year we replaced the French-English language pair with Spanish-English, which allowed us to evaluate the system performance when dealing with null subjects on the source-language side. As in the WMT 2016 task, we provided a lemmatized and POS-tagged reference translation instead of fully inflected text as was used in the DiscoMT 2015 task. This representation, while still artificial, arguably provides a more realistic MT-like setting. MT systems cannot be relied upon to generate correctly inflected surface form words, and thus the lemmatized, POS-tagged representation encourages greater reliance on other information from the source and the target language texts.

## 3 Datasets

### 3.1 Data Sources

The training dataset comprises Europarl, News and TED talks data. The development and the test datasets consist of TED talks. Below we describe the TED talks, the Europarl and News data, the method used for selecting the test datasets, and the steps taken to pre-process the training, the development, and the test datasets.

### 3.1.1 TED Talks

TED is a non-profit organization that "invites the world's most fascinating thinkers and doers [...] to give the talk of their lives". Its website[1] makes the audio and the video of TED talks available under the Creative Commons license. All talks are presented and captioned in English, and translated by volunteers world-wide into many languages.[2] In addition to the availability of (audio) recordings, transcriptions and translations, TED talks pose interesting research challenges from the perspective of both speech recognition and machine translation. Therefore, both research communities are making increased use of them in building benchmarks.

TED talks address topics of general interest and are delivered to a live public audience whose responses are also audible on the recordings. The talks generally aim to be persuasive and to change the viewers' behaviour or beliefs. The genre of the TED talks is transcribed planned speech.

It has been shown in previous analysis that TED talks differ from other text types with respect to pronoun use (Guillou et al., 2014). TED speakers frequently use first- and second-person pronouns (singular and plural): first-person to refer to themselves and their colleagues or to themselves and the audience, and second-person to refer to the audience, the larger set of viewers, or people in general. TED speakers often use the pronoun *they* without a specific textual antecedent, in sentences such as *"This is what they think."* They also use deictic and third-person pronouns to refer to things in the spatio-temporal context shared by the speaker and the audience, such as props and slides. In general, pronouns are common, and anaphoric references are not always clearly defined.

For the WMT 2017 task on cross-lingual pronoun prediction, the TED training and development sets come from either the MT tasks of the IWSLT evaluation campaigns (Cettolo et al., 2016) or from past editions of the task (Hardmeier et al., 2015; Guillou et al., 2016); the test sets are built from 16 TED talks that were never used in any previous evaluation campaign, 8 defining the test sets from English to German and to French, the other 8 those from German and from Spanish to English. More details are provided below.

### 3.1.2 Europarl and News

For training purposes, in addition to TED talks, we further made available the Europarl[3] (Koehn, 2005) and News Commentary[4] corpora for all language pairs but Spanish-English, for which only TED talks and Europarl were available. We used the alignments provided by OPUS, including the document boundaries from the original sources. For Europarl, we used ver. 7 of the data release, and for News Commentary we used ver. 9.

### 3.2 Test Set Selection

We selected the test data from talks added recently to the TED repository such that:

1. The talks have been transcribed (in English) and translated into both German and French.

2. They were not used in the IWSLT evaluation campaigns, nor in the DiscoMT 2015 or WMT 16 test sets.

3. They amount to a number of words suitable for evaluation purposes (tens of thousands).

---



4

Once we found the talks satisfying these criteria, we automatically aligned them at the segment level. Then, we extracted a number of TED talks from the collection, following the criteria outlined in Section 3.1 above. Finally, we manually checked the sentence alignments of these selected TED talks in order to fix potential errors introduced by either automatic or human processing. Table 2 shows some statistics about the test datasets we prepared for each subtask.

| Subtask | Segs | Tokens | |
|---|---|---|---|
| | | source | target |
| German–English | 709 | 11,716 | 13,360 |
| English–German | 704 | 12,624 | 11,859 |
| Spanish–English | 729 | 13,139 | 13,439 |
| English–French | 698 | 12,623 | 13,242 |

Table 2: Statistics about the 2017 test datasets.

In total, we selected 16 TED talks for testing, which we split into two groups as follows: 8 TED talks for the English to French/German direction, and 8 TED talks for the Spanish/German to English direction. Another option would have been to create four separate groups of TED talks, one for each subtask. However, we chose the current setup as using a smaller set of documents reduced the manual effort in correcting the automatic sentence alignment of the documents.

More detailed information about the TED talks that we included in the test datasets is shown in Tables 3 and 4, for translating from and into English, respectively. We used the same English TED talks for the English to French/German and Spanish/German to English subtasks. Note however that differences in alignment of the sentences lead to different segmentation of the parallel texts for the different language pairs. Moreover, minor corrections to the sentence alignment and to the text itself, which we applied manually, resulted in small differences in the number of token for the same English TED talk when paired with the French vs. the German translation.

Note that when selecting these TED talks, we tried to pick such that include more pronouns from the rare classes. For example, for the English to French/German dataset, we wished to include documents that contained more feminine pronouns in the French and in the German translations.

## 3.3 Data Preparation

Next, we processed all datasets following the same procedure as last year. In particular, we extracted examples for pronoun prediction based on automatic word alignment, and we used filtering techniques to exclude non-subject pronouns. We further converted the data to a lemmatized version with coarse POS tags (Petrov et al., 2012). For all languages except Spanish, we used the TreeTagger (Schmid, 1994) with its built-in lemmatizer. Then, we converted the TreeTagger's POS tags to the target coarse POS tags using pre-defined mappings.[5] For French, we clipped the morphosyntactic information and we reduced the number of verb form tags to just one. For Spanish, we used UDPipe (Straka et al., 2016), which includes universal POS tags and a lemmatizer.

In previous years, the automatic alignments used for the task were optimized to improve the precision and recall of pronoun alignments. For the repeated language pairs, we reused the best performing alignment strategies from 2015 and 2016. For English→French and Spanish→English we used GIZA++ (Och and Ney, 2003) model 4 with grow-diag-final-and (Koehn et al., 2005) as symmetrization. For English↔German we used GIZA++ HMM (Vogel et al., 1996) alignment with intersection for symmetrization. In all cases, we used fast_align (Dyer et al., 2013) as backoff for sentences that are longer than the 100-word limit of GIZA++.

### 3.3.1 Example Selection

In order to select the acceptable target classes, we computed the frequencies of pronouns aligned to the ambiguous source-language pronouns based on the POS-tagged training data. Using these statistics, we defined the sets of predicted labels for each language pair. Based on the counts, we also decided to merge small classes such as the demonstrative pronouns *these* and *those*.

For English-French/German and German-English, we identified examples based on the automatic word alignments. We included cases in which multiple words were aligned to the selected pronoun if one of them belonged to the set of accepted target pronouns. If this was not the case, we used the shortest word aligned to the pronoun as the placeholder token.

---

[5] https://github.com/slavpetrov/universal-pos-tags

| ID | Speaker | Segs | Tokens | | Segs | Tokens | |
|---|---|---|---|---|---|---|---|
| | | | English | French | | English | German |
| 2470 | Knut Haanaes | 111 | 1,597 | 1,658 | 114 | 1,596 | 1,465 |
| 2471 | Lisa Nip | 92 | 2,114 | 2,277 | 92 | 2,114 | 1,974 |
| 2476 | Stephen Petranek | 165 | 3,089 | 3,171 | 167 | 3,089 | 2,997 |
| 2482 | Joshua Prager | 43 | 948 | 1,018 | 44 | 950 | 910 |
| 2485 | Chris Anderson | 79 | 1,480 | 1,468 | 79 | 1,480 | 1,348 |
| 2488 | Ameera Harouda | 70 | 1,178 | 1,277 | 70 | 1,178 | 1,055 |
| 2511 | Zaria Forman | 53 | 1,031 | 1,106 | 53 | 1,031 | 959 |
| 2535 | Gill Hicks | 85 | 1,186 | 1,267 | 85 | 1,186 | 1,151 |
| | **Total** | **698** | **12,623** | **13,242** | **704** | **12,624** | **11,859** |

Table 3: TED talks for testing: English→French and English→German.

| ID | Speaker | Segs | Tokens | | Segs | Tokens | |
|---|---|---|---|---|---|---|---|
| | | | Spanish | English | | German | English |
| 2466 | Danielle Feinberg | 118 | 2,129 | 2,201 | 125 | 1,893 | 2,188 |
| 2467 | Paula Hammond | 90 | 1,514 | 1,605 | 82 | 1,247 | 1,581 |
| 2479 | Mary Norris | 93 | 1,750 | 1,750 | 97 | 1,713 | 1,746 |
| 2492 | Sarah Gray | 87 | 1,742 | 1,824 | 86 | 1,534 | 1,824 |
| 2496 | Sanford Biggers | 31 | 760 | 710 | 31 | 683 | 710 |
| 2504 | Laura Indolfi | 50 | 961 | 964 | 50 | 895 | 961 |
| 2505 | Sebastian Junger | 135 | 2,210 | 2,199 | 124 | 1,831 | 2,170 |
| 2508 | Lidia Yuknavitch | 125 | 2,073 | 2,186 | 114 | 1,920 | 2,180 |
| | **Total** | **729** | **12,455** | **13,439** | **709** | **11,716** | **13,360** |

Table 4: TED talks for testing: German→English and Spanish→English.

Finding a suitable position to insert a placeholder on the target-language side for a source-language pronoun that was unaligned required using a heuristic. For this purpose, we first used the alignment links for the surrounding source-language words in order to determine the likely position for the placeholder token. We then expanded the window in both directions until we found an alignment link. We inserted the placeholder before or after the linked token, depending on whether the aligned source-language token was in the left or in the right context of the selected target pronoun. If no link was found in the entire sentence (which was an infrequent case), we used a position similar to the position of the selected pronoun within the source-language sentence.

For Spanish-English, the process was a bit different given that English subject pronouns are often realized as null subjects in Spanish. For this language pair, we identified the examples based on the parse of both the source and the target languages. From the Spanish parse, we took all ver-bal phrases (i.e., phrases that had the POS tags VERB, AUX and ADJ as heads) in the segment and we retained those in the third person without an overt subject, i.e., without an "nsubj" or "nsub-jpass" arc. We then identified the corresponding English verb using the alignment links. Since English pronouns are aligned to the NULL token, we relied on the English parse, looking for previously identified verbs with an overt subject.

Finally, we inserted the placeholder in the position of the English pronoun with the position of the Spanish verb concatenated to it. In the case of verb phrases that include multiple tokens (e.g., *had been reading*), we used the position of the first word in the verb phrase. As before, we used a position similar to the position of the selected pronoun within the source-language sentence. Unfortunately, and contrary to the other language pairs, we found many cases for which there was no alignment link in the entire sentence: 26,277/87,528 for IWSLT, 160/638 for TEDdev, and 187,103/ 712,728 for Europarl.

### 3.3.2 Subject Filtering

As we have explained above, the shared task focused primarily on subject pronouns. However, in English and German, some pronouns are ambiguous between subject and object position, e.g., the English *it* and the German *es* and *sie*. In order to address this issue, in 2016 we introduced filtering of object pronouns based on dependency parsing. This filtering removed all pronoun instances that did not have a subject dependency label.[6] For joint dependency parsing and POS-tagging, we used Mate Tools (Bohnet and Nivre, 2012), with default models. Since in 2016 we found that this filtering was very accurate, this year we performed only automatic filtering for the training and the development, and also for the test datasets. Note that since only subject pronouns can be realized as pro-dropped pronouns in Spanish, subject filtering was not necessary.

## 4 Baseline Systems

The baseline system is based on an $n$-gram language model (LM). The architecture is the same as that used for the WMT 2016 cross-lingual pronoun prediction task.[7] In 2016, most systems outperformed this baseline, and for the sake of comparison, we thought that it was adequate to include the same baseline system this year. Another reason to use an LM-based baseline is that it represents an important component for pronoun translation in a full SMT system. The main assumption here is that the amount of information that can be extracted from the translation table of an SMT system would be insufficient or inconclusive. As a result, pronoun prediction would be influenced primarily by the language model.

We provided baseline systems for each language pair. Each baseline is based on a 5-gram language model for the target language, trained on word lemmata constructed from news texts, parliament debates, and the TED talks of the training/development portions of the datasets. The additional monolingual news data comprises the shuffled news texts from WMT, including the 2014 editions for German and English, and the 2007–2013 editions for French.

The German corpus contains a total of 46 million sentences with 814 million lemmatized tokens, the English one includes 28 million sentences and 632 million tokens, and the French one covers 30 million sentences with 741 million tokens. These LMs are the same ones that we used in 2016.

The baseline system fills the REPLACE token gaps by using a fixed set of pronouns (those to be predicted) and a fixed set of non-pronouns (which includes the most frequent items aligned with a pronoun in the provided test set) as well as the NONE option (i.e., do not insert anything in the hypothesis). The baseline system may be optimized using a configurable NONE penalty that accounts for the fact that $n$-gram language models tend to assign higher probability to shorter strings than to longer ones.

We report two official baseline scores for each subtask. The first one is computed with the NONE penalty set to an unoptimized default value of zero. The second one uses a NONE penalty set to an optimized value, which is different for each subtask. We optimized this value on the TEDdev2 dataset for Spanish–English, and on the WMT2016 data set for the other languages, set by a grid search procedure, where we tried values between 0 and $-4$ with a step of 0.5. The optimized values vary slightly from the optimized values on less balanced data from 2016 (Guillou et al., 2016), but the differences in the resulting evaluation scores are actually minor.

## 5 Submitted Systems

A total of five teams participated in the shared task, submitting primary systems for all subtasks. Most teams also submitted contrastive systems, which have unofficial status for the purpose of ranking, but are included in the tables of results.

### 5.1 TurkuNLP

The TurkuNLP system (Luotolahti et al., 2017) is an improvement of the last year's system by the same team (Luotolahti et al., 2016). The improvement mainly consists of a pre-training scheme for vocabulary embeddings based on the task. The system is based on a recurrent neural network based on stacked Gated Recurrent Units (GRUs). The pretraining scheme involves a modification of WORD2VEC to use all target sequence pronouns along with typical skip-gram contexts in order to induce embeddings suitable for the task.

---

[6] In 2016, we found that this filtering was too aggressive for German, since it also removed expletives, which had a different tag: *EP*. Still, we decided to use the same filtering this year, to keep the task stable and the results comparable.

[7] `https://bitbucket.org/yannick/discomt_baseline`

The neural network model takes eight sequences as an input: target-token context, target-POS context, target-token-POS context, source-token context; each of these sequences is represented twice – once for the right and once for the left context. As a ninth input, the neural network takes the source-language token that is aligned to the pronoun to be predicted. All input sequences are fed in an embedding layer followed by two layers of GRUs. The values in the last layer form a vector, which is further concatenated to the pronoun alignment embeddings, to form a larger vector, which is then used to make the final prediction using a dense neural network. The pretraining is a modification of the skip-gram model of WORD2VEC (Mikolov et al., 2013), in which along with the skip-gram token context, all target sentence pronouns are predicted as well. The process of pretraining is performed using WORD2VECF (Levy and Goldberg, 2014).

## 5.2 Uppsala

The UPPSALA system (Stymne et al., 2017) is based on a neural network that uses a BiLSTM representation of the source and of the target sentences, respectively. The source sentences are preprocessed using POS tagging and dependency parsing, and then are represented by embeddings for words, POS tags, dependency labels, and a character-level representation based on a one-layer BiLSTM. The target sentences are represented by embeddings for the provided lemmata and POS tags. These representations are fed into separate two-layer BiLSTMs. The final layer includes a multi-layer perceptron that takes the BiLSTM representations of the target pronoun, of the source pronoun, of the dependency head of the source pronoun (this is not used for Spanish as it is a pro-drop language) and the original embeddings of the source pronouns.

In order to address the imbalanced class distribution, sampling of 10% of the data is used in each epoch. For the primary system, all classes are sampled equally, as long as there are enough instances for each class. Although this sampling method biases the system towards macro-averaged recall, on the test data the system performed very well in terms of both macro-averaged recall and accuracy. The secondary system uses a sampling method in which the samples are proportional to the class distribution in the development dataset.

## 5.3 NYU

The NYU system (Jean et al., 2017b) uses an attention-based neural machine translation model and three variants that incorporate information from the preceding source sentence. The sentence is added as an auxiliary input using additional encoder and attention models. The systems are not specifically designed for pronoun prediction and may be used to generate complete sentence translations. They are trained exclusively on the data provided for the task, using the text only and ignoring the provided POS tags and alignments.

## 5.4 UU-Hardmeier

The UU-HARDMEIER system (Hardmeier, 2017) is an ensemble of convolutional neural networks combined with a source-aware $n$-gram language model. The neural network models evaluate the context in the current and in the preceding sentence of the prediction placeholder (in the target language) and the aligned pronoun (in the source language) with a convolutional layer, followed by max-pooling and a softmax output layer. The $n$-gram language model is identical to the source-aware $n$-gram model of Hardmeier (2016) and Loáiciga et al. (2016). It makes its prediction using Viterbi decoding over a standard $n$-gram model. Information about the source pronoun is introduced into the model by inserting the pronoun as an extra token before the placeholder. The posterior distributions of the $n$-gram model and of various training snapshots and different configurations of the neural network are linearly interpolated with weights tuned on the development dataset to make the final predictions.

## 5.5 UU-Stymne16

The UU-STYMNE16 system uses linear SVM classifiers, and it is the same system that was submitted for the 2016 shared task (Stymne, 2016). It is based mainly on local features, and anaphora is not explicitly modeled. The features used include source pronouns, local context words/lemmata, target POS $n$-grams with two different POS tagsets, dependency heads of pronouns, alignments, and position of the pronoun. A joint tagger and dependency parser (Bohnet and Nivre, 2012) is used on the source text in order to produce some of the features. Overall, the source pronouns, the local context and the dependency features performed best across all language pairs.

Stymne (2016) describes several variations of the method, including both one-step and two-step variants, but the submitted system is based on one-step classification. It uses optimized features trained on all data. This is the system that is called *Final 1-step (all training data)* in the original system description paper. Note that this system is not identical to the 2016 submission, but it is the system that performed best in a post-task additional experiments on the 2016 test data for most language pairs.

## 6  Evaluation

While in 2015 we used macro-averaged $F_1$ as an official evaluation measure, this year we followed the setup of 2016, where we switched to *macro-averaged recall*, which was also recently adopted by some other competitions, e.g., by SemEval-2016/2017 Task 4 (Nakov et al., 2016; Rosenthal et al., 2017). Moreover, as in 2015 and 2016, we also report *accuracy* as a secondary evaluation measure (but we abandon $F_1$ altogether).

Macro-averaged recall ranges in $[0, 1]$, where a value of 1 is achieved by the perfect classifier,[8] and a value of 0 is achieved by the classifier that misclassifies all examples. The value of $1/C$, where $C$ is the number of classes, is achieved by a trivial classifier that assigns the same class to all examples (regardless of which class is chosen), and is also the expected value of a random classifier.

The advantage of macro-averaged recall over accuracy is that it is more robust to class imbalance. For instance, the accuracy of the majority-class classifier may be much higher than $1/C$ if the test dataset is imbalanced. Thus, one cannot interpret the absolute value of accuracy (e.g., is 0.7 a good or a bad value?) without comparing it to a baseline that must be computed for each specific test dataset. In contrast, for macro-averaged recall, it is clear that a value of, e.g., 0.7, is well above both the majority-class and the random baselines, which are both always $1/C$ (e.g., 0.5 with two classes, 0.33 with three classes, etc.). Similarly to accuracy, standard $F_1$ and macro-averaged $F_1$ are both sensitive to class imbalance for the same reason; see Sebastiani (2015) for more detail and further discussion.

---

[8]If the test data did not have any instances of some of the classes, we excluded these classes from the macro-averaging, i.e., we only macro-averaged over classes that are present in the gold standard.

## 7  Results

The evaluation results are shown in Tables 5-8. The first column in the tables shows the rank of the primary systems with respect to the official metric: macro-averaged recall. The second column contains the team's name and its submission type: primary vs. contrastive. The following columns show the results for each system, measured in terms of macro-averaged recall (official metric) and accuracy (unofficial, supplementary metric).

The subindices show the rank of the primary systems with respect to the evaluation measure in the respective column. As described in Section 4, we provide two official baseline scores for each subtask. The first one is computed with the NONE penalty set to a default value of zero. The second baseline uses a NONE penalty set to an optimized value. Note that these optimized penalty values are different for each subtask; the exact values are shown in the tables.

**German→English.** The results are shown in Table 5. We can see that all five participating teams outperformed the baselines by a wide margin. The top systems, TURKUNLP and UPPSALA scored 68.88 and 68.55 in macro-averaged recall. The unofficial accuracy metric yields quite a different ranking, with TurkuNLP having the lowest accuracy among the five primary systems. All systems performed well above the baselines, which are in the high-mid 30s for macro-averaged recall.

**English→German.** The results are shown in Table 6. For this direction, there is a gap of ten percentage points between the first and the second systems, UPPSALA and TURKUNLP, respectively. The clear winner is UPPSALA, with a macro-averaged recall of 78.38. For the unofficial accuracy metric, UPPSALA is again the winner, closely followed by NYU.

**Spanish→English.** The results are shown in Table 7. This language pair is the most difficult one, with the lowest scores overall, for both evaluation measures. Yet, all teams comfortably outperformed the baseline on both metrics by at least an 8-9 point margin. The best-performing system here is TURKUNLP with a macro-averaged recall of 58.82. However, it is nearly tied with UPPSALA, and both are somewhat close to NYU. Noteworthy, though, is that the highest-scoring system on macro-average recall is the contrastive system of NYU; NYU also has the second-best accuracy, outperformed only by UPPSALA.

| | Submission | Macro-Avg Recall | Accuracy |
|---|---|---|---|
| | TurkuNLP-contrastive | 69.21 | 76.92 |
| 1 | **TurkuNLP-primary** | **68.88**$_1$ | **75.64**$_5$ |
| 2 | **Uppsala-primary** | **68.55**$_2$ | **84.62**$_1$ |
| | Uppsala-contrastive | 67.41 | 85.04 |
| 3 | **NYU-primary** | **65.49**$_3$ | **82.91**$_2$ |
| | NYU-contrastive | 63.30 | 81.20 |
| 4 | **UU-Stymne16-primary** | **63.13**$_4$ | **82.05**$_3$ |
| 5 | **UU-Hardmeier-primary** | **62.18**$_5$ | **79.49**$_4$ |
| | UU-Hardmeier-contrastive | 51.12 | 69.23 |
| | *baseline: null-penalty=−1* | *38.59* | *54.27* |
| | *baseline: null-penalty=0* | *35.02* | *51.71* |

Table 5: Results for German→English.

| | Submission | Macro-Avg Recall | Accuracy |
|---|---|---|---|
| 1 | **Uppsala-primary** | **78.38**$_1$ | **79.35**$_1$ |
| 2 | **TurkuNLP-primary** | **68.95**$_2$ | **66.85**$_5$ |
| | Uppsala-contrastive | 61.72 | 78.80 |
| | TurkuNLP-contrastive | 61.66 | 64.67 |
| 3 | **NYU-primary** | **61.31**$_3$ | **77.72**$_2$ |
| | NYU-contrastive | 60.92 | 77.72 |
| 4 | **UU-Hardmeier-primary** | **58.41**$_4$ | **71.20**$_4$ |
| 5 | **UU-Stymne16-primary** | **57.86**$_5$ | **73.91**$_3$ |
| | UU-Hardmeier-contrastive | 56.80 | 69.02 |
| | *baseline: null-penalty=−1.5* | *54.81* | *55.43* |
| | *baseline: null-penalty=0* | *50.09* | *53.26* |

Table 6: Results for English→German.

**English→French.** The evaluation results for English→French are shown in Table 8. We should note that this is the only language pair and translation direction that was present in all three editions of the shared task on cross-lingual pronoun prediction so far. The best-performing system here is TURKUNLP, with macro-averaged recall of 66.89. Then, there is a gap of 3-4 percentage points to the second and to the third systems, UPPSALA (macro-averaged recall of 63.55) and UU-HARDMEIER (macro-averaged recall of 62.86), respectively. With respect to the secondary accuracy measure, the best-performing system was that of UU-HARDMEIER, followed by UPPSALA and UU-STYMNE16. Note that all participating systems outperformed the baselines on both metrics and by a huge margin of 15-30 points absolute; in fact, this is the highest margin of improvement over the baselines across all four language pairs and translation directions.

**Overall results.** TURKUNLP achieved the highest score on the official macro-averaged recall measure for three out of the four language pairs, except for English→German, where the winner was UPPSALA. However, on accuracy, TURKUNLP was not as strong, and ended up fifth for three language pairs. This is in contrast to UPPSALA, which performed well also on accuracy, being first for three out of the four language pairs. This incongruity between the evaluation measures did not occur in 2016, when macro-averaged recall and accuracy were aligned quite closely.

When we compare the best 2017 scores with the best 2016 scores for the three repeated language pairs, we can note some differences. For German→English, the scores are higher in 2017, but for the other language pairs, the scores are lower. However, we cannot draw any conclusions from this, since the test datasets, and particularly the class distributions, are different.

|   | Submission | Macro-Avg Recall | Accuracy |
|---|---|---|---|
|   | NYU-contrastive | 58.88 | 65.03 |
| **1** | **TurkuNLP-primary** | **58.82**₁ | 60.66₃ |
| **2** | **Uppsala-primary** | **58.78**₂ | 67.76₁ |
| **3** | **NYU-primary** | **56.13**₃ | 61.75₂ |
|   | Uppsala-contrastive | 55.80 | 62.30 |
| **4** | **UU-Hardmeier-primary** | **52.32**₄ | 54.10₄ |
|   | TurkuNLP-contrastive | 52.25 | 50.82 |
|   | UU-Hardmeier-contrastive | 42.19 | 46.45 |
|   | *baseline: null-penalty=−2* | *34.72* | *37.70* |
|   | *baseline: null-penalty=0* | *33.24* | *33.88* |

Table 7: Results for Spanish→English.

|   | Submission | Macro-Avg Recall | Accuracy |
|---|---|---|---|
| **1** | **TurkuNLP-primary** | **66.89**₁ | 67.40₅ |
|   | TurkuNLP-contrastive | 64.74 | 69.06 |
| **2** | **Uppsala-primary** | **63.55**₂ | 70.17₂ |
| **3** | **UU-Hardmeier-primary** | **62.86**₃ | 73.48₁ |
| **4** | **NYU-primary** | **62.29**₄ | 69.61₃ |
|   | UU-Hardmeier-contrastive | 58.95 | 71.82 |
|   | NYU-contrastive | 58.10 | 71.82 |
| **5** | **UU-Stymne16-primary** | **52.32**₅ | 68.51₄ |
|   | Uppsala-contrastive | 50.06 | 65.19 |
|   | *baseline: null-penalty=−1.5* | *37.05* | *48.07* |
|   | *baseline: null-penalty=0* | *36.31* | *48.62* |

Table 8: Results for English→French.

Tables 9–12 show the recall for each participating system, calculated with respect to each pronoun class. Note that for most classes, the LM baselines perform worse than the participating systems. It is also clear that some classes are considerably easier than others, and that rare classes are often difficult.

For German→English (Table 9), no team has managed to predict the single instance of *these*, and only TURKUNLP has found one of the two instances of *this*, which considerably boosted their macro-averaged recall.

For English→German (Table 10), there are eight instances of *er*, but for this class there is a lot of variance, with the best systems having a recall of 75.0, while for several systems it is 0.

For Spanish→English (Table 11), unlike the other pairs, the classes are rather uniformly distributed, the OTHER class, in particular, not being the most frequent one. Besides, although *he, she,* and *it* all have 12–15 instances, *he* and *she* have low overall recall, while for *it* it is quite high.

For English→French (Table 12), the female pronouns *elle* and *elles* have been notoriously difficult to predict in previous work on this task. We can see that this is also the case this year. However, TURKUNLP achieved a better score for the feminine singular *elle* than for the masculine singular *il*, and UPPSALA was better at predicting the feminine plural *elles* than the masculine plural *ils*.

Overall, it is hard to see systematic differences across the participating systems: all systems tend to perform well on some classes and bad on others, even though there is some variation. However, it is clear that Spanish→English is more difficult than the other language pairs: compared to German→English, the scores are considerably lower for the classes *he, she, they* and OTHER, which these two language pairs share. Another clear observation is that for *you* and *there*, the scores are lower for Spanish→English than for the other language pairs for all systems, except for NYU-CONTRASTIVE.

| Systems | Classes | he | she | it | they | you | this | these | there | OTHER |
| --- | --- | --- | --- | --- | --- | --- | --- | --- | --- | --- |
| | Instances | 20 | 17 | 58 | 40 | 24 | 2 | 1 | 8 | 64 |
| TurkuNLP-contrastive | | 100.00 | 82.35 | 62.07 | 92.50 | 75.00 | 50.00 | 0.00 | 87.50 | 73.44 |
| **TurkuNLP-primary** | | 95.00 | 94.12 | 53.45 | 92.50 | 70.83 | 50.00 | 0.00 | 87.50 | 76.56 |
| **Uppsala-primary** | | 100.00 | 94.12 | 77.59 | 90.00 | 83.33 | 0.00 | 0.00 | 87.50 | 84.38 |
| Uppsala-contrastive | | 95.00 | 76.47 | 81.03 | 87.50 | 91.67 | 0.00 | 0.00 | 87.50 | 87.50 |
| **NYU-primary** | | 90.00 | 82.35 | 77.59 | 90.00 | 91.67 | 0.00 | 0.00 | 75.00 | 82.81 |
| NYU-contrastive | | 90.00 | 70.59 | 74.14 | 85.00 | 87.50 | 0.00 | 0.00 | 75.00 | 87.50 |
| **UU-Stymne16** | | 100.00 | 64.71 | 77.59 | 92.50 | 70.83 | 0.00 | 0.00 | 75.00 | 87.50 |
| **UU-Hardmeier-primary** | | 100.00 | 52.94 | 77.59 | 90.00 | 87.50 | 0.00 | 0.00 | 75.00 | 76.56 |
| UU-Hardmeier-contrastive | | 90.00 | 17.65 | 75.86 | 62.50 | 75.00 | 0.00 | 0.00 | 62.50 | 76.56 |
| Baseline -1 | | 30.00 | 17.65 | 63.79 | 40.00 | 45.83 | 0.00 | 0.00 | 75.00 | 75.00 |
| Baseline 0 | | 10.00 | 11.76 | 62.07 | 35.00 | 41.67 | 0.00 | 0.00 | 75.00 | 79.69 |

Table 9: Recall for each class and system for German→English.

| Systems | Classes | er | sie | es | OTHER |
| --- | --- | --- | --- | --- | --- |
| | Instances | 8 | 62 | 52 | 62 |
| **Uppsala-primary** | | 75.00 | 88.71 | 78.85 | 70.97 |
| **TurkuNLP-primary** | | 75.00 | 62.90 | 75.00 | 62.90 |
| Uppsala-contrastive | | 0.00 | 85.48 | 80.77 | 80.65 |
| TurkuNLP-contrastive | | 50.00 | 74.19 | 69.23 | 53.23 |
| **NYU-primary** | | 0.00 | 79.03 | 90.38 | 75.81 |
| NYU-contrastive | | 0.00 | 85.48 | 80.77 | 77.42 |
| **UU-Hardmeier-primary** | | 12.50 | 70.97 | 71.15 | 79.03 |
| **UU-Stymne16** | | 0.00 | 82.26 | 75.00 | 74.19 |
| UU-Hardmeier-contrastive | | 12.50 | 70.97 | 71.15 | 72.58 |
| Baseline -1.5 | | 50.00 | 25.81 | 69.23 | 74.19 |
| Baseline 0 | | 37.50 | 16.13 | 59.62 | 87.10 |

Table 10: Recall for each class and system for English→German. In the test dataset, there were no instances of the pronoun class *man*, and thus this class is not included in the table.

| Systems | Classes | he | she | it | they | you | there | OTHER |
| --- | --- | --- | --- | --- | --- | --- | --- | --- |
| | Instances | 12 | 15 | 63 | 36 | 12 | 22 | 23 |
| NYU-contrastive | | 41.67 | 20.00 | 79.37 | 66.67 | 83.33 | 86.36 | 34.78 |
| **TurkuNLP-primary** | | 66.67 | 26.67 | 60.32 | 75.00 | 66.67 | 77.27 | 39.13 |
| **Uppsala-primary** | | 41.67 | 13.33 | 82.54 | 77.78 | 66.67 | 77.27 | 52.17 |
| **NYU-primary** | | 41.67 | 20.00 | 69.84 | 69.44 | 66.67 | 81.82 | 43.48 |
| Uppsala-contrastive | | 50.00 | 0.00 | 68.25 | 80.56 | 66.67 | 77.27 | 47.83 |
| **UU-Hardmeier-primary** | | 33.33 | 26.67 | 46.03 | 72.22 | 58.33 | 81.82 | 47.83 |
| TurkuNLP-contrastive | | 50.00 | 46.67 | 44.44 | 63.89 | 66.67 | 63.64 | 30.43 |
| UU-Hardmeier-contrastive | | 16.67 | 0.00 | 42.86 | 61.11 | 50.00 | 68.18 | 56.52 |
| Baseline -2 | | 8.33 | 6.67 | 46.03 | 30.56 | 66.67 | 50.00 | 34.78 |
| Baseline 0 | | 0.00 | 6.67 | 34.92 | 22.22 | 66.67 | 50.00 | 52.17 |

Table 11: Recall for each class and system for Spanish→English.

| Systems | Classes | ce | elle | elles | il | ils | cela | on | OTHER |
| | Instances | 32 | 12 | 12 | 29 | 35 | 5 | 5 | 51 |
|---|---|---|---|---|---|---|---|---|---|
| **TurkuNLP-primary** | | 87.50 | 66.67 | 58.33 | 48.28 | 65.71 | 60.00 | 80.00 | 68.63 |
| TurkuNLP-contrastive | | 96.88 | 41.67 | 66.67 | 41.38 | 88.57 | 40.00 | 80.00 | 62.75 |
| **Uppsala-primary** | | 87.50 | 33.33 | 83.33 | 51.72 | 80.00 | 40.00 | 60.00 | 72.55 |
| **UU-Hardmeier-primary** | | 90.62 | 8.33 | 66.67 | 72.41 | 94.29 | 60.00 | 40.00 | 70.59 |
| **NYU-primary** | | 84.38 | 50.00 | 25.00 | 65.52 | 82.86 | 60.00 | 60.00 | 70.59 |
| UU-Hardmeier-contrastive | | 81.25 | 16.67 | 25.00 | 82.76 | 91.43 | 60.00 | 40.00 | 74.51 |
| NYU-contrastive | | 84.38 | 33.33 | 25.00 | 72.41 | 97.14 | 20.00 | 60.00 | 72.55 |
| **UU-Stymne16** | | 81.25 | 16.67 | 0.00 | 68.97 | 97.14 | 40.00 | 40.00 | 74.51 |
| Uppsala-contrastive | | 84.38 | 16.67 | 0.00 | 51.72 | 97.14 | 40.00 | 40.00 | 70.59 |
| Baseline -1.5 | | 87.50 | 8.33 | 0.00 | 75.86 | 0.00 | 0.00 | 60.00 | 64.71 |
| Baseline 0 | | 87.50 | 0.00 | 0.00 | 72.41 | 0.00 | 0.00 | 60.00 | 70.59 |

Table 12: Recall for each class and system for English→French.

## 8 Discussion

Unlike 2016, this year all participating teams managed to outperform the corresponding baselines. Note, however, that these baselines are based on $n$-gram language models, which are conceived to be competitive to SMT, while most systems this year used neural architectures. In fact, four of the systems used neural networks and they all outperformed the SVM-based UU-STYMNE system, which was among the best in 2016.

Moreover, the systems used language-independent approaches which they applied to all language pairs and translation directions. With the exception of dependency parsers, none of the systems made use of additional tools, nor tried to address coreference resolution explicitly. Instead, they relied on modeling the sentential and intersentential context. Table 13 summarizes the sources of information that the systems used.

One of the original goals of the task was to improve our understanding of the process of pronoun translation. In this respect, however, we can only suggest that context should be among the most important factors, since this is what neural methods are very good at learning. Interestingly, the two best-performing systems, TURKUNLP and UPP-SALA, used only intra-sentential context, but still performed better than the two systems that used inter-sentence information. Linguistically, it is easy to motivate using inter-sentential information for resolving anaphora; yet, none of the current systems targeted anaphora explicitly. We can conclude that making use of inter-sentential information for the task remains an open challenge.

Last year, the participating systems had difficulties with language pairs that had English on the *source* side. However, this year the hardest language pair was Spanish→English, which has English on the *target* side. This result reflects the difficulty of translating null subjects, which are as underspecified as the pronouns *it* and *they* when translating into French or German. We should further note that the example extraction process for Spanish focused on cases of third person verbs with null subjects. In other words, the use of Spanish pronouns vs. null subjects is not considered since overt Spanish pronouns were excluded.

As mentioned earlier, the macro-averaged recall and the accuracy metrics did not correlate well this year, suggesting that the official metric may need some re-thinking. The motivation for using macro-averaged recall was to avoid rewarding too much a system that performs well on high frequency classes. It is not clear, however, that a system optimized to favor macro-averaged recall is strictly better than one that has higher accuracy.

Another question is how realistic our baselines are with respect to NMT systems. Our $n$-gram language model-based baselines were competitive with respect to phrase-based SMT systems trained with fully inflected target text, as evidenced by the higher scores achieved by the baselines with English on the source side. Given the recent rise of NMT and also in view of the strong performance of the NYU team, who submitted a full-fledged NMT system that uses intra-sentential information, it might be a good idea to adopt a similar system as a baseline in the future.

|                                   | TurkuNLP | NYU | Uppsala | UU-Hardmeier | UU-Stymne16 |
| --------------------------------- | -------- | --- | ------- | ------------ | ----------- |
| SVM                               |          |     |         |              | X           |
| Neural networks                   | X        | X   | X       | X            |             |
|    -Convolutions   | X        |     |         | X            |             |
|    -GRUs           | X        | X   |         |              |             |
|    -BiLSTMs        |          |     | X       |              |             |
| Source pronoun representation     | X        |     | X       | X            | X           |
| Target POS tags                   | X        |     | X       |              | X           |
| Head dependencies                 |          |     | X       |              | X           |
| Pre-trained word embeddings       | X        |     |         |              |             |
| Source intra-sentential context   | X        | X   | X       | X            | X           |
| Source inter-sentential context   |          | X   |         | X            |             |
| Target intra-sentential context   | X        |     | X       | X            | X           |
| Target inter-sentential context   |          |     |         | X            |             |

Table 13: Sources of information and key characteristics of the submitted systems.

We should note however that full-fledged NMT systems present challenges with respect to automatic evaluation, just like full-fledged phrase-based SMT systems do. The problem is that we cannot just compare the pronouns that a machine translation system has generated to the pronouns in a reference translation, as in doing so we might miss the legitimate variation of certain pronouns, as well as variations in gender or number of the antecedent itself. Human judges are thus required for reliable evaluation. In particular, the DiscoMT 2015 shared task on *pronoun-focused translation* (Hardmeier et al., 2015) included a protocol for human evaluation. This approach, however, has a high cost, which grows linearly with the number of submissions to the task, and it also makes subsequent research and direct comparison to the participating systems very hard.

This is why in 2016, we reformulated the task as one about cross-lingual pronoun prediction, which allows us to evaluate it as a regular classification task; this year we followed the same formulation. While this eliminates the need for manual evaluation, it yielded a task that is only indirectly related to machine translation, and one that can be seen as artificial, e.g., because it does not allow an MT system to generate full output, and because the provided output is lemmatized.

In future editions of the task, we might want to go back to machine translation, but to adopt a specialized evaluation measure that would focus on pronoun translation, so that we can automate the process of evaluation at least partially, e.g., as proposed by Luong and Popescu-Belis (2016).

## 9 Conclusions

We have described the design and the evaluation of the shared task on cross-lingual pronoun prediction at DiscoMT 2017. We offered four subtasks, each for a different language pair and translation direction: English→French, English→German, German→English, and Spanish→English. We followed the setup of the WMT 2016 task, and for Spanish→English, we further introduced the prediction of null subjects, which proved challenging.

We received submissions from five teams, with four teams submitting systems for all language pairs. All participating systems outperformed the official $n$-gram-based language model-based baselines by a sizable margin. The two top-performing teams used neural networks and only intra-sentential information, ignoring the rest of the document. The only non-neural submission was ranked last, indicating the fitness of neural networks for this task. We hope that the success in the cross-lingual pronoun prediction task will soon translate into improvements in pronoun translation by end-to-end MT systems.

## 10 Acknowledgements

The organization of this task has received support from the following project: Discourse-Oriented Statistical Machine Translation funded by the Swedish Research Council (2012-916). We thank Andrei Popescu-Belis and Bonnie Webber for their advice in organizing this shared task. The work of Chistian Hardmeier and Sara Stymne is part of the Swedish strategic research programme eSSENCE.

## References

Dzmitry Bahdanau, Kyunghyun Cho, and Yoshua Bengio. 2015. Neural machine translation by jointly learning to align and translate. In *Proceedings of the 3rd International Conference on Learning Representations*, ICLR '15, San Diego, California, USA.

Bernd Bohnet and Joakim Nivre. 2012. A transition-based system for joint part-of-speech tagging and labeled non-projective dependency parsing. In *Proceedings of the Joint Conference on Empirical Methods in Natural Language Processing and Computational Natural Language Learning*, EMNLP-CoNLL '12, pages 1455–1465, Jeju Island, Korea.

Mauro Cettolo, Jan Niehues, Sebastian Stüker, Luisa Bentivogli, Roldano Cattoni, and Marcello Federico. 2016. The IWSLT 2016 evaluation campaign. In *Proceedings of the International Workshop on Spoken Language Translation*, IWSLT '16, Seattle, Washington, USA.

Kyunghyun Cho, Bart van Merrienboer, Caglar Gulcehre, Dzmitry Bahdanau, Fethi Bougares, Holger Schwenk, and Yoshua Bengio. 2014. Learning phrase representations using RNN encoder–decoder for statistical machine translation. In *Proceedings of the Conference on Empirical Methods in Natural Language Processing*, EMNLP '14, pages 1724–1734.

Joseph Clancy Clemens. 2001. Ergative Patterning in Spanish. In Javier Gutiérrez-Rexach and Luis Silva-Villar, editors, *Current Issues in Spanish Syntax*, pages 271–290. Mouton de Gruyter.

Chris Dyer, Victor Chahuneau, and Noah A. Smith. 2013. A simple, fast, and effective reparameterization of IBM model 2. In *Proceedings of the Conference of the North American Chapter of the Association for Computational Linguistics: Human Language Technologies*, NAACL-HLT '13, pages 644–648, Atlanta, Georgia, USA.

Liane Guillou. 2012. Improving pronoun translation for statistical machine translation. In *Proceedings of the Student Research Workshop at the 13th Conference of the European Chapter of the Association for Computational Linguistics*, EACL-SRW '12, pages 1–10, Avignon, France.

Liane Guillou. 2016. *Incorporating Pronoun Function into Statistical Machine Translation*. Ph.D. thesis, University of Edinburgh.

Liane Guillou, Christian Hardmeier, Preslav Nakov, Sara Stymne, Jörg Tiedemann, Yannick Versley, Mauro Cettolo, Bonnie Webber, and Andrei Popescu-Belis. 2016. Findings of the WMT shared task on cross-lingual pronoun prediction. In *Proceedings of the First Conference on Machine Translation*, WMT '16, pages 525–542, Berlin, Germany.

Liane Guillou, Christian Hardmeier, Aaron Smith, Jörg Tiedemann, and Bonnie Webber. 2014. ParCor 1.0: A parallel pronoun-coreference corpus to support statistical MT. In *Proceedings of the 9th International Conference on Language Resources and Evaluation*, LREC '14, pages 3193–3198, Reykjavik, Iceland.

Christian Hardmeier. 2014. *Discourse in Statistical Machine Translation*. Ph.D. thesis, University of Uppsala.

Christian Hardmeier. 2016. Pronoun prediction with latent anaphora resolution. In *Proceedings of the First Conference on Machine Translation*, WMT '16, pages 576–580, Berlin, Germany.

Christian Hardmeier. 2017. Predicting pronouns with a convolutional network and an n-gram model. In *Proceedings of the Third Workshop on Discourse in Machine Translation*, DiscoMT '17, Copenhagen, Denmark.

Christian Hardmeier and Marcello Federico. 2010. Modelling pronominal anaphora in statistical machine translation. In *Proceedings of the 7th International Workshop on Spoken Language Translation*, IWSLT '10, pages 283–289, Paris, France.

Christian Hardmeier, Preslav Nakov, Sara Stymne, Jörg Tiedemann, Yannick Versley, and Mauro Cettolo. 2015. Pronoun-focused MT and cross-lingual pronoun prediction: Findings of the 2015 DiscoMT shared task on pronoun translation. In *Proceedings of the 2nd Workshop on Discourse in Machine Translation*, DiscoMT '15, pages 1–16, Lisbon, Portugal.

Sébastien Jean, Stanislas Lauly, Orhan Firat, and Kyunghyun Cho. 2017a. Does neural machine translation benefit from larger context? *CoRR*, abs/1704.05135.

Sébastien Jean, Stanislas Lauly, Orhan Firat, and Kyunghyun Cho. 2017b. Neural machine translation for cross-lingual pronoun prediction. In *Proceedings of the Third Workshop on Discourse in Machine Translation*, DiscoMT '17, Copenhagen, Denmark.

Philipp Koehn. 2005. Europarl: A Parallel Corpus for Statistical Machine Translation. In *Proceedings of the Tenth Machine Translation Summit*, MT Summit '05, pages 79–86, Phuket, Thailand.

Philipp Koehn, Amittai Axelrod, Alexandra Birch Mayne, Chris Callison-Burch, Miles Osborne, and David Talbot. 2005. Edinburgh system description for the 2005 IWSLT speech translation evaluation. In *Proceedings of the International Workshop on Spoken Language Translation*, IWSLT '05, Pittsburgh, Pennsylvania, USA.

Philipp Koehn, Franz Josef Och, and Daniel Marcu. 2013. Statistical phrase-based translation. In *Proceedings of the Conference of the North American Chapter of the Association for Computational Linguistics on Human Language Technology*, NAACL-HLT '03, pages 48–54, Edmonton, Canada.

Ronan Le Nagard and Philipp Koehn. 2010. Aiding pronoun translation with co-reference resolution. In *Proceedings of the Joint Fifth Workshop on Statistical Machine Translation and MetricsMATR*, WMT-MetricsMATR '10, pages 252–261, Uppsala, Sweden.

Omer Levy and Yoav Goldberg. 2014. Dependency-based word embeddings. In *Proceedings of the 52nd Annual Meeting of the Association for Computational Linguistics*, ACL '14, pages 302–308, Baltimore, Maryland, USA.

Sharid Loáiciga, Liane Guillou, and Christian Hardmeier. 2016. It-disambiguation and source-aware language models for cross-lingual pronoun prediction. In *Proceedings of the First Conference on Machine Translation*, WMT '16, pages 581–588, Berlin, Germany.

Ngoc Quang Luong and Andrei Popescu-Belis. 2016. Improving pronoun translation by modeling coreference uncertainty. In *Proceedings of the First Conference on Machine Translation*, WMT '16, pages 12–20, Berlin, Germany.

Thang Luong, Hieu Pham, and Christopher D. Manning. 2015. Effective approaches to attention-based neural machine translation. In *Proceedings of the Conference on Empirical Methods in Natural Language Processing*, EMNLP '15, pages 1412–1421, Lisbon, Portugal.

Juhani Luotolahti, Jenna Kanerva, and Filip Ginter. 2016. Cross-lingual pronoun prediction with deep recurrent neural networks. In *Proceedings of the First Conference on Machine Translation*, WMT '16, pages 596–601, Berlin, Germany.

Juhani Luotolahti, Jenna Kanerva, and Filip Ginter. 2017. Cross-lingual pronoun prediction with deep recurrent neural networks v2.0. In *Proceedings of the Third Workshop on Discourse in Machine Translation*, DiscoMT '17, Copenhagen, Denmark.

Tomas Mikolov, Ilya Sutskever, Kai Chen, Greg S Corrado, and Jeff Dean. 2013. Distributed representations of words and phrases and their compositionality. In *Proceedings of the Twenty-Seventh Annual Conference on Neural Information Processing Systems*, NIPS '13, pages 3111–3119, Lake Tahoe, Nevada, USA.

Preslav Nakov, Alan Ritter, Sara Rosenthal, Veselin Stoyanov, and Fabrizio Sebastiani. 2016. SemEval-2016 task 4: Sentiment analysis in Twitter. In *Proceedings of the 10th International Workshop on Semantic Evaluation*, SemEval '16, pages 1–18, San Diego, California, USA.

Ad Neeleman and Kriszta Szendői. 2005. Pro drop and pronouns. In *Proceedings of the 24th West Coast Conference on Formal Linguistics*, pages 299–307, Somerville, Massachusetts, USA.

Michal Novák. 2011. Utilization of anaphora in machine translation. In *Proceedings of Contributed Papers, Week of Doctoral Students 2011*, pages 155–160, Prague, Czech Republic.

Franz Josef Och and Hermann Ney. 2003. A systematic comparison of various statistical alignment models. *Computational Linguistics*, 29(1):19–51.

Slav Petrov, Dipanjan Das, and Ryan McDonald. 2012. A universal part-of-speech tagset. In *Proceedings of the Eight International Conference on Language Resources and Evaluation*, LREC '12, pages 2089–2096, Istanbul, Turkey.

Sara Rosenthal, Noura Farra, and Preslav Nakov. 2017. SemEval-2017 task 4: Sentiment analysis in Twitter. In *Proceedings of the 11th International Workshop on Semantic Evaluation*, SemEval '17, Vancouver, Canada.

Helmut Schmid. 1994. Probabilistic part-of-speech tagging using decision trees. In *Proceedings of International Conference on New Methods in Language Processing*, pages 44–49, Manchester, United Kingdom.

Fabrizio Sebastiani. 2015. An axiomatically derived measure for the evaluation of classification algorithms. In *Proceedings of the 5th ACM International Conference on the Theory of Information Retrieval*, ICTIR '15, pages 11–20, Northampton, Massachusetts, USA.

Milan Straka, Jan Hajič, and Jana Straková. 2016. UDPipe: Trainable pipeline for processing CoNLL-U files performing tokenization, morphological analysis, POS tagging and parsing. In *Proceedings of the Tenth International Conference on Language Resources and Evaluation*, LREC '16, pages 4290–4297, Portorož, Slovenia.

Sara Stymne. 2016. Feature exploration for cross-lingual pronoun prediction. In *Proceedings of the First Conference on Machine Translation*, WMT '16, pages 609–615, Berlin, Germany.

Sara Stymne, Sharid Loáiciga, and Fabienne Cap. 2017. A BiLSTM-based system for cross-lingual pronoun prediction. In *Proceedings of the Third Workshop on Discourse in Machine Translation*, DiscoMT '17, Copenhagen, Denmark.

Ilya Sutskever, Oriol Vinyals, and Quoc V. Le. 2014. Sequence to sequence learning with neural networks. In *Proceedings of the 27th International Conference on Neural Information Processing Systems*, NIPS'14, pages 3104–3112, Montreal, Canada.

Stephan Vogel, Hermann Ney, and Christoph Tillman. 1996. HMM-based word alignment in statistical translation. In *Proceedings of the 16th International Conference on Computational Linguistics*, COLING '16, pages 836–841, Copenhagen, Denmark.

# Validation of an Automatic Metric for the
# Accuracy of Pronoun Translation (APT)


**Lesly Miculicich Werlen** and **Andrei Popescu-Belis**
Idiap Research Institute
Rue Marconi 19, CP 592
1920 Martigny, Switzerland
{lmiculicich,apbelis}@idiap.ch



## Abstract

In this paper, we define and assess a reference-based metric to evaluate the accuracy of pronoun translation (APT). The metric automatically aligns a candidate and a reference translation using GIZA++ augmented with specific heuristics, and then counts the number of identical or different pronouns, with provision for legitimate variations and omitted pronouns. All counts are then combined into one score. The metric is applied to the results of seven systems (including the baseline) that participated in the DiscoMT 2015 shared task on pronoun translation from English to French. The APT metric reaches around 0.993–0.999 Pearson correlation with human judges (depending on the parameters of APT), while other automatic metrics such as BLEU, METEOR, or those specific to pronouns used at DiscoMT 2015 reach only 0.972–0.986 Pearson correlation.


## 1 Introduction

The machine translation of pronouns has long been known as a challenge, especially for pro-drop languages. The correct translation of pronouns often requires non-local information, which is one of the reasons it is quite challenging for statistical or neural MT systems. Still, the problem has attracted new interest in recent years (Hardmeier, 2014; Guillou, 2016), in particular through the organization of three shared tasks: at the EMNLP DiscoMT 2015 and 2017 workshops (Hardmeier et al., 2015; Loáiciga et al., 2017), and at the First Conference on Machine Translation (WMT) (Guillou et al., 2016).

As often with MT evaluation issues at the semantic and discourse levels, measuring the accuracy of pronoun translation was found difficult, due to the interplay between the translation of pronouns and of their antecedents, and to variations in the use of non-referential pronouns. Therefore, the DiscoMT 2015 shared task on pronoun-focused translation resorted to human evaluation, to compare the candidate translations of pronouns with the options deemed correct by human judges who did not see the candidate translations. However, this approach came at a significant cost, and its principle does not allow repeated evaluations with new candidate sentences. On the other hand, it is commonly considered that a reference-based approach to pronoun evaluation in MT is too restrictive, as the amount of legitimate variation is too high: for instance, if a candidate translation uses a different genre than the reference for the translation of an antecedent, then the subsequent pronouns should follow the same genre.

In this paper, we show that a simple, reference-based metric that estimates the accuracy of pronoun translation (hence called 'APT') reaches high correlations with human judgments of quality. In relation to the above-mentioned shared tasks, the APT metric targets the translation of third person English pronouns *it* and *they* into French. These pronouns have a large number of possible translations, depending on the referential status of each occurrence, and on the gender and number of its antecedent. The metric compares the candidate translation of each occurrence of *it* and *they* with the reference one, an operation that requires in the first place a precise alignment of pronouns between these texts. Then, the metric counts the number of identical, equivalent, or different translations in the candidate vs. the reference, as well as cases when one of the translations is absent or cannot be identified. Several combinations of




*Proceedings of the Third Workshop on Discourse in Machine Translation*, pages 17–25,
Copenhagen, Denmark, September 8, 2017. ©2017 Association for Computational Linguistics.

counts are considered – the most straightforward one gives credit for identical matches and discards all other ones.

As we will show, the APT scores correlate strongly with the human scores on the data from the DiscoMT 2015 shared task on pronoun-focused translation (0.993–0.999 Pearson and 1.000 Spearman rank correlation). This is considerably higher than general purpose automatic metrics such as BLEU and METEOR, and than the automatic metrics used at DiscoMT. The code for the APT metric, with the best settings of this paper for English/French translation, is freely available.[1]

The paper is organized as follows. We first define the APT metric, including the alignment procedure and the options to aggregate counts into one score (Section 2). Then, we present the dataset used to validate APT, along with the other metrics and the correlation measures (Section 3). Finally, we present the results showing that APT has a higher correlation with human judgments than the other existing metrics (Section 4).

## 2 Definition of the APT Metric

### 2.1 Terminology

To clarify our terminology, we distinguish *referential* pronouns from non-referential ones, which are also called pleonastic or impersonal. Referential pronouns are also called *anaphoric*, as they point back to a previous item in the discourse, typically but not necessarily a noun phrase, which is called their *antecedent*. An anaphoric pronoun and its antecedent both refer to the same (discourse) entity and are therefore *co-referent*. Guillou (2016) argues that a correct translation of pronouns, in case several options are possible (i.e. in the case of translation divergences), requires the identification of their function, and then of their antecedent (if they are referential), with which they typically agree in gender and number. The automatic identification of the antecedent of a referential pronoun is called anaphora resolution (Mitkov, 2002).

### 2.2 Overview of the Approach

The APT metric relies on a reference human translation and on a comparison of the candidate translation (i.e. produced by the MT system) with the reference translation to compute the evaluation scores. Given the word-level alignment of the source, reference, and candidate translations,

APT first identifies triples of pronouns: (*source pronoun, reference pronoun, candidate pronoun*). Then, it compares each candidate against the corresponding reference, assuming that a pronoun is well translated when it is identical to the reference. (This assumption is validated below by comparing APT scores with human ones, averaged over a large number of instances.) Partial matches defined using equivalence classes can also contribute to the score, but these classes depend of course on the target language and need to be defined *a priori*.

"Equivalent" pronouns are those that can be exchanged in most contexts without affecting the meaning of the sentence. Also, in some languages, one should consider the possibility of identical pronouns with different forms. For example, French has pronoun contractions such as *c'* for *ce*, in the expletive construction *c'est* (meaning *it is*).

### 2.3 Pronoun Alignment

Given the list of source pronouns considered for evaluation, the first step is to obtain their corresponding alignments in the target language texts. In the case of the candidate translation, the alignment can be directly obtained from the MT system if such an option is available. However, in the case of the reference, it is necessary to perform automatic word alignment. We use here the GIZA++ system (Och and Ney, 2003), including the sentences to be scored in a larger corpus to ensure an acceptable accuracy, since GIZA++ has no separate training vs. testing stages. The alignment is made both in direct (source-target) and reverse (target-source) directions, which are then merged using the *grow-diag-final* heuristic from Moses (Koehn et al., 2007).

Accurate pronoun alignment is essential to APT. To estimate its accuracy, we manually evaluated 100 randomly selected sentences from the WIT3 parallel corpus of English-French TED Talks (Cettolo et al., 2012), containing the pronouns *it* and *they*. We found that the alignments of 19 out of 100 pronoun were missing, and that 4 pronouns were incorrectly aligned. As expected, the majority of misalignments involved infrequently-used target pronouns.

We defined several pronoun-specific heuristics to improve the alignment. Our four-step procedure is exemplified in Table 1 below, where the alignment between the pronouns *it* and *il* was not

---

[1] https://github.com/idiap/APT

| Step | Example |
| --- | --- |
| 0 | E: *The system is so healthy that **it** purifies the water.*<br>F: *Le système est si sain qu' **il** purifie l' eau.* |
| 1 | E: *The system is so healthy <u>that</u> it purifies the water.*<br>F: *Le système est si sain <u>qu' il purifie l'</u> eau.* |
| 2 | F: *Le système est si [ sain <u>qu' il purifie l'</u> ] eau.* |
| 3 | F: *Le système est si [ sain$_2$ <u>qu' **il**$_1$ purifie **l'**$_2$</u> ] eau.* |
| 4 | From the list $\{il, l'\}$, the closest to the center: *il*. |

Table 1: Example of applying the heuristics to improve pronoun alignment: *it* in the English source.

identified by GIZA++. First, we identify possible misalignments: source pronouns which are not aligned to any word, or which are aligned to a non-pronoun, or to multiple target words. This task can be performed by using a predefined list of pronouns or a POS tagger. If among the multiply-aligned target words there is a pronoun, then it is considered the alignment. If not, we identify the corresponding alignments (called markers) of the words preceding and following the pronoun (position -1 and +1). Second, we define a range in the target-side neighborhood by considering one word before the first marker and one after the second one, to expand the range of options. Third, we test whether this range includes any likely translations of the source pronoun. Finally, we choose as the aligned word the closest word to the center of the range. An example of application of this algorithm is shown in Table 1. The proposed procedure helped to correctly address 22 out of the 23 misalignments found in the WIT3 test data described above.

## 2.4 Computing APT Scores

The first step of the evaluation is to compare each pair of candidate and reference translations of each source pronoun. We define six cases based on those from a similar metric for discourse connectives (Hajlaoui and Popescu-Belis, 2013):

1. Identical pronouns.
2. Equivalent pronouns (specified below in 2.5).
3. Different (incompatible) pronouns.
4. Candidate translation not found.
5. Reference translation not found.
6. Both translations not found.

To each case, from 1 to 6, we associate a score or weight that reflects how correct is a candidate translation in that case, given the reference. For instance, the first case (candidate identical to reference) is likely a correct translation and its weight should be 1. These scores thus indicate the contribution to the final score of each occurrence of a pronoun in the respective case.

Let $C = c_1, .., c_m$ be the set of $m = 6$ cases defined above, $n_{c_i}$ the number of pronoun translation pairs that belong to case $c_i$, and $w_i \in [0, 1]$ the weight or score associated with case $c_i$. We denote the subset of discarded cases as $C_d \subseteq C$, for instance if we want to discard from the final score those cases where there was no reference pronoun to compare with. The APT score is computed as the number of correctly translated pronouns over the total number of pronouns, formally expressed as:

$$APT = \left( \sum_{i=1, c_i \notin C_d}^{m} w_i n_{c_i} \right) / \left( \sum_{i=1, c_i \notin C_d}^{m} n_{c_i} \right).$$

The input parameters for the APT metric are the weights, the discarded cases if any, and the lists of equivalent and identical pronouns in the target language. The weights for our experiments on evaluating English to French pronoun translation are set as follows:

**Case 1:** Candidate pronouns identical to the reference are considered correct, $w_1 = 1$.

**Case 2:** In this case, the candidate pronoun is only deemed "equivalent" to the reference one according to a predefined list (see Section 2.5). Counting them always as correct may lead to an indulgent metric, while the contrary might unduly penalize the candidate. We experiment with three options: counted as incorrect ($w_2 = 0$), as partially correct ($w_2 = 0.5$), or as correct ($w_2 = 1$).

**Case 3:** Candidate pronouns different from the reference are considered as incorrect ($w_3 = 0$).

**Case 4:** When the reference pronoun is found but not the candidate one, which is then likely absent, the pair is counted as incorrect ($w_4 = 0$), although in some cases omitting a pronoun may still be correct.

**Case 5:** This is a special scenario because there is no reference pronoun to compare with, therefore we assume two possibilities: either discard these cases, or consider them for evaluation. With the second option, case 5 is necessarily considered as incorrect ($w_5 = 0$), but contributes to the denominator in the definition of APT above.

**Case 6:** Similar to case 5, we have two possibilities: discard entirely these cases, or evaluate them. If we evaluate them, there are situations when neither the reference nor the candidate translation of a source pronoun could be found, which can often be supposed to be correct, but sometimes reflect complex configurations with wrong candidate translations. Due to this uncertainty, we experiment with three possibilities: counted as incorrect ($w_6 = 0$), as partially correct ($w_6 = 0.5$), or as correct ($w_6 = 1$).

### 2.5 Equivalent Pronouns

The pronouns considered as identical were defined based on insights from a French grammar book (Grevisse and Goosse, 2007), which were verified and optimized based on the following quantitative study of observed equivalents.

We built a baseline MT system using Moses (Koehn et al., 2007), and then performed a manual evaluation with 100 randomly selected sentences from the parallel dataset of English-French TED Talks WIT3 (Cettolo et al., 2012), containing the pronouns *it* and *they*. Each translation of pronoun was marked as correct or incorrect. The probability of a correct equivalence of different pronouns is defined as $p(c = 1|t, r)$ where $t$ and $r$ are the candidate and reference pronouns, $r \neq t$, and $c \in \{0, 1\}$ corresponds to the manual evaluation (0 incorrect, 1 correct). First we filtered all pairs $(t, r)$ with a frequency of appearance smaller than 5% of the total sample. Then, we calculated the probability by counting the number of correct samples given a particular pair $(t, r)$. Finally, we selected all pairs where $p(c = 1|t, r) > 0.5$, which indicates that the two pronouns are more likely to be correct translation alternatives than not. The final lists found for French are shown in Table 2. Two examples of pronoun equivalence in English/French translation are: *"it is difficult . . ."* translated to *"il / c' est difficile . . ."*, and *"it would be nice . . ."* to *"ce / ça serait beau . . ."*.

## 3 Experimental Settings

### 3.1 DiscoMT Data Set and Metrics

The data set we use for our experiments was generated during the shared task on pronoun-focused

| Identical | Equivalent |
|---|---|
| *ce, c'* | *ce, il* ($p = 0.6$) |
| *ça, ç', cela* | *ce, ça* ($p = 0.6$) |

Table 2: APT lists of identical and equivalent pronouns in French, constructed from a data set where the translation options for *it* and *they* were limited to *il, elle, ils, elles, ce, on, ça,* and *cela*.

translation at the DiscoMT 2015 workshop (Hardmeier et al., 2015). The systems participating in this task were given 2,093 English sentences to translate into French. The evaluation was focused on the correctness of the translation of the English pronouns *it* and *they* into French. Only a sample of 210 pronouns was manually evaluated for each of the six submitted systems plus a baseline one. The methodology of evaluation was gap-filling annotation: instead of correcting the translation, the annotators were asked to fill the gaps of hidden French candidate sentences with one or more of the following options: *il, elle, ils, elles, ce, on, ça/cela, other* or *bad translation*.

The accuracy of each submitted translation was calculated with respect to the human annotations using several metrics: accuracy with or without the *other* category, pronoun-specific F-scores (harmonic mean of precision and a lenient version of recall), and general F-score (based on micro-averages of pronoun-specific recall and precision). Additional possible metrics are presented hereafter.

### 3.2 Other Metrics for Comparison

We compare the results of APT with two well-known automatic metrics for MT: BLEU (Papineni et al., 2002) and METEOR (Denkowski and Lavie, 2014). Additionally, we include the METEOR score restricted to the French pronouns present in the manual annotation. For this purpose, we set the *function words list* of METEOR to the list of French pronouns defined in DiscoMT (listed above), and its $\delta$ parameter to 0 to give preference to the evaluation of the function words (in our case, pronouns).

Additionally, we include the *AutoP*, *AutoR* and *AutoF* metrics proposed by Hardmeier and Federico (2010) for automatic evaluation of pronoun translation. These metrics were inspired by BLEU score. First, they extracts a list $C$ of all words aligned to the source pronouns from the candidate

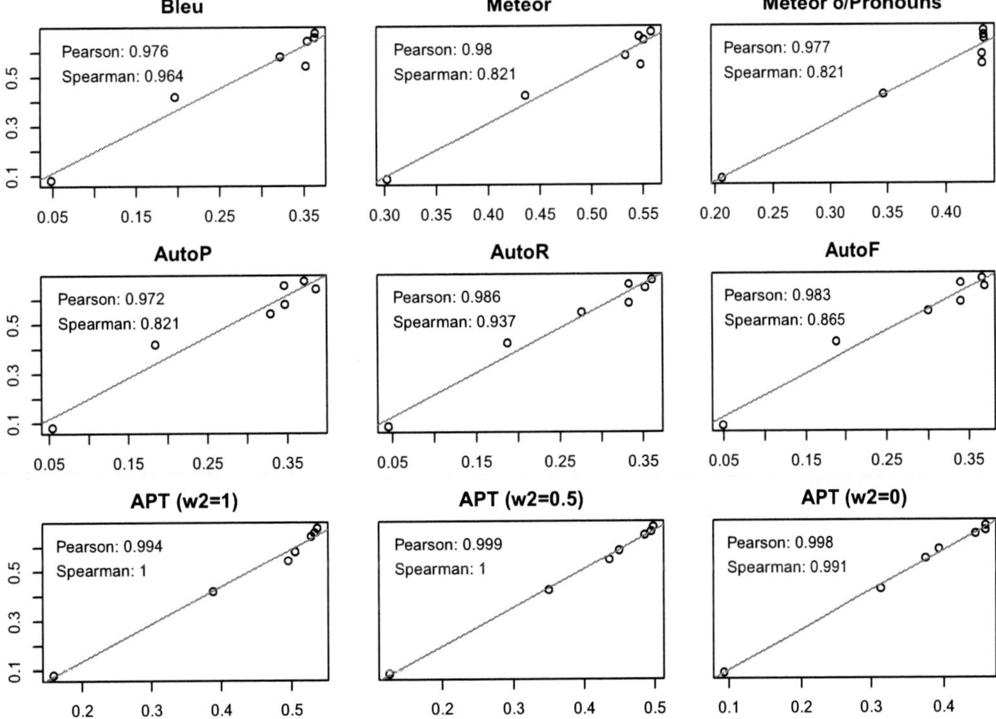

Figure 1: Correlation between the manual evaluation (vertical axis) and different automatic metrics (horizontal axis). The red line is the linear regression model. Pearson's and Spearman's correlations values are showed. The values of APT correspond to the setting: $w_6 = 0$ and $C_d = \{\emptyset\}$ i.e. all cases are counted in the APT score.

text, and similarly a list $R$ from the reference text. Then, they compute a clipped count of a candidate word $w$, defined as the minimum value between the number of times it occurs in $C$ and $R$: $c_{clip}(w) = min(c_{C(w)}, c_{R(w)})$. Finally, all the clipped counts from the words in $C$ are summed up, in order to calculate the precision and recall as follows: $AutoP = \sum_{w \in C} c_{clip}(w)/|C|$ and $AutoR = \sum_{w \in C} c_{clip}(w)/|R|$.

### 3.3 Method for Metric Assessment

We use for the assessment of the correlation between each automatic metric and the human judgments the Pearson and Spearman correlation coefficients. Pearson's correlation coefficient $r$ measures the linear dependency between two variables. The formulation we use for our data is:

$$r = \frac{\sum_{i=1}^{n}(h_i - \bar{h})(a_i - \bar{a})}{\sqrt{\sum_{i=1}^{n}(h_i - \bar{h})^2}\sqrt{\sum_{i=1}^{n}(a_i - \bar{a})^2}}$$

where $\{h_1, .., h_n\}$ and $\{a_1, .., a_n\}$ represent the human and automatic scores for the $n = 7$ systems, and $\bar{h}$ and $\bar{a}$ are the means of those scores.

Spearman's rank correlation coefficient is a non-parametric measure of the possibility to express the relation between two variables as a monotonic function. In contrast to Pearson's correlation coefficient, it does not measure to what extent the metrics are linearly dependent, but compares only the rankings resulting from each metric. The formulation we use is the same as for $r$ where we replaced $\{h_1, .., h_n\}$, $\{a_1, .., a_n\}$, $\bar{h}$ and $\bar{a}$ with the rankings given by the human and automatic metrics and their means.

In the pronoun-focused translation shared task at DiscoMT 2015 (Hardmeier et al., 2015), three different human evaluation metrics were used: accuracy including the category *others*, accuracy without *others*, and precision. The organizers selected the first one for the official ranking of the systems, because it allows evaluating the whole sample, and penalizes MT systems that tend to classify many difficult cases as *others*. Therefore, we also use this metric in our correlation experiments hereafter.

## 4   Results of the Experiments

### 4.1   Comparison of Correlation Coefficients

Figure 1 shows the correlations of several automatic metrics with the human evaluation scores (i.e. accuracy with *other*, the official DiscoMT 2015 shared task metric): three versions of APT (at the bottom, with $w_2 \in \{0, 0.5, 1\}$), and six previous metrics: BLEU, METEOR (general and restricted to pronouns), and recall/precision/F-score from Hardmeier and Federico (2010). The plots display the values of Pearson's and Spearman's correlation coefficients and the linear regression model fitted for the first coefficient.

For all automatic metrics, Pearson's correlation is over 0.97, which is a rather high value. METEOR has the lowest Spearman correlation, and contrary to what we expected, METEOR evaluated only over pronouns does not perform better than its generic version. Although BLEU and METEOR are not specialized for the evaluation of pronouns, their Pearson's correlation with human judgments is quite high. These values should be considered as lower bounds when studying metrics dedicated to pronouns. Another interpretation of the high correlations of BLEU and METEOR with human judgments of pronouns is that MT systems which are good at translation in general, are also good at translating pronouns.

The performance of the metric proposed by Hardmeier and Federico (2010) is better than that of the generic metrics, especially for its recall *AutoR*. Therefore, this specific metric appears to model better the human evaluation for this particular task.

As shown in the lowest row of Figure 1, the three tested versions of APT have the best performance, regardless of the weight $w_2$ given to case 2 occurrences, namely "equivalent" pronouns. If data for metric tuning were available, we could actually tune $w_2$ to reach optimal scores on tuning data. However, this not being available, we show here that several assumptions on the weights outperform the other metrics in terms of correlation with human judgments.

Finally, one can argue that the linear correlation between the manual evaluation and the dif-

ferent metrics is inflated because we included an obvious outlier system. This system, coded 'A3-108' in Hardmeier et al. (2015), shows a markedly poor performance at predicting pronouns with respect to the other systems. Thus, we also present the correlation values without the outlier, in Table 3, and observe that in comparison with the values shown in Figure 1, APT remains almost the same while the correlation of the other metrics have a small degradation. Therefore, our conclusions hold regardless of the outlier system.

|           | **Bleu** | **Meteor** | **Meteor o/Pron.** |
|-----------|----------|------------|--------------------|
| Pearson   | 0.902    | 0.893      | 0.863              |
| Spearman  | 0.943    | 0.714      | 0.714              |
|           | **AutoP** | **AutoR** | **AutoF** |
| Pearson   | 0.923    | 0.965      | 0.955              |
| Spearman  | 0.714    | 0.919      | 0.804              |
|           | **APT** $(w_2 = 1)$ | **APT** $(w_2 = 0.5)$ | **APT** $(w_2 = 0)$ |
| Pearson   | 0.994    | 0.999      | 0.998              |
| Spearman  | 1.000    | 1.000      | 0.989              |

Table 3: Correlation between the manual evaluation and different automatic metrics without the outlier system. The values of APT are obtained with $w_6 = 0$ and $C_d = \{\emptyset\}$, i.e. all cases are counted in the APT score.

### 4.2   Role of APT Weights for Cases 2 and 6

Table 4 shows the correlation values between APT and other metrics for different values of the weights of cases 2 and 6, with two alignment options. When applying APT with the basic alignment method, always considering equivalent pronouns (case 2) as incorrect translations $w_2 = 0$ has better performance than considering them as partially incorrect $w_2 = 0.5$ or totally correct $w_2 = 1$. The same observation can be made for the weight of case 6, i.e. when considering missing pronoun pairs as correct or not.

Nevertheless, the situation changes when applying APT with the heuristics for pronoun alignment described above. Here, the partially correct scenarios present better performance than the others. There is a balanced percentage of correct and incorrect samples for case 2 (as seen in Table 5, with heuristic-based alignment), which could explain why $w_2 = 0.5$ leads to a slightly better correlation than other values. On the contrary, all occurrences in case 6 are found to be incorrect according to the manual evaluation. Although this could lead us to set $w_6 = 0$, this does not lead to the best correlation value; a possible explanation is the fact that all MT systems are compared against the same reference.

In general, the differences among each configuration are too small to lead to firm conclusions about the weights. If more data with human judgments were available, then the weights could be optimized on such a set.

|  | $w_2$ | $w_6$ | Pearson | Spearman |
|---|---|---|---|---|
| | 0 | 0 | **0.999** | **1.000** |
| Basic | 1 | 0 | 0.992 | 0.987 |
| alignment | 0.5 | 0 | 0.998 | 1.000 |
| | 1 | 1 | 0.994 | 0.964 |
| | 0.5 | 0.5 | 0.999 | 0.987 |
| | 0 | 0 | 0.998 | 0.989 |
| Alignment | 1 | 0 | 0.994 | 1.000 |
| with | 0.5 | 0 | **0.999** | **1.000** |
| heuristics | 1 | 1 | 0.995 | 0.964 |
| | 0.5 | 0.5 | **0.999** | **1.000** |

Table 4: Correlation between the manual evaluation and APT scores for different values of the parameters of APT, namely the $w_2$ and $w_6$ weights of cases 2 and 6.

### 4.3 Analysis of APT Scores

Figure 2 shows the distribution of cases identified by APT. Most of the samples are identified as case 1 (equal to reference) or case 3 (different from it). This indicates that most candidate translations are either correct or incorrect, and that the number of missing pronouns (on either sides) is much smaller.

Moreover, the heuristics for pronoun alignment help to reduce the number of reference misaligned pronouns (mainly cases 5 and 6, but not exclusively). As a result, when comparing the reference and the manual annotation, the proportion of perfect matches increases from 61% to 66% after applying the heuristics.

Table 5 shows a breakdown of the comparison between APT scores and manual evaluation into the six different cases. The result of the comparison is: *Correct* when the manual annotator's choice of pronoun coincides with the system's translation; *Incorrect* when it doesn't coincide; and *Bad Translation* when the annotator indicated that the entire sentence is poorly translated and the pronoun cannot be scored. Table 5 provides the total number of judgments for the six systems and the baseline.

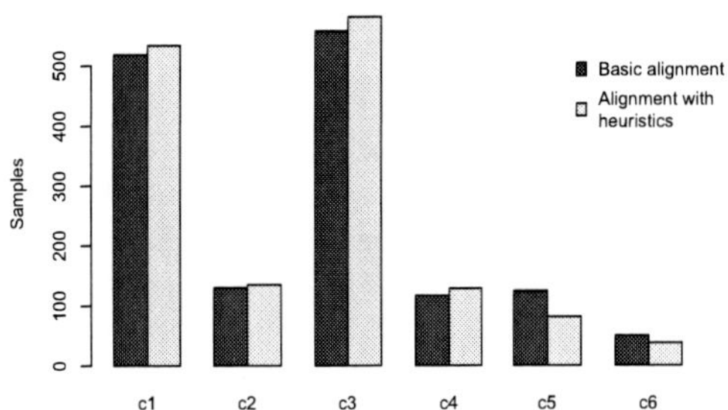


Figure 2: Distribution of pronoun occurrences in each of APT's six cases, with and without heuristics for alignment.

| Cases | Manual Evaluation | | | |
|---|---|---|---|---|
| | Correct | Incorr. | Bad Tr. | Total |
| $c1$ (same) | **84%** | 13% | 3% | 534 |
| $c2$ (similar) | **43%** | 47% | 10% | 135 |
| $c3$ (different) | 26% | **60%** | 14% | 581 |
| $c4$ (not in cand.) | 0% | **76%** | 24% | 129 |
| $c5$ (not in ref.) | 53% | **36%** | 11% | 81 |
| $c6$ (not in both) | 0% | **76%** | 24% | 38 |
| Total | 47% | 43% | 10% | 1498 |

Table 5: Comparison between APT and the manual evaluation for each case identified by APT.

We observe that 84% of the instances in case 1 (candidate identical to reference) are considered correct, which is a fairly large proportion. Conversely, for case 3 (different pronouns) and case 4 (candidate translation not found), a vast majority of occurrences were indeed judged as incorrect, although a sizable 26% of case 3 occurrences were considered as correct translations by the annotator – presumably due to legitimate variations which cannot be captured by a reference-based metric such as APT.

As for case 2 ("equivalent" translations), the percentages of actually correct vs. incorrect translations are quite balanced. This indicates that the definition of equivalent pronouns is quite problematic, as there are equal chances that "equivalent" pronouns are actually substitutable or not.

Another direction for improvement are the cases with no reference pronoun to which to compare a candidate: 53% of occurrences in case 5 are considered correct by humans, but APT cannot evaluate them correctly for lack of a comparison term. These cases could be discarded for APT evaluation, but if the goal is to compare several systems with the same reference, they will all be equally penalized by these cases.

## 5 Conclusion

In this paper, we have shown that a simple reference-based metric for the accuracy of pronoun translation (APT) had a high correlation with human judgments of correctness, over the scores of seven systems submitted to the DiscoMT 2015 shared task on pronoun-focused translation. While intrinsically the APT metric seems to set strong constraints on the correctness of the pronouns, when averaged over a large number of translations, it appears that improved APT scores reflect quite accurately an improvement in the human perception of pronoun translation quality. A precise alignment of source and target pronouns, for the reference and the candidate translations, appears to be an essential requirement for the accuracy of APT, and should be improved in the future. Similarly, a better understanding of "equivalent" pronouns and their proper weighing in the APT score should improve the quality of the metric, as well as better models of omitting pronouns in translation.

APT has been used for evaluating Spanish-to-English pronoun translation (Rios Gonzales and Tuggener, 2017; Luong et al., 2017; Miculicich Werlen and Popescu-Belis, 2017), showing that it can be adapted to other language pairs.

While it is not likely that large shared tasks such as the WMT Metrics Task (Stanojević et al., 2015) can be designed for assessing pronoun evaluation metrics only, we believe that, in the future, the availability of larger amounts of human ratings from new shared tasks on pronoun translation will offer new opportunities to confirm the accuracy of APT and possibly to tune its parameters for an even increased correlation.

## Acknowledgments

We are grateful for support to the Swiss National Science Foundation (SNSF) under the Sinergia MODERN project (grant n. 147653, see `www.idiap.ch/project/modern/`) and to the European Union under the Horizon 2020 SUMMA project (grant n. 688139, see `www.summa-project.eu`). We thank the DiscoMT anonymous reviewers for their helpful suggestions.

## References

Mauro Cettolo, Christian Girardi, and Marcello Federico. 2012. WIT$^3$: Web inventory of transcribed and translated talks. In *Proceedings of the 16$^{th}$ Conference of the European Association for Machine Translation (EAMT)*. Trento, Italy, pages 261–268.

Michael Denkowski and Alon Lavie. 2014. Meteor universal: Language specific translation evaluation for any target language. In *Proceedings of the 9th Workshop on Statistical Machine Translation (WMT)*. Baltimore, MD.

Maurice Grevisse and André Goosse. 2007. *Le bon usage et son édition Internet*. Grevisse de la langue française. De Boeck Supérieur, Louvain-la-Neuve.

Liane Guillou. 2016. *Incorporating Pronoun Function into Statistical Machine Translation*. PhD thesis, University of Edinburgh, UK.

Liane Guillou, Christian Hardmeier, Preslav Nakov, Sara Stymne, Jörg Tiedemann, Yannick Versley, Mauro Cettolo, Bonnie Webber, and Andrei Popescu-Belis. 2016. Findings of the 2016 WMT shared task on cross-lingual pronoun prediction. In *Proceedings of the First Conference on Machine Translation*. Association for Computational Linguistics, Berlin, Germany, pages 525–542.

Najeh Hajlaoui and Andrei Popescu-Belis. 2013. Assessing the accuracy of discourse connective translations: Validation of an automatic metric. In *Proceedings of Computational Linguistics and Intelligent Text Processing (CICLing)*, Springer-Verlag, LNCS 7817, Samos, Greece, pages 236–247.

Christian Hardmeier. 2014. *Discourse in Statistical Machine Translation*. PhD thesis, Uppsala University, Sweden.

Christian Hardmeier and Marcello Federico. 2010. Modelling pronominal anaphora in statistical machine translation. In *Proceedings of the International Workshop on Spoken Language Translation (IWSLT)*. Paris, France, pages 283–289.

Christian Hardmeier, Preslav Nakov, Sara Stymne, Jörg Tiedemann, Yannick Versley, and Mauro Cettolo. 2015. Pronoun-focused MT and cross-lingual pronoun prediction: Findings of the 2015 DiscoMT shared task on pronoun translation. In *Proceedings of the 2nd Workshop on Discourse in Machine Translation (DiscoMT)*. Lisbon, Portugal, pages 1–16.

Philipp Koehn, Hieu Hoang, Alexandra Birch, Chris Callison-Burch, Marcello Federico, Nicola Bertoldi, Brooke Cowan, Wade Shen, Christine Moran, Richard Zens, et al. 2007. Moses: Open source toolkit for statistical machine translation. In *Proceedings of the 45th Annual Meeting of the ACL on Interactive Poster and Demonstration Sessions*. Association for Computational Linguistics, pages 177–180.

Sharid Loáiciga, Sara Stymne, Preslav Nakov, Christian Hardmeier, Jörg Tiedemann, Mauro Cettolo, and Yannick Versley. 2017. Findings of the 2017 DiscoMT shared task on cross-lingual pronoun prediction. In *Proceedings of the 3rd Workshop on Discourse in Machine Translation (DiscoMT)*. Copenhagen, Denmark.

Ngoc Quang Luong, Andrei Popescu-Belis, Annette Rios Gonzales, and Don Tuggener. 2017. Machine translation of spanish personal and possessive pronouns using anaphora probabilities. In *Proceedings of the 15th Conference of the European Chapter of the Association for Computational Linguistics: Volume 2, Short Papers*. Association for Computational Linguistics, Valencia, Spain, pages 631–636.

Lesly Miculicich Werlen and Andrei Popescu-Belis. 2017. Using coreference links to improve spanish-to-english machine translation. In *Proceedings of the 2nd Workshop on Coreference Resolution Beyond OntoNotes (CORBON 2017)*. Association for Computational Linguistics, Valencia, Spain, pages 30–40.

Ruslan Mitkov. 2002. *Anaphora Resolution*. Longman, London, UK.

Franz Josef Och and Hermann Ney. 2003. A systematic comparison of various statistical alignment models. *Computational Linguistics* 29(1):19–51.

Kishore Papineni, Salim Roukos, Todd Ward, and Wei-Jing Zhu. 2002. BLEU: a method for automatic evaluation of machine translation. In *Proceedings of the 40th Annual Meeting of the Association for Computational Linguistics (ACL)*. Philadelphia, PA, pages 311–318.

Annette Rios Gonzales and Don Tuggener. 2017. Coreference resolution of elided subjects and possessive pronouns in spanish-english statistical machine translation. In *Proceedings of the 15th Conference of the European Chapter of the Association for Computational Linguistics: Volume 2, Short Papers*. Association for Computational Linguistics, Valencia, Spain, pages 657–662.

Miloš Stanojević, Amir Kamran, Philipp Koehn, and Ondřej Bojar. 2015. Results of the WMT15 metrics shared task. In *Proceedings of the Tenth Workshop on Statistical Machine Translation (WMT)*. Lisbon, Portugal, pages 256–273.

# Using a Graph-based Coherence Model in
# Document-Level Machine Translation


**Leo Born[†], Mohsen Mesgar[‡]** and **Michael Strube[‡]**
† Department of Computational Linguistics, Heidelberg University
Heidelberg, Germany
`born@cl.uni-heidelberg.de`

‡ Heidelberg Institute for Theoretical Studies gGmbH
Heidelberg, Germany
`(mohsen.mesgar|michael.strube)@h-its.org`



## Abstract

Although coherence is an important aspect of any text generation system, it has received little attention in the context of machine translation (MT) so far. We hypothesize that the quality of document-level translation can be improved if MT models take into account the semantic relations among sentences during translation. We integrate the graph-based coherence model proposed by Mesgar and Strube (2016) with Docent[1] (Hardmeier et al., 2012; Hardmeier, 2014) a document-level machine translation system. The application of this graph-based coherence modeling approach is novel in the context of machine translation. We evaluate the coherence model and its effects on the quality of the machine translation. The result of our experiments shows that our coherence model slightly improves the quality of translation in terms of the average Meteor score.


## 1 Introduction

Coherence represents semantic connectivity of texts with regard to grammatical and lexical relations between sentences. It is an essential part of natural texts and important in establishing structure and meaning of documents as a whole.

It is crucial for any text generation system to generate coherent texts. For instance in real machine translation systems, we desire to translate a document, which consists of several sentences, from a source language to a target language. Current machine translation systems (as an instance of text generation systems) mostly focus on the sentence-level translation. Indeed, the state-of-the-art machine translation models perform well on sentence-level translation (Bahdanau et al., 2015; Sennrich et al., 2017). However, it is insufficient to just sequentially and independently translate sentences of the source document and concatenate them as the translated version. The translated sentences should be coherently connected to each other in the target document as well.

From a linguistic point of view also the discourse-wide context must be taken into account to have a high-quality translation (Hatim and Mason, 1990; Hardmeier et al., 2012). The current paradigm of machine translation needs to be improved as it does not consider any discourse coherence phenomena that establish a text's connectedness (Sim Smith et al., 2015).

One of the active research topics in modeling coherence focuses on entity connections over sentences based on Centering Theory (Grosz et al., 1995). Previous research on coherence modeling shows its application mainly in readability assessment (Barzilay and Lapata, 2008; Pitler and Nenkova, 2008). Recently, Parveen et al. (2016) showed that the graph-based coherence model can be utilized to generate more coherent summaries of scientific articles.

The main goal of this paper is to integrate coherence features with a statistical machine translation system to improve the quality of the output translation. To achieve this goal, we combine the graph-based coherence representation by Guinaudeau and Strube (2013) and its extensions (Mesgar and Strube, 2015, 2016) into the document-level machine translation decoder *Docent* (Hardmeier et al., 2012, 2013).

*Docent* defines an initial translation of the source document and modifies the translation of sentences aiming to maximize an objective function. This function measures the quality of the

---

[1]https://github.com/chardmeier/docent




*Proceedings of the Third Workshop on Discourse in Machine Translation*, pages 26–35,
Copenhagen, Denmark, September 8, 2017. ©2017 Association for Computational Linguistics.

**S1:** But the noise didn't disappear.

**S2:** The mysterious noise that Penzias and Wilson were listening to turned out to be the oldest and most significant sound that anyone had ever heard.

**S3:** It was cosmic radiation left over from the very birth of the universe.

**S4:** This was the first experimental evidence that the Big Bang existed and the universe was born at a precise moment some 14.7 billion years ago.

**S5:** So our story ends at the beginning – the beginning of all things, the Big Bang.

Table 1: Excerpt of a TED talk (ID: 1177) from the DiscoMT 2015 training data.

translated document after each modification. We propose to update the objective function of Docent such that it takes into account the coherence of the translated document too. We quantify the coherence level of the translated document using graph-based coherence features. We show that integrating coherence features improves the quality of the translation in terms of the Meteor score.

We start with the relevant background literature (Section 2). We then describe the graph-based coherence model and how we integrate its coherence features with Docent (Section 3). Section 4 outlines the datasets and the experimental setup. We discuss results in Section 5. Conclusions and possible future work are in Section 6.

## 2 Related Work

### 2.1 Entity Graph

Guinaudeau and Strube (2013) present a graph-based version of the entity grid (Barzilay and Lapata, 2008). It models the interaction between entities and sentences as a bipartite graph. In this representation, one set of nodes corresponds to sentences, whereas the other set of nodes corresponds to entities in a document. Table 1 shows a sample text from our training data and Figure 1 the bipartite entity-graph representation of it.

Coherence is measured over the one-mode projection on sentence nodes. The one-mode projection is the graph in which the sentence nodes are connected to each other if and only if they have at least one entity in common (see Figure 2). The coherence of a text $T$ can then be measured by computing the average outdegree of the projection graph. Outdegree of a node is the number of edges that leave the node. The average outdegree is the sum of outdegree of all nodes in the one-mode pro-

jection graph divided by the number of sentences.

Mesgar and Strube (2015) evaluate this model for readability assessment. They show that the average outdegree is not the best choice for quantifying the coherence. They propose to encode coherence as the connectivity structure of sentence nodes in a projection graph. So they represent the connections among sentences of each document in the corpus with its projection graph; then they mine all possible subgraphs of these graphs. These subgraphs resemble what the linguistic literature terms *thematic progression* (Daneš, 1974) as subgraphs represent connections between sentences following a certain pattern. Mesgar and Strube (2015) call these subgraphs *coherence patterns*. The connectivity structure of a projection graph can be modeled by the frequency of subgraphs in each graph. These frequencies are called *coherence features*. Mesgar and Strube (2015) show that these coherence features, obtained from frequency of subgraphs of projection graphs of the entity graphs, can assess readability better. Figure 3 illustrates four possible subgraphs with three nodes. The pool of possible subgraphs can be expanded to encompass any arbitrary number of nodes, so-called $k$-node subgraphs.

Mesgar and Strube (2016) extend the entity graph to the lexical graph: two sentences may be semantically connected because at least two words of them are semantically associated to each other. They compute semantic relatedness between all content word pairs using *GloVe* word embeddings (Pennington et al., 2014). If there is a word pair whose word vectors have a cosine relatedness greater than a threshold, two sentences are considered to be connected. They quantify the coherence of texts via frequency of subgraphs of the lexical graphs. It outperforms the entity graph coherence model on readability assessment.

Parveen et al. (2016) show that coherence patterns can be mined from a corpus and those can get weighted based on their frequencies in the corpus. They use the extracted coherence patterns and their weights to generate a coherent summary from scientific documents. Using a human evaluation, they show that coherence patterns are more powerful than average outdegree to encode coherence for automatic summarization.

Here we check if these coherence features (i.e., average outdegree and frequency of coherence patterns) of graph-based models can assist

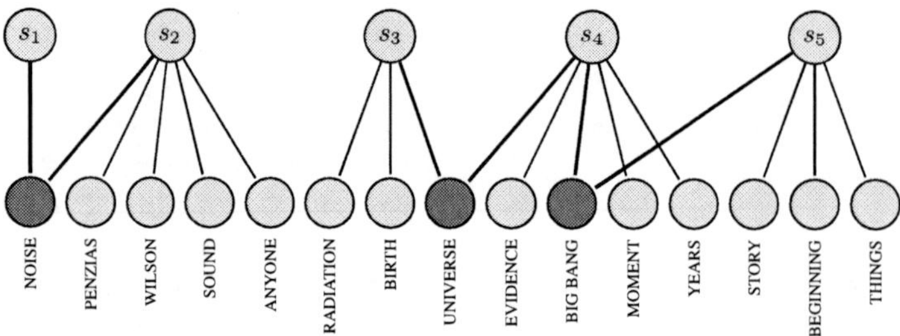

Figure 1: The entity graph representation of the text in Table 1. Dark entities are shared by the sentences.

Figure 2: Unweighted projection graph of the entity graph in Figure 1. The nodes are connected based on whether sentences share an entity or not, whereas the edge direction follows sentence order.

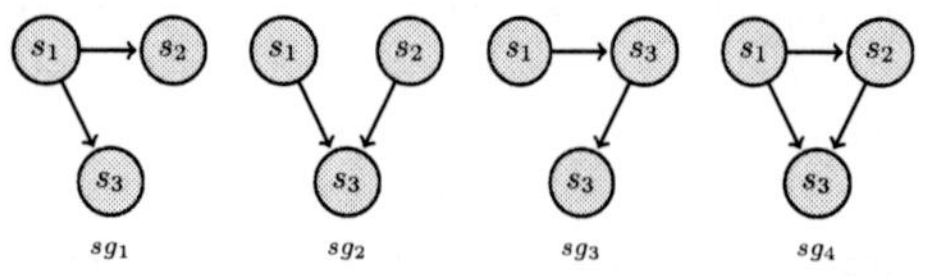

Figure 3: All possible directed 3-node subgraphs. The edge directions indicate the order of sentences in the text.

document-level machine translation as another, and more difficult, text generation system. We can also evaluate which feature is more beneficial for machine translation.

### 2.2 Coherence in Machine Translation

Coherence modeling in machine translation is an (almost) desideratum . To the best of our knowledge, there are only a handful of publications in this direction. The one relevant to our approach is the work by Lin et al. (2015) as it constitutes an application of a coherence model in the context of machine translation, as opposed to more theoretical papers on the state of coherence in machine translation (Sim Smith et al., 2016).

Lin et al. (2015) develop a sentence-level Recurrent Neural Network Language Model (RNNLM) that takes a sentence as input and tries to predict the next one based on the sentence history vector. By modeling sequences of sentences, the vector is able to model local coherence within RNNLM.[2] Given the 10-best results of all sen-

tences from the decoder, their system then selects the best translation for the first sentence. Given that translation, they score all translation candidates of the second sentence based on coherence and select the best one. They repeat this for all sentences in the document.

This approach, however, can be considered linguistically weak as it only measures coherence after the translation and does not consider it as a part of the text generation process. As coherence, however, is a fundamental need for any text generation system (Barzilay and Lapata, 2008), this motivates us to go beyond a simple re-ranking approach and integrate the coherence measure directly into the decoding process of machine translation.

## 3 Method

### 3.1 Docent

We use *Docent* (Hardmeier et al., 2012, 2013) as the baseline. It explicitly has no notion of coherence. Docent is a document-level decoder that treats a translation not as a bag of sentences but instead has a translation hypothesis for the whole document at each step. The initial hypothesis can either be generated randomly from the translation table or it can be initialized with the result of any standard sentence-level decoder such as Moses (Koehn et al., 2007).

Docent first independently translates all sentences of the input document. Then it starts to modify the translation of sentences with respect to the other translated sentences. Three basic operations modify the translation of sentences: *change-phrase-translation*, *swap-phrases*, and *resegment*. *Change-phrase-translations* replaces the translation of a single phrase with a random translation for the same source phrase. *Swap-phrases* changes the word order without affecting the phrase translations by exchanging two phrases in a sentence.

---

[2]They consider the "log probability of a given document as its coherence score" (Lin et al., 2015).

The third operation, *resegment*, is able to generate from a number of phrases a new set of phrases covering the same span. Docent checks the quality of the modified translation by an objective function that takes the modified translation of the document (the so-called state of the translated document) as its input and maps it to a real number. If the value of the objective function increases then Docent accepts the applied operation.

The main advantage of Docent is that the objective function can be defined over the whole document (Hardmeier et al., 2012). This allows us to integrate our new document-level coherence features with Docent. More formally, the overall document state $S$ is modeled as a sequence of sentence states:

$$S = S_1 S_2 ... S_N, \tag{1}$$

where $N$ is the number of sentences and $S_i$ is the translation (hypothesis) of the $i^{th}$ source sentence. A scoring function $f(S)$ maps a state to a real number. The scoring function can be further decomposed into a linear combination of $K$ feature functions $h_k(S)$, each with a constant weight $\lambda_k$, such that

$$f(S) = \sum_{k=1}^{K} \lambda_k h_k(S). \tag{2}$$

Docent uses *simulated annealing*, a stochastic variant of the hill climbing algorithm (Khachaturyan et al., 1981), for either accepting or rejecting operations for maximizing its objective function (Hardmeier, 2012) .

Docent already implements some sentence-local feature models that are similar to those found in traditional sentence-level decoders. These include phrase translation scores provided by the phrase table (Koehn et al., 2003), $n$-gram language model scores implemented with *KenLM* (Heafield, 2011), a word penalty score, and an unlexicalised distortion cost model with geometric decay (Koehn et al., 2003).

Our idea is to add a new document-level coherence function $h_{coh}(S)$, namely a graph-based coherence model to the objective function represented in Equation. 2. In the next subsection, we describe this model in more detail.

## 3.2 Graph-based Coherence Model

Our coherence model is based on the lexical graph representation (Mesgar and Strube, 2016). For any given document, we first filter out stop words using the provided stop word list by Salton (1971).

Then, we calculate the cosine relatedness of all remaining word pairs of all sentence pairs using the 840 billion token pre-trained word embeddings of *GloVe* (Pennington et al., 2014). For every out-of-vocabulary word, we assign a random 300-dimensional vector that is memorized for its next occurrence. Based on this, we represent the lexical relations among sentences via graphs. If at least two words in the sentences are related, we choose the relation between those two words whose embeddings have the maximum cosine value. In order to make the graph not too dense, we filter out those edges whose strengths are below a certain threshold.

However, in contrast to Mesgar and Strube (2016), we use a different threshold for graph construction. They use a threshold of 0.9, but we find this too strict on allowing the graph structure to change in the direction of more coherent texts. We choose a lower threshold, 0.85, to let the model consider more connections and more lexical variations (i.e., synonyms) in the translation.

We encode coherence by frequency of coherence patterns in these graphs.

## 3.3 Integrating the Coherence Model With Docent

For extracting coherence patterns we use the target documents[3] of the training set of the DiscoMT dataset. We extract all $k$-node subgraphs for $k \in \{3, 4, 5\}$. We limit the size of subgraphs to 3-, 4-, and 5-node as Mesgar and Strube (2016) report declining results for subgraphs with $k > 5$.

We also calculate a respective weight for each pattern from lexical graph representations of DiscoMT training target documents.

We base our coherence patterns on the characteristics of the target language as there is a theory within Translation Studies that "textual relations obtaining in the original are often modified [...] in favour of (more) habitual options offered by a target culture" (Toury, 1995). Toury (1995) calls this the *law of growing standardization* which seeks to describe and explain the acceptability of the translation in the receiving culture (Venuti, 2004). This law seems suitable in the context of subgraph mining as it is also already reflected in the language model of any MT system (Lembersky et al., 2012).

For computing the weights of subgraphs, we divide the count of each $k$-node subgraph by the to-

---

[3] We experiment on translation from French to English.

tal counts of subgraphs for that $k$. For each $k$, this gives the following vector:

$$\varphi(sg^k, G) = (w(sg_1^k, G), ..., w(sg_m^k, G)), \quad (3)$$

where formally

$$w(sg_i^k, G) = \frac{count(sg_i^k, G)}{\sum_{sg_j^k \in (sg_1^k, ..., sg_m^k)} count(sg_j^k, G)}. \quad (4)$$

These weights are then used as weights of coherence features in the coherence function, $h_{coh}(S)$, that quantifies the connectivity structure of sentences of an intermediate state of the translated document in Docent during evaluation on the test set of DiscoMT.

So, given the coherence graph representation of an intermediate state of the translated document (during the test phase), $G_S$, and the set of all extracted subgraphs of the training documents, $FSG = \{sg_1^k, sg_2^k, ..., sg_m^k\}$ where $k \in \{3, 4, 5\}$, and their weights, $h_{coh}(S)$ is defined as follow:

$$h_{coh}(S) = \sum_{sg_i^k \in FSG} count(sg_i^k, G_S) \cdot w(sg_i^k). \quad (5)$$

We use this score – which multiplies the frequency of each subgraph in each state (coherence feature) of the translated document with its weight according to its frequency in the training documents and sums this up for all subgraphs – as our feature model score of our coherence model.

## 4 Experiments

### 4.1 Datasets

We use the WMT 2015 (Bojar et al., 2015) dataset for training and development of the sentence-level translation and language models[4], and the DiscoMT 2015 Shared Task (Hardmeier et al., 2015) dataset for mining subgraphs (coherence patterns) and as our test data (Table 2). We run experiments on the language pair French-English. Coherence patterns are extracted from the 1551 DiscoMT *training* documents using *GloVe* word embeddings. We extract all $k$-node subgraphs for $k \in \{3, 4, 5\}$ using *GASTON*[5] (Nijssen and Kok, 2004, 2005).

---

[4]We use Moses to translate sentences independently and initialize the translation state in Docent.

[5]`http://liacs.leidenuniv.nl/~nijssensgr/gaston/iccs.html`.

We use the twelve test documents of DiscoMT as the test data because these are much longer, on the document level, than the WMT test data. The average number of sentences of the WMT test data is 20, whereas for DiscoMT it is 174 sentences. Thus it is a more difficult test set for our experiments.

|  | train | dev | test |
|---|---|---|---|
| # of docs | - | - | 12 |
| # of sent. | 200,239 | 3,003 | 2,093 |
| avg. # of sent. per doc | - | - | 174 |
| # of tokens | 4,458,256 | 63,778 | 48,122 |

Table 2: Statistics on the datasets used. *train* is the news commentary v10 corpus, *dev* is the 2012 newstest development data, and *test* is the DiscoMT 2015 test data. The number (#) of tokens corresponds to the English (target) side.

### 4.2 Experimental Setup

We train our systems using the *Moses* decoder (Koehn et al., 2007). After standard preprocessing of the data, we train a 3-gram language model using *KenLM* (Heafield, 2011). We use the *MGIZA++* (Gao and Vogel, 2008) word aligner and employ standard *grow-diag-fast-and* symmetrization. Tuning is done on the development data via *minimum error rate training* (Och, 2003).

After training the language model and creating the phrase table with Moses, we use these to initialize our translation systems. We use the *lcurve-docent* binary of Docent, which outputs Docent's learning curve, i.e., files for the intermediate decoding states. This additionally allows us to investigate the learning curves with regard to how our coherence feature behaves over time.

We prune the translation table by only retaining all phrase translations with a probability greater than 0.0001 during training. In our configuration file for Docent, we set to use the simulated annealing algorithm with a maximum number of 16,384 steps[6] and the following features: *geometric distortion model, word penalty cost, OOV-penalty cost, phrase table*, and the *3-gram language model*.

---

[6]We choose this threshold to make a balance between processing time and translation performance.

### 4.3 Evaluation Metrics

We follow the standard machine translation procedure of evaluation, measuring *BLEU* (Papineni et al., 2002) for every system. BLEU is an *n*-gram based co-occurrence metric that operates with modified *n*-gram precision scores. The document *n*-gram precision scores are averaged using the geometric mean of these scores with *n*-grams up to length $N$ and positive weights summing to one. The result is multiplied by an exponential *brevity penalty factor* that penalizes a translation if it does not match the reference translations in length, word choice, and word order.

We also calculate *Meteor* (Lavie et al., 2004; Denkowski and Lavie, 2014) as it is a widely used evaluation metric as well. In contrast to BLEU, Meteor is a word-based metric that takes recall into account as well. Meteor creates a word alignment between a pair of strings that is incrementally produced using a sequence of various word-mapping modules, including the *exact* module, the *Porter stem* module, and the *WordNet synonymy* module (Lavie and Agarwal, 2007).

Because Meteor has been shown to have a higher correlation with human judgements than BLEU (Lavie et al., 2004), it is a useful alternative evaluation metric for our purposes. As it also considers stemmed words and information from WordNet to determine synonymous words between a candidate and a reference translation, the metric is interesting with regard to surface variation with the same semantic content and how this affects the evaluation of our coherence model (as its graph construction is semantically grounded).

## 5 Results

### 5.1 Mined Coherence Patterns Analysis

We represent each English document of the training set of the DiscoMT dataset by a graph (as described in Section 3.2). As a result, instead of a set of documents we have a set of graphs. Then we extract all occurring subgraphs in these graphs as coherence patterns. We mine subgraphs with $3, 4, 5$ nodes.

All 3-node subgraphs exist in the graph representation of the training documents. It is because these subgraph are small and it is very likely that they occur in the graph representation of the large DiscoMT documents.

The mined 4-node subgraphs are shown in Figure 4. Although the frequency of these patterns

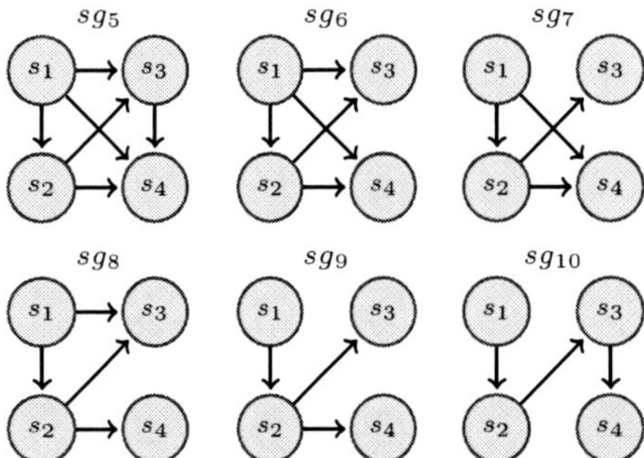

Figure 4: The mined 4-node subgraphs.

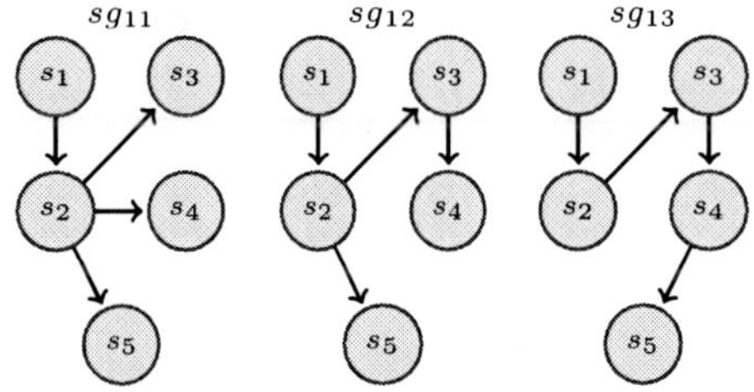

Figure 5: The mined 5-node subgraphs.

encode coherence in our model, the existence of these patterns can be linguistically interpreted too. For example, $sg_{10}$ models the smooth shift in the topic of a sequence of sentences (Mesgar and Strube, 2015). The rest of the patterns have a common property: a sentence introduces some topic and the following sentences are about this topic. For instance, in $sg_6$, topics in the first sentence are developed by the rest of the sentences.

The mined 5-node subgraphs are shown in Figure 5. The expansion of a topic is much clearer here in $sg_{11}$. The subgraph $sg_{13}$ is very similar to $sg_{10}$ following the notion of the topic shift. This is somehow expected because the DiscoMT documents are obtained from TED talks. These talks are mostly given by professional speakers. They have to move smoothly from one topic to the next topic in a short sequence of sentences. This confirms the existence of the linear chain pattern in the 4-node and 5-node patterns.

We analyze the change of the frequencies of the subgraphs during the MT decoding phase. For example, on document 9 the subgraph $sg_1$ of the 3-node subgraphs occurs one more time in the CM model. It is worthwhile to note that the increase of the frequency of $sg_1$ is compatible with its positive correlation with readability scores of documents

| Document ID | BLEU (BL) | BLEU (CM) | Meteor (BL) | Meteor (CM) |
|---|---|---|---|---|
| (#1) 1756 | 21.87 | **21.93** | 61.47 | **61.52** |
| (#2) 1819 | 16.49 | 16.49 | 62.25 | 62.25 |
| (#3) 1825 | 24.86 | 24.86 | **66.34** | 66.32 |
| (#4) 1894 | 17.08 | 17.08 | 57.20 | 57.20 |
| (#5) 1935 | 20.11 | 20.11 | 62.83 | 62.83 |
| (#6) 1938 | **20.43** | 20.41 | **63.53** | 63.48 |
| (#7) 1950 | **23.27** | 23.26 | **63.48** | 63.46 |
| (#8) 1953 | **20.78** | 20.66 | **61.65** | 61.64 |
| (#9) 1979 | 15.25 | **15.26** | 55.68 | **55.69** |
| (#10) 2043 | 18.27 | 18.27 | 56.42 | **56.47** |
| (#11) 2053 | 30.65 | 30.65 | 69.13 | 69.13 |
| (#12) 205 | 13.79 | 13.79 | 52.68 | 52.68 |
| Average | **20.24** | 20.23 | 61.01 | **61.06** |

Table 3: Results of the coherence model (*CM*) compared to the baseline (*BL*) on the DiscoMT test set (highest values are marked in bold). The scores of the entity graph model using average outdegree as coherence feature are identical to the baseline model. The differences are not statistically significant ($p = 0.05$) using Student's $t$-test (Student, 1908).

in the readability assessment experiment done by Mesgar and Strube (2015). For the documents 1 and 10 the frequency of subgraphs are constant during decoding. It might be because the connectivity of sentences is already compatible with the training documents and our coherence features push the Docent model to reject operations that might disturb the structure. The decrease in the number of accepted operations for these two documents by the CM model (represented in Table 4) supports this.

### 5.2 Machine Translation Metrics Analysis

We evaluate the model on the test set of the DiscoMT dataset. As the baseline, we use the coherence-blind Docent and compare it against a system with the additional document-level coherence features.

First we try the entity graph model with the average outdegree as the coherence feature. The BLEU and Meteor scores of this model are identical to the baseline. This means that the average outdegree is not a good representative of coherence. That was also shown by Mesgar and Strube (2015) for the readability assessment task.

Next, we try the lexical graph representation of documents and frequency of coherence patterns as the coherence features.

The results of the baseline (BL) and our coherence model (CM) in terms of BLEU and Meteor scores are shown in Table 3.

Compared to the baseline, results for about half of the documents do not change in terms of BLEU. For two documents, the coherence model improves the BLEU score, whereas for three documents it diminishes. Overall, the average BLEU score of the coherence model is slightly lower than that of the baseline.

The Meteor score of the coherence model is better on three documents. The coherence model achieves the best overall result in terms of the averaged Meteor score. The coherence model does not improve the Meteor score on four documents.

We interpret these observations as follows: First, the coherence patterns can model the coherence property of texts better than average outdegree. This is compatible with the reported results by Mesgar and Strube (2015) and Parveen et al. (2016) that, respectively, show that coherence patterns are more informative for readability assessment and multi-document summarization. However, our results also indicate that they are not that powerful for a more difficult task like machine translation (Sim Smith et al., 2016).

Second, the obtained improvement of our coherence model, which is augmented with some document-level features, especially on the Meteor score confirms this hypothesis that the quality of the machine translation can be improved if the MT model is informed by the document-level context.

The third interpretation is about the validity of these traditional metrics that were constructed in the context of sentence-level decoding. This means that these MT scores might not be that much appropriate to measure the global translation quality, especially with regard to discourse coherence. As a future work, we are going to do a human evaluation on this.

Table 4 indicates the number of accepted *change-phrase-translation* operations by Docent in a comparison between the baseline and the coherence model. For both models, the number of accepted operations is very close.

Document 1 is one of the documents where the coherence model outperforms the baseline and it is tempting to assume that the score difference stems from the one operation not accepted by the coherence model. Indeed, the only detectable difference in the two translations is in one sentence only (see its output translations in Table 5). The coherence features might prevent the translation model to change the translation of *thought for*, which is identical with the reference translation.

Similarly, for document 10 the CM model accepts one less operation than the baseline model and it, again, helps the model to obtain a higher Meteor score. Interestingly, the BLEU score on these two documents remains the same, so the score difference is likely a result of a more semantic change in translation. For the document 9 the CM model improves the MT scores by accepting more operations than the baseline model. For documents 3, 6 and 8 the accepted operations by the CM model reduce the MT scores.

Finally, supported operations in Docent seem

| Document ID | # of accepted operations | |
|---|---|---|
| | BL | CM |
| (#1) 1756 | 22 | 21 |
| (#2) 1819 | 18 | 18 |
| (#3) 1825 | 22 | 21 |
| (#4) 1894 | 25 | 25 |
| (#5) 1935 | 21 | 21 |
| (#6) 1938 | 30 | 33 |
| (#7) 1950 | 59 | 59 |
| (#8) 1953 | 29 | 32 |
| (#9) 1979 | 25 | 26 |
| (#10) 2043 | 9 | 8 |
| (#11) 2053 | 12 | 12 |
| (#12) 205 | 4 | 4 |

Table 4: Comparison of the number of accepted *change-phrase-translation* operations.

| Baseline |
|---|
| I demanderais qu' what he thought to this qu' it was doing? **Sue has watched the soil, has ponder a minute.** It has watched of new and said, "I demanderais I forgive d' have been his mother and n' have ever known what was happening in its head". |

| Coherence Model |
|---|
| I demanderais qu' what he thought to this qu' it was doing? **Sue has watched the soil, has thought for a minute.** It has watched of new and said, "I demanderais I forgive d' have been his mother and n' have ever known what was happening in its head". |

| Reference |
|---|
| I'd want to ask him what the hell he thought he was doing." **And Sue looked at the floor, and she thought for a minute.** And then she looked back up and said, "I would ask him to forgive me for being his mother and never knowing what was going on inside his head." |

Table 5: Comparison of the baseline (*BL*), coherence model (*CM*), and reference (*REF*) translations for document 1 (ID: 1756) for one differing sentence between *BL* and *CM* (marked in bold).

insufficient to change the structure of graphs. From the three basic operations Docent uses, the two operations *swap-phrases* and *resegment* may not change the graph structure. *Change-phrase-translation*, however, has the potential to actually change the graph structure by either choosing an alternative translation of a word that is either not connected to any other words anymore or that conversely connects to another word within the text.

## 6 Conclusions

In this paper, we employed the graph-based representation of local coherence by Mesgar and Strube (2016) for the machine translation task by integrating the graph-based coherence features with the document-level MT decoder Docent (Hardmeier et al., 2012, 2013). The usage of these coherence features has been shown for readability assessment and multi-document summarization (Parveen et al., 2016; Mesgar and Strube, 2016). We are the first who utilize these coherence features for document-level translation. Our coherence model using subgraph frequencies as coherence features improves the performance of Docent as a document-level MT decoder. For future work, we are going to check if the connectivity structure of the source document can help the translation system to improve the translation quality of each sentence. This idea is inspired from the application of topic-based coherence modeling in machine translation before (Xiong and Zhang, 2013).

## Acknowledgments

This work has been funded by the Klaus Tschira Foundation, Heidelberg, Germany. The second author has been supported by a HITS Ph.D. scholarship. We are grateful to the anonymous reviewers for their insightful comments.

## References

Dzmitry Bahdanau, Kyunghyun Cho, and Yoshua Bengio. 2015. Neural machine translation by jointly learning to align and translate. In *Proceedings of the International Conference on Learning Representations (ICLR)*.

Regina Barzilay and Mirella Lapata. 2008. Modeling Local Coherence: An Entity-Based Approach. *Computational Linguistics* 34(1):1–34.

Ondrej Bojar, Rajen Chatterjee, Christian Federmann, Barry Haddow, Matthias Huck, Chris Hokamp, Philipp Koehn, Varvara Logacheva, Christof Monz, Matteo Negri, Matt Post, Carolina Scarton, Lucia Specia, and Marco Turchi. 2015. Findings of the 2015 Workshop on Statistical Machine Translation. In *Proceedings of the Tenth Workshop on Statistical Machine Translation*. Lisbon, Portugal, pages 1–46.

František Daneš. 1974. Functional Sentence Perspective and the Organization of the Text. In František Daneš, editor, *Papers on Functional Sentence Perspective*, Academia, Prague, pages 106–128.

Michael Denkowski and Alon Lavie. 2014. Meteor Universal: Language Specific Translation Evaluation for Any Target Language. In *Proceedings of the EACL 2014 Workshop on Statistical Machine Translation*. pages 376–380.

Qin Gao and Stephan Vogel. 2008. Parallel Implementations of Word Alignment Tool. In *Proceedings of the ACL 2008 Software Engineering, Testing, and Quality Assurance Workshop*. pages 49–57.

Barbara J. Grosz, Aravind Joshi, and Scott Weinstein. 1995. Centering: A Framework for Modeling the Local Coherence of Discourse. *Computational Linguistics* 21(2):203–225.

Camille Guinaudeau and Michael Strube. 2013. Graph-based Local Coherence Modeling. In *Proceedings of the 51st Annual Meeting of the Association for Computational Linguistics*. Sofia, Bulgaria, pages 93–103.

Christian Hardmeier. 2012. Discourse in Statistical Machine Translation: A Survey and a Case Study. *Discours* 11:3–30.

Christian Hardmeier. 2014. *Discourse in Statistical Machine Translation*. Ph.D. thesis, Uppsala University.

Christian Hardmeier, Preslav Nakov, Sara Stymne, Jörg Tiedemann, Yannick Versley, and Mauro Cettolo. 2015. Pronoun-Focused MT and Cross-Lingual Pronoun Prediction: Findings of the 2015 DiscoMT Shared Task on Pronoun Translation. In *Proceedings of the Second Workshop on Discourse in Machine Translation (DiscoMT)*. Lisbon, Portugal, pages 1–16.

Christian Hardmeier, Joakim Nivre, and Jörg Tiedemann. 2012. Document-Wide Decoding for Phrase-Based Statistical Machine Translation. In *Proceedings of the 2012 Joint Conference on Empirical Methods in Natural Language Processing and Computational Natural Language Learning*. Jeju Island, Korea, pages 1179–1190.

Christian Hardmeier, Sara Stymne, Jörg Tiedemann, and Joakim Nivre. 2013. Docent: A Document-Level Decoder for Phrase-Based Statistical Machine Translation. In *Proceedings of the 51st Annual Meeting of the Association for Computational Linguistics*. Sofia, Bulgaria, pages 193–198.

Basil Hatim and Ian Mason. 1990. *Discourse and the Translator*. Language in Social Life Series. Longman, London.

Kenneth Heafield. 2011. KenLM: Faster and Smaller Language Model Queries. In *Proceedings of the Sixth Workshop on Statistical Machine Translation*. pages 187–197.

A. Khachaturyan, S. Semenovsovskaya, and B. Vainshtein. 1981. The thermodynamic approach to the structure analysis of crystals. *Acta Crystallographica Section A* 37(5):742–754.

Philipp Koehn, Hieu Hoang, Alexandra Birch, Chris Callison-Burch, Marcello Federico, Nicola Bertoldi, Brooke Cowan, Wade Shen, Christine Moran, Richard Zens, Chris Dyer, Ondrej Bojar, Alexandra Constantin, and Evan Herbst. 2007. Moses: Open Source Toolkit for Statistical Machine Translation. In *Proceedings of the ACL 2007 Demo and Poster Sessions*. Prague, Czech Republic, pages 177–180.

Philipp Koehn, Franz Josef Och, and Daniel Marcu. 2003. Statistical Phrase-Based Translation. In *Proceedings of HLT-NAACL 2003*. pages 48–54.

Alon Lavie and Abhaya Agarwal. 2007. METEOR: An Automatic Metric for MT Evaluation with Improved Correlation with Human Judgments. In *Proceedings of the Second Workshop on Statistical Machine Translation*. Prague, Czech Republic, pages 228–23.

Alon Lavie, Kenji Sagae, and Shyamsundar Jayaraman. 2004. The Significance of Recall in Automatic Metrics for MT Evaluation. In *Proceedings of the 6th Conference of the Association for Machine Translation in the Americas (AMTA-2004)*. pages 134–143.

Gennadi Lembersky, Noam Ordan, and Shuly Wintner. 2012. Language Models for Machine Translation: Original vs. Translated Texts. *Computational Linguistics* 38(4):799–825.

Rui Lin, Shujie Liu, Muyun Yang, Mu Li, Ming Zhou, and Sheng Li. 2015. Hierarchical Recurrent Neural Network for Document Modeling. In *Proceedings of the 2015 Conference on Empirical Methods in Natural Language Processing*. Lisbon, Portugal, pages 899–907.

Mohsen Mesgar and Michael Strube. 2015. Graph-based Coherence Modeling For Assessing Readability. In *Proceedings of the Fourth Joint Conference on Lexical and Computational Semantics (*SEM 2015)*. Denver, Col., pages 309–318.

Mohsen Mesgar and Michael Strube. 2016. Lexical Coherence Graph Modeling Using Word Embeddings. In *Proceedings of the 2016 Conference of the North American Chapter of the Association for Computational Linguistics: Human Language Technologies*. San Diego, Cal., pages 1414–1423.

Siegfried Nijssen and Joost N. Kok. 2004. A Quick-start in Frequent Structure Mining Can Make a Difference. In *The Proceedings of the tenth ACM SIGKDD international conference on Knowledge discovery and data mining*. pages 647–652.

Siegfried Nijssen and Joost N. Kok. 2005. The Gaston Tool for Frequent Subgraph Mining. *Electronic Notes in Theoretical Computer Science* 127(1):77–87.

Franz Josef Och. 2003. Minimum Error Rate Training in Statistical Machine Translation. In *Proceedings of the 41st Annual Meeting of the Association for Computational Linguistics*. Sapporo, Japan, pages 160–167.

Kishore Papineni, Salim Roukos, Todd Ward, and Wei-Jing Zhu. 2002. BLEU: a Method for Automatic Evaluation of Machine Translation. In *Proceedings of the 40th Annual Meeting of the Association for Computational Linguistics*. Philadelphia, pages 311–318.

Daraksha Parveen, Mohsen Mesgar, and Michael Strube. 2016. Generating Coherent Summaries of Scientific Articles Using Coherence Patterns. In *Proceedings of the 2016 Conference on Empirical Methods in Natural Language Processing*. Austin, Texas, pages 772–783.

Jeffrey Pennington, Richard Socher, and Christopher D. Manning. 2014. GloVe: Global Vectors for Word Representation. In *Proceedings of the 2014 Conference on Empirical Methods in Natural Language Processing*. Doha, Qatar, pages 1532–1543.

Emily Pitler and Ani Nenkova. 2008. Revisiting readability: A unified framework for predicting text quality. In *Proceedings of the 2008 Conference on Empirical Methods in Natural Language Processing*. Waikiki, Honolulu, Hawaii, pages 186–195.

Gerard Salton. 1971. *The SMART Retrieval System—Experiments in Automatic Document Processing*. Prentice-Hall, Inc., Upper Saddle River, NJ, USA.

Rico Sennrich, Orhan Firat, Kyunghyun Cho, Alexandra Birch, Barry Haddow, Julian Hitschler, Marcin Junczys-Dowmunt, Samuel Läubli, Antonio Valerio Miceli Barone, Jozef Mokry, and Maria Nadejde. 2017. Nematus: a toolkit for neural machine translation. In *Proceedings of the Software Demonstrations of the 15th Conference of the European Chapter of the Association for Computational Linguistics*. Valencia, Spain, pages 65–68.

Karin Sim Smith, Wilker Aziz, and Lucia Specia. 2015. A Proposal for a Coherence Corpus in Machine Translation. In *Proceedings of the Second Workshop on Discourse in Machine Translation (DiscoMT)*. Lisbon, Portugal, pages 52–58.

Karin Sim Smith, Wilker Aziz, and Lucia Specia. 2016. The Trouble with Machine Translation Coherence. *Baltic Journal of Modern Computing* 4(2):178–189.

Student. 1908. The Probable Error of a Mean. *Biometrika* 6(1):1–25.

Gideon Toury. 1995. *Descriptive Translation Studies – and beyond*. John Benjamins Publishing.

Lawrence Venuti, editor. 2004. *The Translation Studies Reader*. Routledge, London, 2nd edition.

Deyi Xiong and Min Zhang. 2013. A Topic-Based Coherence Model for Statistical Machine Translation. In *Proceedings of the Twenty-Seventh AAAI Conference on Artificial Intelligence*. pages 977–983.

# Treatment of Markup in Statistical Machine Translation

**Mathias Müller**

Institute of Computational Linguistics, University of Zurich

`mmueller@cl.uzh.ch`



## Abstract

We present work on handling XML markup in Statistical Machine Translation (SMT). The methods we propose can be used to effectively preserve markup (for instance inline formatting or structure) and to place markup correctly in a machine-translated segment. We evaluate our approaches with parallel data that naturally contains markup or where markup was inserted to create synthetic examples. In our experiments, hybrid reinsertion has proven the most accurate method to handle markup, while alignment masking and alignment reinsertion should be regarded as viable alternatives. We provide implementations of all the methods described and they are freely available as an open-source framework[1].


## 1 Introduction

It is very common for machine translation to be used in workflows where the source documents contain XML markup. If a document was originally written in Microsoft Word, then in a line like

```
Ich bitte Sie, sich zu einer
Schweigeminute zu erheben.

[Please rise, then, for this
minute's silence.]
```

the inline formatting (**boldface**) will internally be represented as inline XML markup, similar to:

```
Ich bitte Sie, sich zu einer
Schweigeminute zu <b>erheben</b>.
```

---



Before translation, such a document would probably be converted to a more flexible and interoperable format that is ubiquitous in the translation industry, XLIFF, which is also an XML standard.

Nevertheless, inline XML elements will remain in the source segments and in theory could actually be sent to a machine translation system. But in practice, standard machine translation systems are unable to properly deal with markup and delegate markup handling to downstream applications like computer-assisted translation (CAT) tools. For instance, the machine translation framework Moses (Koehn et al., 2007) does not have a standard solution for markup handling.

Using a standard, phrase-based SMT system trained with Moses, the translation of markup breaks as early as during tokenization. Standard tokenization is not aware of XML markup and will tear apart XML element tags:

```
Ich bitte Sie , sich zu einer
Schweigeminute zu < b > erheben <
/ b > .
```

No subsequent step during translation will be able to undo the damage and since the XML standard enforces strict rules, the output is very likely a malformed XML fragment. But even if tokenization were aware of XML markup (we provide an implementation of markup-aware tokenization) another problem remains: XML markup does not need to be translated at all since it has clear-cut, language-independent semantics and a statistical system should not be trusted to copy the markup to the target segment unchanged.

So, if a machine translation system is given a source segment that contains inline markup, it should be able to detect the markup and not treat it as text. But simply stripping the markup from the source segment is not satisfactory. If, for instance, a translation system would offer




*Proceedings of the Third Workshop on Discourse in Machine Translation*, pages 36–46,
Copenhagen, Denmark, September 8, 2017. ©2017 Association for Computational Linguistics.

as a translation, we argue that part of the information present in the source segment (the formatting encoded in the markup tags <b> and </b>) was "lost in translation".

From the point of view of translators, losing the markup during translation has inconvenient consequences. In many translation projects, automatic pre-translation of the source segments is an obligatory step and human translators, instead of translating from scratch, will post-edit the pre-translations. There is reason to believe that wrongly translated markup has an impact on *translator productivity* (OBrien, 2011).

Tezcan and Vandeghinste (2011, 56) argue that an MT system should handle XML markup correctly to avoid inefficient translation workflows. In the same vein, Joanis et al. (2013, 74) say that "post-editing SMT output without the formatting information found in the source may represent a serious loss of productivity". Parra and Arcedillo (2015, 142) state "that inline tags have a big impact on productivity, a fact which is not reflected in any of the known metrics and which has not yet received much attention in research".

We agree with this assessment and would like to work towards the goal of implementing markup handling in standard machine translation frameworks. Several solutions have been put forward, but there is no consensus as to which strategy should be employed in standard use cases. Studies that *compare* different approaches are currently lacking.

In order to facilitate those comparisons, we have implemented different markup handling strategies in the same machine translation framework. We have then carried out experiments to gauge the usefulness of each markup strategy, which we will describe in the remainder of this paper.

## 2  Related Work

Known methods to handle markup in machine translation belong to one of two general paradigms:

- **reinsertion:** markup is stripped from segments prior to training and translation, and reinserted after translation.

- **masking:** markup is not removed entirely,

but replaced with a placeholder (a "mask") before training and translation. After translation, the original content is restored.

Both methods ensure that the actual markup is hidden during training and decoding. In the case of our introductory example that includes two XML element tags <b> and </b>:

```
Ich bitte Sie, sich zu einer
Schweigeminute zu <b>erheben</b>.
```

reinsertion would remove markup from the segment alltogether:

```
Ich bitte Sie, sich zu einer
Schweigeminute zu erheben.
```

while masking would replace the tags with placeholders (appearance of mask token may vary):

```
Ich bitte Sie, sich zu einer
Schweigeminute zu _MASK_ erheben
_MASK_ .
```

Du et al. (2010) present three methods to process TMX markup in an SMT system. The first two methods simply vary the behaviour of the tokenizer with respect to XML markup. The third method, "markup transformation", removes markup before training and translation – and thus is a **reinsertion** strategy. After translation, the markup is restored with the help of phrase segmentation reported by the decoder. They report that XML-aware tokenization yielded the best results, albeit by very small margins.

Zhechev and van Genabith (2010) are the first to describe a **masking** strategy. They are aware that "letting any MT system deal with these tags in a probabilistic manner can easily result in ill-formed, mis-translated and/or out-of-order meta-tags in the translation" (ibid.). To avoid this problem, they replaced XML tags with IDs that act as a placeholder for the actual markup. All IDs were unique on a global level, i.e. throughout the whole corpus. Since markup handling is not the primary goal of this paper, they do not evaluate their approach in any way.

Hudík and Ruopp (2011) further develop the idea of removing the markup before training and translation alltogether. They see their work as a follow-up to Du et al. (2010), trying to improve their **reinsertion** method. They improved the method in the sense that they solved problems related to reordering and provide an algorithm that reinserts markup into translated segments on the basis of *word alignment* instead of phrase segmentation. Intuitively, reinsertion that uses word alignment will be more precise since reinsertion using phrase segmentation can only insert at phrase boundaries, but no experimental results are presented.

Tezcan and Vandeghinste (2011) experiment with several variants of **masking**. Mainly, what is varied is the specificity of the mask tokens. Mask tokens can be unique identifiers for stretches of markup (resulting in a high number of different mask tokens) or can be more generic (in the extreme case, one single mask token). The main outcome of their experiments is that according to automatic metrics of translation quality, a masking method that assigns masks based on the XML element name performed best.

Finally, Joanis et al. (2013) describe a **reinsertion** strategy that uses both phrase segmentation and word alignment to decide where markup tags should be reinserted. They performed a "mini evaluation" of their approach, manually annotating roughly 1500 segments. The results showed that "most tags are placed correctly" (ibid., 79), because 93 % of TMX tags and 90 % of XLIFF tags were perfect according to the human annotators.

The authors themselves identify an important limitation of their work, namely that they "do not carry out an experimental comparison between the [masking] and [reinsertion] approaches, though this would certainly be a worthwile next step" (ibid., 74). Such an evaluation would indeed be advisable, and the goal of the current work is exactly that: providing reimplementations of different approaches and comparing them to each other in controlled experiments.

## 3  Data

For our experiments, we have used two data sets with parallel text in German and English:

- **XLIFF:** a real-world collection of XLIFF documents in which inline markup occurs naturally

- **Euromarkup:** a large set of synthetic examples we ourselves have created by inserting inline markup into the Europarl corpus[2]

|  | English | German |
|---|---|---|
| Number of segments | 427k | 425k |
| Number of tokens | 3.5m | 3m |
| Segments with markup | 98k | 97k |

Table 1: Descriptive statistics of the **XLIFF** data set, markup tags count as 1 token

|  | English | German |
|---|---|---|
| Number of segments | 1.7m | 1.7m |
| Number of tokens | 52m | 50m |
| Segments with markup | 893k | 893k |

Table 2: Descriptive statistics of the **Euromarkup** data set, markup tags count as 1 token

The documents in the **XLIFF** data set are so-called "introductory checklists" used for parameterization of banking software, similar to software manuals, so the texts are from a very technical domain and were actually post-edited by translators. But although the data set is a real use case and typical of machine translation and industry settings, its suitability for markup handling is questionable.

After performing initial experiments with the XLIFF data set, it became clear that handling the markup in this data is relatively easy: segments are short (8 tokens on average), which means that the translation and additional information like word alignment will be accurate, and there is little reordering that could involve markup tags. In short, there are few hard problems for markup handling methods to tackle in the XLIFF data.

In order to discriminate better between the methods, we introduce a second data set, **Euromarkup**, a blend of Europarl (Koehn, 2005) and markup tags. Because it is a synthetic data set that we built ourselves, it has the following desired properties: longer segments (more than 20 tokens on average) and a lot of reordering. We have introduced markup in a way that is consistent with word alignment and ensured that half of the markup was inserted where reordering takes place.

Tables 1 and 2 show the size of both data sets and, importantly, how much markup they contain. Markup is abundant in both sets and in this respect, both are suitable for testing markup handling approaches.

---

[2]An implementation of an algorithm that inserts random inline markup into parallel, word-aligned data is available upon request.

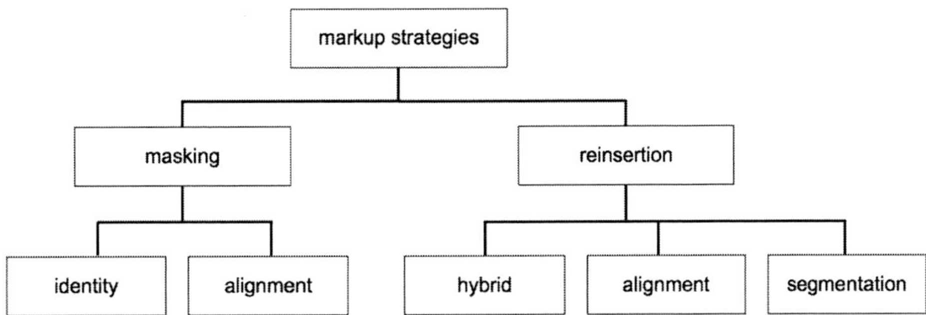

Figure 1: Overview of implemented strategies to process markup

## 4 Methods

We have implemented five different methods of handling markup in the same machine translation framework, `mtrain`. All methods are described in Section 4.1. Section 4.2 explains the experimental setup and how the results were evaluated.

### 4.1 Implementation of markup handling methods

Inspired by previous work, we have designed five different ways to treat markup in machine translation (see Figure 1 for an overview). In `mtrain`, two variants of **masking** are available:

- **identity masking:** before training and translation, markup is replaced by mask tokens that are *unique* within the segment. After translation, the original content can be restored without any additional information.

- **alignment masking:** before training and translation, markup is replaced by mask tokens that are *identical* to each other. After translation, word alignment is used to guide the unmasking process.

In all masking approaches, the mapping between the mask tokens and the original markup content must be held in memory until after translation. Stretches of markup are identified by means of a regular expression. Therefore, masking is actually not limited to markup, but is implemented as a general method to mask any string that can be described by a regular expression.

On the other hand, there are three implementations of **reinsertion** that roughly work as follows:

- **segmentation reinsertion:** before training and translation, markup is removed completely from the segments. After translation, the original markup is reinserted into the translation using phrase segmentation.

- **alignment reinsertion:** identical to segmentation reinsertion, except that word alignment is used instead of phrase segmentation.

- **hybrid reinsertion:** both phrase segmentation and word alignment are used for reinsertion, together with a set of rules. A reimplementation of Joanis et al. (2013).

All strategies assume ideal conditions. Masking methods assume that the translation did not necessitate any reordering of mask tokens (this assumption is specific to identity masking) and that the decoder did not omit any mask tokens. Methods that rely on word alignment (alignment masking, alignment reinsertion and hybrid reinsertion) assume ideal, maximally informative word alignment. Methods that rely on phrase segmentation (segmentation reinsertion and hybrid reinsertion) assume that markup only occurs at the boundaries of phrases and that phrase segmentation is available in the first place.

In practice, these assumptions do not always hold. For instance, reordering may take place or the word alignment might be inaccurate and for those cases, the framework offers flexibility. If the placement of a markup tag is uncertain, any method can be instructed to insert the tag anyway at the end of the segment (aggressive behaviour) or not to introduce this markup tag at all (conservative behaviour).

An important difference between masking and reinsertion methods is the nature of the training data: if a masking method is used, then the training data will contain mask tokens and the system derived from the data will know about mask tokens. If a reinsertion method is used, the training data will not contain any markup. In this regard, reinsertion is more flexible since it can be used with any machine translation system.

### 4.2 Experiments

We compare the overall performance of all 5 implemented markup handling strategies by training a series of SMT systems. The systems are identical except for their method of markup handling.

What all systems have in common is the data sets, preprocessing (except for markup handling), model training and translation parameters. We have randomly divided the data sets into training (roughly 400k segments for XLIFF data, roughly 1.7m for Euromarkup data), tuning (2000 segments) and testing (1000 segments) sets that were fixed for all systems, the direction of translation is always from German to English.

We train a fairly standard, phrase-based SMT system with Moses: a maximum phrase length of 7, a 5-gram KenLM language model with modified Kneser-Ney smoothing, lexicalized reordering model, standard Moses recasing and standard tokenization. Word alignment and symmetrization is performed by `fast_align` and `atools` (Dyer et al., 2013). The phrase and reordering table are compressed with the `cmph` library. The weights of the model are tuned with MERT (Och, 2003).

For all of the five implemented strategies, such a system was trained, varying only the markup handling. Since our framework allows more fine-grained control over the algorithms, we have used the following settings: if there is uncertainty about where a markup tag should be placed, it must still be inserted into the translation at the very end. The translation of mask tokens is not enforced ("forced decoding"), instead the decision is left to the decoder.

In addition to the five systems above, we have trained the following baseline system:

- **strip:** markup is stripped entirely from the training, tuning and evaluation corpus.

in order to have an estimate of the overall quality of machine translation when no markup is involved.

Finally, we have measured the outcome of our experiments automatically and manually. Automatic metrics should never be used to evaluate the performance of markup handling methods, and we have employed them only to answer a preliminary question: do mask tokens in the training data have an impact on the overall quality of machine translation? It is unclear whether mask tokens affect negatively the overall output of the system and if that were the case, developers should refrain from using masking to handle markup.

We measure the effect of mask tokens by comparing the machine-translated test set with the human reference **after removing markup on both sides**. Then, the `MultEval` tool is used (Clark et al., 2011) to report BLEU (Papineni et al., 2002), METEOR (Lavie and Agarwal, 2007), TER (Snover et al., 2006) and length scores.

While the automatic evaluation translates all of the 1000 segments in the test set, the manual evaluation only looks at the segments where both the source and target reference have tags in them. Markup tags were inspected manually and assigned one of the following categories (inspired by Joanis et al., 2013):

- **good**: correct markup is present, correctly placed,

- **reasonable**: correct markup is present, but needs to be moved,

- **wrong**: markup is broken or not present at all,

- **garbage-in**: the decoder output is unintelligible and there is no proper place for markup.

In general, it is always preferable to transfer markup tags to the target segment, even if the correct position cannot be determined. From the point of view of the post-editor, it is more efficient to move a markup tag instead of going back to the source segment. Therefore, markup tags that are in the wrong place are described as "reasonable". In theory, there are scenarios where markup tags should be dropped entirely (because all tokens related to them have no translation) but in the vast majority of cases, missing markup tags are "wrong".

In this manual evaluation we will focus on evaluating the markup handling, not the performance

| | XLIFF | | | | Euromarkup | | | |
|---|---|---|---|---|---|---|---|---|
| | **BLEU** | **METEOR** | **TER** | **Length** | **BLEU** | **METEOR** | **TER** | **Length** |
| strip | 60.5 | 46.3 | 26.6 | 93.9 | 32.4 | 34.2 | 52.4 | 98.7 |
| IM | 61.0 | 46.7 | 26.4 | 94.3 | 30.9 | 33.9 | 53.8 | 99.3 |
| AM | 60.4 | 46.3 | 26.9 | 94.2 | 31.4 | 34.0 | 54.1 | 99.8 |
| SR | 60.5 | 46.4 | 26.8 | 94.9 | 32.6 | 34.5 | 52.1 | 98.7 |
| AR | 60.5 | 46.4 | 26.9 | 94.9 | 32.3 | 34.6 | 52.1 | 98.7 |
| HR | 60.4 | 46.3 | 26.8 | 94.8 | 32.2 | 34.5 | 52.5 | 99.0 |

Table 3: Automatic evaluation of the overall performance of markup handling methods, after markup was removed completely. The metrics reported are BLEU (higher is better), METEOR (higher is better) and TER (lower is better). IM = identity masking, AM = alignment masking, SR = segmentation reinsertion, AR = alignment reinsertion, HR = hybrid reinsertion.

of the systems in general. For each data set, we decided to look at a maximum of 200 parallel segments from the test set that contain markup. In the XLIFF test set, only 176 segments contain markup, so all of them were evaluated, which amounts to a total of 658 tags.

In the Euromarkup test set, we annotated the first 200 segments that contain markup, and they contain 584 tags in total. We only look at the lowercased, tokenized version of the translation output, after processing the reference accordingly.

## 5 Results

The automatic evaluation in Table 3 shows the overall performance of systems on "normal" text, that is, after markup was stripped from both the machine-translated hypothesis and the human reference. All systems trained on XLIFF data have a performance comparable to the baseline system that did not see any markup at all ("strip"). For instance, the BLEU scores range from 60.4 to 61.0. The systems that use a variant of reinsertion and the "strip" system are expected to produce exactly the same translation since they are trained on the same data, but non-deterministic tuning has caused slight fluctuations in all scores.

For the XLIFF data set, both masking systems perform as good as the baseline system. But in general, the scores for this data set are high and it is clear that the data set is easy to translate. For the Euromarkup data, the behaviour of the reinsertion methods does not change since they are still very close to the baseline. However, using this synthetic data set, masking indeed decreases the overall quality of machine translation in terms of BLEU scores.

Moving on to the manual evaluation, Table 4 shows that for the XLIFF data set, identity masking clearly performs best, because it places correctly 658 out of 658 tags. Alignment masking and alignment reinsertion are not too far behind, both have led to 4 cases of "reasonable" tags (tags are present but in the wrong place). Hybrid reinsertion could not determine the correct position for markup in 34 cases. Even segmentation reinsertion placed markup correctly in 582 out of 658 cases. Using XLIFF data, no tags were omitted ("wrong") and the decoder never produced unusable output ("garbage-in").

Using Euromarkup, the "harder" data set, shifts the picture: hybrid reinsertion performs best on this data set as it placed correctly 437 out of 584 tags. Another 133 were in the wrong place, but all output segments were still well-formed and markup was not broken. Alignment masking and alignment reinsertion still work reasonably well, transferring markup correctly in 412 and 415 cases, respectively. Identity masking on the other hand is now well behind, and segmentation reinsertion performed worst, as expected.

Another striking result is that both masking methods lead to a number of "wrong" tags, i.e. tags that make the whole segment a malformed XML fragment. Malformed content is likely to cause problems, depending on the application that processes the translation output. Finally, the systems trained on Euromarkup data also produced a few cases where the decoder output is unintelligible (i.e. not even a human annotator could have placed markup correctly).

In summary, identity masking solved the task of markup handling perfectly given a corpus of

| | XLIFF (tags in total: 658) | | | | Euromarkup (tags in total: 584) | | | |
|---|---|---|---|---|---|---|---|---|
| | **good** | **reasonable** | **wrong** | **garbage-in** | **good** | **reasonable** | **wrong** | **garbage-in** |
| **IM** | **658** | **0** | **0** | **0** | 372 | 167 | 29 | 16 |
| **AM** | 654 | 4 | 0 | 0 | 412 | 123 | 39 | 10 |
| **SR** | 582 | 76 | 0 | 0 | 252 | 318 | 0 | 14 |
| **AR** | 654 | 4 | 0 | 0 | 415 | 148 | 7 | 14 |
| **HR** | 624 | 34 | 0 | 0 | **437** | **133** | **0** | **14** |

Table 4: Manual evaluation of the performance of markup handling methods, by tags. IM = identity masking, AM = alignment masking, SR = segmentation reinsertion, AR = alignment reinsertion, HR = hybrid reinsertion.

short and relatively monotone segments. In that case, both alignment masking and alignment reinsertion are viable alternatives. However, the second, synthetic data set with longer segments and "harder" markup emphasizes better the differences between the methods. Hybrid reinsertion has outperformed all other methods on the second data set. Alignment reinsertion and alignment masking are still viable, but identity masking struggled with the second data set.

## 6 Discussion

In Section 6.1, we discuss whether masking methods for markup handling have merit. Section 6.2 discusses the performance of all reinsertion methods.

### 6.1 Masking methods

Mask tokens in the training data can lead to a decrease in overall translation quality and thus "make the translation itself worse" (Joanis et al., 2013, 78). More concretely, Table 3 shows that on the Euromarkup data set, masking systems perform worse (e.g. BLEU score of around 31) than the baseline and the reinsertion systems (e.g. BLEU score of around 32). One possible explanation is that mask tokens in the training data potentially dilute the phrase statistics derived from that corpus. In the training data, a segment like

```
i am delighted to hear that
```

can be interrupted by mask tokens in arbitrary ways:

```
i am __MASK__ delighted __MASK__
__MASK__ to hear __MASK__ that

__MASK__ i __MASK__ am delighted
__MASK__ to hear that __MASK__
```

But at translation time, the same phrase can contain masks in different places:

```
i am __MASK__ __MASK__ delighted to
__MASK__ hear __MASK__ that
```

and since this sequence of words is unseen, the segment will be broken up into smaller phrases, despite the fact that the underlying phrase `i am delighted to hear that` is actually known to the system and could be translated as a single phrase.

This does not hold in general, since we only observed this effect in synthetic data and therefore, this finding does not invalidate masking as a whole. Still, we would only want to tolerate such a degradation in overall translation quality if it comes with superior markup handling performance.

Identity masking worked well on the XLIFF data set, but not on the Euromarkup data. The method is very lean because it does not rely on any kind of auxiliary information (such as phrase segmentation or word alignment), but also it is unable to cope with any amount of reordering on a fundamental level. Unique IDs are assigned to markup tags according to their position in the segment going from left to right, and therefore, reordering is not modelled at all. This means that if translation involves reordering of markup tags, identity masking will fail (see Table 5 for an example).

The reordering problem is overcome by alignment masking, where reordering is explicitly modelled and word alignment is used as a proxy. Handling the markup present in the XLIFF data set did not cause any difficulty for alignment masking and word alignment was sufficient to solve the problem in all but 4 cases. On the Euromarkup data, alignment masking proved to be robust and still placed correctly most tags. Using word alignment

```
source segment            Leider <i/> war <g/> <b> dies </b> von kurzer Dauer.
target reference          sadly , <b> it </b> <i/> was <g/> short @-@ lived .

identity masking          unfortunately , <i/> this <g/> <b> was </b> a short time .
alignment masking         unfortunately , <b> this </b> <i/> was <g/> a short time .
segmentation reinsertion  <i/> <g/> <b> unfortunately , this was </b> a short time .
```

Table 5: Examples of markup handling that show 1) the inability of identity masking to deal properly with markup that needs reordering and 2) that segmentation reinsertion can only insert markup at phrase boundaries.

enables the unmasking algorithm to track reordering, at the cost of depending on word alignment.

Both identity masking and alignment masking have led to a number of cases where the placement of tags resulted in the whole segment being malformed XML. On the one hand, this is because the default behaviour of the algorithms is to insert tags at the very end of the segment if the correct place cannot be determined. If, for instance, an opening element tag is placed at the very end in this manner, the whole segment will be malformed. On the other hand, both masking methods do not understand the notion of *tag pairs* (pairs of opening and closing tags) – which is necessary to guarantee that the output will be well-formed XML.

A clear advantage of masking is that it is not limited to markup at all: anything that can be described with a regular expression can be masked and unmasked in our framework[3]. In this respect, masking methods are more versatile than reinsertion methods and for certain use cases, this might outweigh the limitations we have mentioned.

## 6.2 Reinsertion methods

Looking at the results on the XLIFF data, segmentation reinsertion cannot be said to have failed the task of reinserting markup. Quite on the contrary, it is remarkable that segmentation reinsertion could act on the markup in such a precise way, given that phrase segmentation is imprecise to begin with: it can only insert tags at phrase boundaries, which is bound to lead to errors (see Table 5 for an example). A further analysis of the XLIFF data revealed that markup is frequently present at the very beginning and very end of segments. If there is no reordering, markup at the beginning and end of segments can always be inserted in the right place by segmentation reinsertion, regardless of phrase boundaries.

Still, segmentation reinsertion is very limited and the results on the Euromarkup data set confirm that it leads to a very high number of misplaced ("reasonable") tags: 318 out of 584 tags were not placed correctly. In fact, segmentation reinsertion is downright paradoxical: it works better if phrases are short, while longer phrases typically lead to better translations, and by extension, segmentation reinsertion works well if the machine translation system is feeble. If word alignment is available, there is probably no reason to implement or use segmentation reinsertion at all.

The performance of alignment reinsertion is very similar to alignment masking, which is not surprising, given that they make use of the same additional information from the decoder. On the XLIFF data set, alignment reinsertion solves the problem almost perfectly, all scores are identical to alignment masking. On the Euromarkup data set, the number of correctly placed tags ("good" tags) is very similar, but alignment masking is prone to break markup structures, while alignment reinsertion is not. The alignment reinsertion algorithm generally keeps together pairs of tags and actively avoids placements that would break the markup, yet not breaking the markup is not a hard requirement in our implementation.

Turning to the most promising strategy, hybrid reinsertion coped well with both data sets. On the XLIFF data, it placed correctly 624 out of 658 markup tags, but more importantly, it outperformed all other methods on the Euromarkup data. A possible explanation for its superior performance is that, as a hybrid method, it can overcome deficiencies in phrase segmentation with word alignment and vice versa. Similar to the other reinsertion methods, hybrid reinsertion also models pairs of tags explicitly and ensures the well-formedness of the segment.

In addition, our experiments very likely underestimate the method presented in Joanis et al. (2013) since there, "some care is taken to preserve

---

[3]Incidentally, this is also the explanation for why masking methods do not insert tags in pairs: most strings that can be masked do not come in pairs.

the source order when multiple tags end up between the same two target language words" (ibid., 78). Our implementation does not guarantee the order of adjacent tags.

The strength of reinsertion in general is that it can be used with any machine translation system, while masking must be used together with a system trained on mask tokens. If masked segments are given to a system that did not see mask tokens during training, the results are quite unpredictable. In the case of phrase-based SMT systems, this would likely lead to all mask tokens being moved to the end of the segment, because language models prefer grouping together unknown words (Fishel and Sennrich, 2014).

Put another way, the decision to use masking as the markup handling method must be made at training time, reinsertion can be introduced at translation time. In both cases, the nature of the decoder is another limiting factor: systems that cannot report phrase segmentation make it impossible to use segmentation reinsertion, but also rule out the best-performing method, hybrid reinsertion. Word alignment, however, can be supplied by an additional tool in case the decoder is unable to report this information. This means that methods relying on word alignment are broadly applicable across machine translation paradigms.

## 7 Conclusion

We have presented work on handling markup in statistical machine translation. In our experiments we have compared the usefulness of five different markup handling strategies. The main findings are: hybrid reinsertion outperformed all other methods and was found to cope best with the markup in a synthetic data set. Alignment masking and alignment reinsertion also placed correctly two out of three tags and should be regarded as viable alternatives.

However, alignment masking led to more cases of malformed XML and masking methods can only be used with systems that are trained with mask tokens. For new projects that have to decide on a method to handle markup we therefore recommend to use hybrid reinsertion (if phrase segmentation is available) or alignment reinsertion (otherwise).

In recent years, neural approaches have dominated the field of machine translation and it is therefore worth considering whether our results carry over to neural machine translation systems. Encoder-decoder networks with attention (Bahdanau et al., 2014), a popular architecture for translation, do not report phrase segmentation of course, which rules out both segmentation reinsertion and hybrid reinsertion. On the other hand, alignment information can still be derived from attention weights.

Future work could investigate whether alignment masking or alignment reinsertion are feasible in the context of neural machine translation. But neural networks also lend themselves to more innovative experiments: anecdotal evidence suggests that character-level recurrent neural networks (Hochreiter and Schmidhuber, 1997) are capable of generating well-formed markup[4]. This is a remarkable achievement and to our knowledge, this property of neural networks has never been investigated in earnest.

Also, our implementations currently do not properly model two important aspects of the data: whitespace inside and outside of XML elements is not handled properly and our algorithms never regard dropping tags from the translation as a correct action. Addressing those two shortcomings would also be a worthwhile continuation of our work.

## Acknowledgments

We thank the anonymous reviewers for their valuable comments and suggestions.

## References

Dzmitry Bahdanau, Kyunghyun Cho, and Yoshua Bengio. 2014. Neural machine translation by jointly learning to align and translate. *arXiv preprint arXiv:1409.0473* .

Jonathan H Clark, Chris Dyer, Alon Lavie, and Noah A Smith. 2011. Better hypothesis testing for statistical machine translation: Controlling for optimizer instability. In *Proceedings of the 49th Annual Meeting of the Association for Computational Linguistics: Human Language Technologies: short papers-Volume 2*. Association for Computational Linguistics, pages 176–181.

Jinhua Du, Johann Roturier, and Andy Way. 2010. TMX markup: a challenge when adapting smt to the localisation environment. In *EAMT - 14th Annual Conference of the European Association for Machine Translation*. European Association for Machine Translation.

---

[4]See `http://karpathy.github.io/2015/05/21/rnn-effectiveness/`.

Chris Dyer, Victor Chahuneau, and Noah A. Smith. 2013. A simple, fast, and effective reparameterization of ibm model 2. In *Proceedings of the 2013 Conference of the North American Chapter of the Association for Computational Linguistics: Human Language Technologies*. Association for Computational Linguistics, Atlanta, Georgia, pages 644–648. http://www.aclweb.org/anthology/N13-1073.

Mark Fishel and Rico Sennrich. 2014. Handling technical OOVs in SMT. In *Proceedings of The Seventeenth Annual Conference of the European Association for Machine Translation (EAMT)*. pages 159–162.

Sepp Hochreiter and Jürgen Schmidhuber. 1997. Long short-term memory. *Neural computation* 9(8):1735–1780.

Tomáš Hudík and Achim Ruopp. 2011. The integration of Moses into localization industry. In *15th Annual Conference of the EAMT*. pages 47–53.

Eric Joanis, Darlene Stewart, Samuel Larkin, and Roland Kuhn. 2013. Transferring markup tags in statistical machine translation: A two-stream approach. In Sharon O'Brien, Michel Simard, and Lucia Specia, editors, *Proceedings of MT Summit XIV Workshop on Post-editing Technology and Practice*. pages 73–81.

Philipp Koehn. 2005. Europarl: A parallel corpus for statistical machine translation. In *Proceedings of MT Summit*. volume 5, pages 79–86. http://mt-archive.info/MTS-2005-Koehn.pdf.

Philipp Koehn, Hieu Hoang, Alexandra Birch, Chris Callison-Burch, Marcello Federico, Nicola Bertoldi, Brooke Cowan, Wade Shen, Christine Moran, Richard Zens, Chris Dyer, Ondřej Bojar, Alexandra Constantin, and Evan Herbst. 2007. Moses: Open source toolkit for statistical machine translation. In *Proceedings of the 45th Annual Meeting of the ACL on Interactive Poster and Demonstration Sessions*. pages 177–180. http://www.aclweb.org/anthology/P07-2045.pdf.

Alon Lavie and Abhaya Agarwal. 2007. METEOR: An automatic metric for mt evaluation with high levels of correlation with human judgments. In *Proceedings of the Second Workshop on Statistical Machine Translation*. pages 228–231.

Franz Josef Och. 2003. Minimum error rate training in statistical machine translation. In *Proceedings of the 41st Annual Meeting on Association for Computational Linguistics-Volume 1*. pages 160–167. http://www.aclweb.org/anthology/P03-1021.pdf.

Sharon OBrien. 2011. Towards predicting post-editing productivity. *Machine translation* 25(3):197–215.

Kishore Papineni, Salim Roukos, Todd Ward, and Wei-Jing Zhu. 2002. Bleu: a method for automatic evaluation of machine translation. In *Proceedings of the 40th annual meeting on association for computational linguistics*. Association for Computational Linguistics, pages 311–318.

Carla Parra Escartín and Manuel Arcedillo. 2015. Machine translation evaluation made fuzzier: A study on post-editing productivity and evaluation metrics in commercial settings. In *Proceedings of MT Summit XV*. Association for Machine Translation in the Americas, pages 131–144.

Matthew Snover, Bonnie Dorr, Richard Schwartz, Linnea Micciulla, and John Makhoul. 2006. A study of translation edit rate with targeted human annotation. In *Proceedings of Association for Machine Translation in the Americas*. pages 223–231.

Arda Tezcan and Vincent Vandeghinste. 2011. SMT-CAT integration in a Technical Domain: Handling XML Markup Using Pre & Post-processing Methods. *Proceedings of EAMT 2011* .

Ventsislav Zhechev and Josef van Genabith. 2010. Seeding statistical machine translation with translation memory output through tree-based structural alignment. In *Proceedings of the 4th Workshop on Syntax and Structure in Statistical Translation*. Coling 2010 Organizing Committee, Beijing, China, pages 43–51. http://www.aclweb.org/anthology/W10-3806.

## Appendix

Listings 1, 2 and 3 show how different components of `mtrain` can be used to pre- and post-process markup. Although `mtrain` is a full-fledged wrapper around the Moses framework, its markup handling modules can also be used as standalone components.

Both masking methods are implemented in the module `mtrain.preprocessing.masking`, while three reinsertion methods are available in `mtrain.preprocessing.reinsertion`.

```
1  >>> from mtrain.preprocessing.masking import Masker
2  >>> masker = Masker('alignment')
3  >>> masked_segment = 'Message moi a __email__ ou __xml__ __url__ __xml__'
4  # after translation
5  >>> translated_segment = 'Email me at __email__ or __xml__ __url__ __xml__'
6  >>> mapping = [('__email__', 'an@ribute.com'),
7      ('__url__', 'http://www.statmt.org'),
8      ('__xml__', '<a>'), ('__xml__', '</a>')]
9  >>> alignment = {0:[0], 1:[1], 2:[2], 3:[3], 4:[4], 5:[5], 6:[6], 7:[7]}
10 >>> masker.unmask_segment(masked_segment, translated_segment, mapping, alignment)
11 'Email me at an@ribute.com or <a> http://www.statmt.org </a>'
```

Listing 1: A case of successful alignment masking and unmasking. The unmasking step crucially depends on alignment information reported by the decoder. Unmasking succeeds in this case because all mask tokens are present in the translation and because the alignment is perfect.

```
1  >>> from mtrain.preprocessing.reinsertion import Reinserter
2  >>> reinserter = Reinserter('alignment')
3  >>> source_segment = 'Hello <g id="1" ctype="x-bold;"> World ! </g>'
4  # markup removal, then translation...
5  >>> translated_segment = 'Hallo Welt !'
6  >>> alignment = {0:[0], 1:[1], 2:[2]}
7  >>> reinserter._reinsert_markup_alignment(source_segment, translated_segment,
8      alignment)
9  'Hallo <g ctype="x-bold;" id="1"> Welt ! </g>'
```

Listing 2: Alignment reinsertion based on the original source segment that contains markup, the translated segment and, most importantly, the alignment between the source segment without markup and the translation.

```
1  >>> from mtrain.preprocessing.reinsertion import Reinserter
2  >>> reinserter = Reinserter('hybrid')
3  >>> source_segment = 'Hello <g id="1" ctype="x-bold;"> World ! </g>'
4  # markup removal, then translation...
5  >>> translated_segment = 'Hallo Welt !'
6  >>> alignment = {0:[0], 1:[1], 2:[2]}
7  >>> segmentation = {(0,1):(0,1), (2,2):(2,2)}
8  >>> reinserter._reinsert_markup_full(source_segment, translated_segment,
9      segmentation, alignment)
10 'Hallo <g ctype="x-bold;" id="1"> Welt ! </g>'
```

Listing 3: Hybrid reinsertion given perfect segmentation and alignment.

# A BiLSTM-based System for Cross-lingual Pronoun Prediction

**Sara Stymne, Sharid Loáiciga** and **Fabienne Cap**
Department of Linguistics and Philology
Uppsala University
`firstname.lastname@lingfil.uu.se`

## Abstract

We describe the Uppsala system for the 2017 DiscoMT shared task on cross-lingual pronoun prediction. The system is based on a lower layer of BiLSTMs reading the source and target sentences respectively. Classification is based on the BiLSTM representation of the source and target positions for the pronouns. In addition we enrich our system with dependency representations from an external parser and character representations of the source sentence. We show that these additions perform well for German and Spanish as source languages. Our system is competitive and is in first or second place for all language pairs.

## 1 Introduction

Cross-lingual pronoun prediction is a classification approach to directly estimate the translation of a pronoun, without generating a full translation of the segment containing the pronoun. The task is restricted to pronouns at subject positions only and it is defined as a "fill-in-the-gap-task": given an input text and a translation with placeholders, replace the placeholders with pronouns. Word alignment links of the placeholders to the source sentence are also given. This setting allows to analyze both the source and the target languages to create features, potentially providing the means to understand the different aspects involved in pronoun translation.

First formalized by Hardmeier (2014), the approach was introduced as a shared task at the DiscoMT 2015 Workshop (Hardmeier et al., 2015). In 2016, the shared task included more language pairs and lemmatized target data (Guillou et al., 2016). This year's edition (Loáiciga et al., 2017)

| src | *me ayudan a ser escuchada*<br>"me help$_{3.Pers.Pl}$ to be heard" |
|---|---|
| trg | REPLACE help me to be heard |
| pos | PRON VERB PRON PART AUX VERB |
| ref | They help me to be heard |

Figure 1: Spanish-English example.

also features lemmatized target data and it includes the Spanish-English language pair, which introduces pro-drops or null subjects to the task. These refer to omitted subject pronouns whose interpretation is recovered through the verb's morphology, as shown in Figure 1.

Given the success of neural networks for cross-lingual pronoun classification (Hardmeier et al., 2013; Luotolahti et al., 2016; Dabre et al., 2016), we wanted to explore this type of system architecture. Our system is based on BiLSTMs enhanced with information about the source pronoun, the pronoun's syntactic head dependency and character-level representations of the source words. Our system ranked first for English–German, with 10 percentage points of macro recall ahead of the second best team. For the other three language pairs, the system obtained the second best macro recall. In addition, our system reached the highest accuracy for three out of the four language pairs.

## 2 Related Work

Our system architecture draws inspiration from several sources, most prominently from the pronoun prediction system by Luotolahti et al. (2016) and the parser architecture by Kiperwasser and Goldberg (2016).

Luotolahti et al. (2016) built the winning system for the 2016 edition of this shared task. The system is based on two stack levels of GRU units and it relies almost uniquely on context. Other

47

*Proceedings of the Third Workshop on Discourse in Machine Translation*, pages 47–53,
Copenhagen, Denmark, September 8, 2017. ©2017 Association for Computational Linguistics.

than representations of the source pronouns, its input contains up to 50 tokens of context, reading away from the pronoun to be predicted, to the left and the right, both for the source and the target language. It uses a weighted loss which penalizes classification errors on low frequency classes. Our system mainly differs from this in that we use BiLSTM units reading from the sentence boundaries towards the pronoun and we rely on sampling strategies instead of weighting the losses.

Kiperwasser and Goldberg (2016) describe a dependency parser based on a BiLSTM layer representing the input sentence. The input to the BiLSTMs are word and POS-tag embeddings. Each word is then represented by the BiLSTM representation at this position, which forms a basis for both a graph-based and a transition-based parser. We use the same underlying BiLSTM layer for word representations, but in our case, we feed the representation of selected words to a pronoun classifier. de Lhoneux et al. (2017) describe several additions to this parser, including character embeddings as part of the word representation. Given their value to capture morphological information, we include character embeddings for the source language in our system.

Loáiciga (2015) reports that pronoun prediction benefits from syntactic features when using a Maximum Entropy classifier. Similarly, but using an SVM classifier, Stymne (2016) provides evidence in favor of including information about dependency heads for pronoun classification, especially for the source languages German and French. We followed these findings and included head dependency information into our current system.

## 3 Data and Evaluation

We use only the training data provided by the shared task (Loáiciga et al., 2017).[1] For development data, we concatenate all available development data for each language pair. Test data is the official shared task test data. For training data we either concatenate all available training data, or use only the in-domain IWSLT data, which contains TED talks. In addition, we perform experiments with a very simple domain adaptation technique in the spirit of Zoph et al. (2016), but applying it to different domains instead of to different languages. We first train models on all available data, then continue training these models for additional epochs using only in-domain IWSLT data.

While the source side sentences are regular inflected words, the target side sentences are given as lemmas with POS-tags. In order to utilize richer representations for the source side we tag and parse the source data. For English and German we use Mate Tools (Bohnet and Nivre, 2012) and for Spanish we use UD-Pipe (Straka et al., 2016). To achieve a flat representation, we represent each source word by its word form, POS-tag and the dependency label for its head (e.g. *woman|NOUN|SBJ, false|JJ|NMOD*). After parsing, all input words and lemmas are lowercased, and all numerals are replaced by a single token.

### 3.1 Sampling

One of the inherent difficulties of the task is the imbalance in the distribution of the classes. Every language pair is different, but in general the OTHER class is large in comparison to all other classes, and masculine pronouns are more frequent than feminine pronouns. The feminine plural pronouns is one of the most extreme cases, since they are only used whenever their referent points to a group containing exclusively feminine members.

During training, we sample the sentences to use in each epoch, in order to handle the imbalance in the data, which in addition also reduces the memory needed to handle all training data. For each epoch we use a small proportion of the training data that we randomly sample by selecting each sentence based on a different probability for each pronoun class. In case a sentence has several pronoun instances, we use the probability of the rarest class in the sentence.[2] We use several sampling schemes. **Equal sampling** optimizes macro-recall, it accommodates an equal number of instances for each pronoun class per sample. In case a class has fewer instances than required, all available instances for that class are used. **Proportional sampling** optimizes accuracy by sampling based on the class proportions in the development data. We also investigated an **offline sampling** scheme, which is similar to proportional sampling. In this case the sample has the same distribution of classes as the development data and also the same size. Because the sample size is small, this

---



[2]Using all pronoun instances of a sentence improves training efficiency, but at the cost of making the sample proportions less precise.

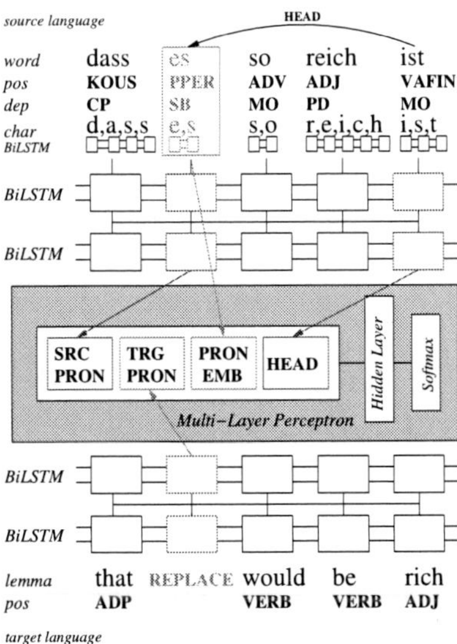


Figure 2: System architecture overview.

| Parameter | Value |
| --- | --- |
| Word embedding dimensions | 100 |
| Lemma embedding dimensions | 100 |
| POS-tag embedding dimensions | 10 |
| Dep label embedding dimensions | 15 |
| Character embedding dimensions | 12 |
| Character BiLSTM dimensions | 100 |
| BiLSTM Layers | 2 |
| BiLSTM hidden dimensions | 200 |
| BiLSTM output dimensions | 200 |
| Hidden units in MLP | 100 |
| $\alpha$ (for word dropout) | 0.25 |
| LSTM dropout | 0.33 |

Table 1: Hyper-parameter values.

sampling method requires training for many more epochs. In order to have exact sample proportions, rather than the inexact proportions from choosing each example with a specified probability, we pre-compute and store the samples in this scheme.

## 3.2 Evaluation

We give results on two metrics, macro-recall (macro-R) and accuracy. Macro-R is the official shared task metric. It gives the average recall for each pronoun class, thus giving the same importance to rare classes as to common classes. We also give unofficial accuracy scores, to give a more balanced view of system performance. All scores are given on both the official test data and dev data.

## 4   System Description

Our system is a neural network architecture with a multi-layer perceptron (MLP) classifier fed with BiLSTM (Hochreiter and Schmidhuber, 1997) representations of tokens, which in turn are based on embeddings for word forms, lemmas, POS-tags, dependency labels, and character representations. The system is depicted in Figure 2.

Each token in the target sentence is represented as the concatenation of an embedding of its lemma and its POS-tag. Each source token is represented as the concatenation of embeddings for the input word, POS-tag, dependency label, and a character representation based on a separate character BiL-STM, reading the sequence of characters in the token. Character representations were only used in the source, since we believe that they can capture morphology, which is not meaningful for the lemmatized target sentence. All embeddings are initialized randomly. The source and target token representations are then fed to a separate two-level BiLSTM that reads the sentence backwards and forwards. No cross-sentence information is used.

On top of this architecture we have an MLP, using `tanh` for activation, that for each pronoun instance takes as input the BiLSTM representation of the target pronoun, the source pronoun, the dependency head word of the source pronoun, and in addition takes the token representation of the source pronoun. For Spanish-English, we did not use the dependency head word, since the source pronoun is already encoded in a verb, because of pro-drop, see Figure 1. The MLP consists of this input layer, a hidden layer and a softmax output layer, representing all pronoun classes for the given target language.

We use dropout on all LSTMs. In addition, we use the word dropout of Iyyer et al. (2015) for words and lemmas, where we randomly replace a word with the UNKNOWN token with a frequency inversely proportional to the word frequency. Moreover, we replace all words occurring only once in the training data with the UN-KNOWN token. Table 1 shows the values of the hyper parameters used in the system. We did not perform any optimization of hyper parameter values. Our system is implemented using DyNet (Neubig et al., 2017), and re-uses code from Kiperwasser and Goldberg (2016) and de Lhoneux et al. (2017).

We train the full model jointly, using a log loss on the final pronoun classification and Adam (Kingma and Ba, 2015) as the optimizer. Training the BiLSTMs as part of the full classification

| System | de-en | | en-de | | en-fr | | es-en | |
|---|---|---|---|---|---|---|---|---|
| | mac-R | acc | mac-R | acc | mac-R | acc | mac-R | acc |
| **All** components | 0.67 | 0.84 | 0.47 | 0.73 | 0.51 | 0.73 | 0.72 | 0.83 |
| No char emb | 0.65 | 0.83 | 0.47 | 0.73 | 0.52 | 0.73 | 0.69 | 0.82 |
| No dep emb | 0.67 | 0.84 | 0.47 | 0.74 | 0.53 | 0.74 | 0.70 | 0.83 |
| No pos+dep emb | 0.67 | 0.82 | 0.46 | 0.72 | 0.51 | 0.72 | 0.68 | 0.82 |
| No dep emb/head | 0.57 | 0.80 | 0.47 | 0.74 | 0.53 | 0.74 | – | – |
| No pron emb (MLP) | 0.65 | 0.81 | 0.46 | 0.73 | 0.53 | 0.74 | 0.69 | 0.82 |
| **None** of the above | 0.49 | 0.73 | 0.46 | 0.72 | 0.50 | 0.71 | 0.67 | 0.81 |

Table 2: Development results with different system settings, training with IWSLT data, and proportional sampling. Scores are Macro-R and accuracy.

| System | de-en | | en-de | | en-fr | | es-en | |
|---|---|---|---|---|---|---|---|---|
| | mac-R | acc | mac-R | acc | mac-R | acc | mac-R | acc |
| **All** components | 0.65 | 0.84 | 0.48 | 0.76 | 0.47 | 0.65 | 0.56 | 0.65 |
| No char emb | 0.59 | 0.77 | 0.47 | 0.75 | 0.48 | 0.67 | 0.55 | 0.66 |
| No dep emb | 0.63 | 0.81 | 0.48 | 0.76 | 0.45 | 0.66 | 0.54 | 0.62 |
| No pos+dep emb | 0.62 | 0.78 | 0.46 | 0.73 | 0.46 | 0.65 | 0.48 | 0.50 |
| No dep emb/head | 0.54 | 0.74 | 0.50 | 0.80 | 0.46 | 0.66 | – | – |
| No pron emb (MLP) | 0.63 | 0.80 | 0.48 | 0.76 | 0.46 | 0.67 | 0.56 | 0.65 |
| **None** of the above | 0.51 | 0.71 | 0.46 | 0.73 | 0.47 | 0.64 | 0.44 | 0.47 |

Table 3: Test results with different system settings, training with IWSLT data, and proportional sampling. Scores are Macro-R and accuracy.

instead of training them separately allows them to adapt better to the pronoun classification task. We use no mini-batching, so in order to stabilize the system to some extent, we follow Kiperwasser and Goldberg (2016) and only update the parameters after collecting several non-zero losses, in our case, 25. In all cases we choose the best epoch based on the average of macro-R and accuracy on the development data. We believe that using both metrics for choosing the best epoch will give us a system that can predict rare classes well, while not sacrificing the overall accuracy across classes.

## 5   Experiments and Results

First we performed experiments to evaluate the different components of our network, using only IWSLT data. These experiments are run for 100 epochs with proportional sampling and 10% of the training data in each epoch. Table 2 shows the results on development data and Table 3 shows the results on test data. We can note a marked difference in performance for English as a target language on the one hand, and English as a source language on the other hand, which interestingly mirrors previous results with an SVM classifier (Stymne, 2016). With German or Spanish as the source, nearly all the components are useful, and discarding them all results in a large performance drop on both metrics. Using the source pronoun head in the MLP was highly useful for German,

but not used for Spanish, where the source pronoun is already encoded in the verb. When English is the source language, we see little effect of any component; some of them even hurt performance slightly. The **all** system did give slightly better scores than the **none** system even in this direction, though, so we decided to use the all components system for all languages in our submission.

For our main experiments, we used all training data and different sampling schemes. For the equal and proportional sampling schemes we used samples containing 10% of the data and ran the system for 72 hours, which resulted in 36–66 epochs, depending on the language pair and sampling scheme. When domain adaptation is used, we ran an additional 100 epochs with the same settings but only IWSLT data, as a final step. For offline sampling, we precomputed 500 samples per training file, and ran 860–1204 epochs.

Tables 4 and 5 shows the results of these experiments for development and test data. Using all data and proportional sampling improves over using only IWSLT, but to different degrees for the different language pairs. Overall we see that for several language pairs the scores are quite different on dev and test data. For English–German, macro-R on test is higher, which can be explained by the missing rare class *man* in the test data. For German–English macro-R is lower on test, which can be explained by our system failing to predict

| Sampling | DA | de-en | | en-de | | en-fr | | es-en | |
|---|---|---|---|---|---|---|---|---|---|
| | | mac-R | acc | mac-R | acc | mac-R | acc | mac-R | acc |
| Equal | no | 0.80 | 0.81 | 0.64 | 0.72 | 0.64 | 0.75 | 0.75 | 0.82 |
| **Equal** | **yes** | 0.81 | 0.86 | 0.62 | 0.73 | 0.66 | 0.77 | 0.79 | 0.82 |
| Proportional | no | 0.69 | 0.85 | 0.48 | 0.76 | 0.58 | 0.75 | 0.71 | 0.83 |
| *Proportional* | *yes* | 0.71 | 0.87 | 0.51 | 0.75 | 0.60 | 0.76 | 0.72 | 0.84 |
| Offline | no | 0.67 | 0.83 | 0.49 | 0.73 | 0.59 | 0.76 | 0.70 | 0.83 |

Table 4: Final development results on all training data with different types of sampling, with and without domain adaptation (DA). Scores are Macro-R and accuracy.

| Sampling | DA | de-en | | en-de | | en-fr | | es-en | |
|---|---|---|---|---|---|---|---|---|---|
| | | mac-R | acc | mac-R | acc | mac-R | acc | mac-R | acc |
| Equal | no | 0.65 | 0.78 | 0.73 | 0.76 | 0.64 | 0.69 | 0.59 | 0.64 |
| **Equal** | **yes** | 0.69 | 0.85 | 0.78 | 0.79 | 0.64 | 0.70 | 0.59 | 0.68 |
| Proportional | no | 0.66 | 0.85 | 0.62 | 0.79 | 0.53 | 0.65 | 0.58 | 0.66 |
| *Proportional* | *yes* | 0.67 | 0.85 | 0.62 | 0.79 | 0.50 | 0.65 | 0.56 | 0.62 |
| Offline | no | 0.66 | 0.83 | 0.59 | 0.74 | 0.48 | 0.65 | 0.51 | 0.65 |
| Shared task baseline | – | 0.38 | 0.54 | 0.54 | 0.55 | 0.37 | 0.48 | 0.34 | 0.37 |

Table 5: Final test results on all training data with different types of sampling, with and without domain adaptation (DA). The last line shows the official shared task baseline scores. Scores are Macro-R and accuracy.

the very few instances of two rare classes. For Spanish–English, the scores on both metrics are overall lower for all classes in test, for which we can see no clear explanation.

We expected to see a trade-off between macro-R and accuracy for the equal sampling compared with the other sampling methods, like for Luotolahti et al. (2016) who used weighted loss. For the dev data we see clearly higher macro-R with equal sampling, but, less of a difference for accuracy. For the test data with domain adaption, though, scores on both metrics are either better or similar with equal sampling compared to the other sampling methods. This means that the system with equal sampling performs strongly on both metrics, contrary to our expectations, making it clearly the best choice for this task. We believe that one partial reason for this could be that we choose the best epoch based on the average of the two metrics.

Domain adaptation improved the results slightly in most cases on dev data. On the test data, we also saw improvements or stable results in most cases, the exceptions being proportional sampling for English-French and Spanish-English, where we saw a small drop in results. We also note that all of our systems are considerably better than the shared task LM-based baseline (Loáiciga et al., 2017), shown in Table 5, on both metrics.

For our shared task submission we used the system with equal sampling and domain adaptation as our primary system, **bold** in Table 4, since it had the best macro-R scores on the development set. We used the system with proportional sampling with domain adaptation as our secondary system, *italic* in Table 4. Our systems perform well in the shared task, achieving first and second places for both macro-R and accuracy in all cases. Our primary systems have high scores on both macro-R and accuracy, in contrast to most other systems in the shared task.

## 6 Conclusions

We have presented the Uppsala system for the 2017 DiscoMT shared task on cross-lingual pronoun prediction. It is a neural network with BiLSTMs as backbone representations of words and lemmas. We show that for German and Spanish as source languages it is useful to add information from characters, POS-tags and dependencies, whereas this has little effect for English as a source language. We define effective sampling schemes to optimize macro-R and accuracy. Our primary systems have high scores on both macro-R and accuracy, when we use sampling schemes with an equal distribution of classes, and choose the best epoch based on the average of macro-R and accuracy. We also show that simple domain adaptation where we train on only in-domain data in the last epochs can improve results. Our system has the highest or second highest score for both macro-R and accuracy for all language pairs in the official evaluation.

## Acknowledgments

We would like to thank Eliyahu Kiperwasser and Miryam de Lhoneux for sharing their code and for valuable discussions. SL was supported by the Swedish Research Council under project 2012-916 *Discourse Oriented Statistical Machine Translation*. FC was funded by a VINNMER Marie Curie Incoming Grant within VINNO-VAs Mobility for Growth programme. Computations were completed in the Taito-CSC cluster in Helsinki through NeIC-NLPL (www.nlpl.eu).

## References

Bernd Bohnet and Joakim Nivre. 2012. A transition-based system for joint part-of-speech tagging and labeled non-projective dependency parsing. In *Proceedings of the 2012 Joint Conference on Empirical Methods in Natural Language Processing and Computational Natural Language Learning*. Jeju Island, Korea, pages 1455–1465.

Raj Dabre, Yevgeniy Puzikov, Fabien Cromieres, and Sadao Kurohashi. 2016. The Kyoto university cross-lingual pronoun translation system. In *Proceedings of the First Conference on Machine Translation*. Berlin, Germany, pages 571–575.

Miryam de Lhoneux, Yan Shao, Ali Basirat, Eliyahu Kiperwasser, Sara Stymne, Yoav Goldberg, and Joakim Nivre. 2017. From raw text to universal dependencies – look, no tags! In *Proceedings of the CoNLL 2017 Shared Task: Multilingual Parsing from Raw Text to Universal Dependencies*. Vancouver, Canada.

Liane Guillou, Christian Hardmeier, Preslav Nakov, Sara Stymne, Jörg Tiedemann, Yannick Versley, Mauro Cettolo, Bonnie Webber, and Andrei Popescu-Belis. 2016. Findings of the 2016 WMT shared task on cross-lingual pronoun prediction. In *Proceedings of the First Conference on Machine Translation*. Berlin, Germany, pages 525–542.

Christian Hardmeier. 2014. *Discourse in Statistical Machine Translation*. Ph.D. thesis, Uppsala University, Uppsala, Sweden.

Christian Hardmeier, Preslav Nakov, Sara Stymne, Jörg Tiedemann, Yannick Versley, and Mauro Cettolo. 2015. Pronoun-focused MT and cross-lingual pronoun prediction: Findings of the 2015 DiscoMT shared task on pronoun translation. In *Proceedings of the Second Workshop on Discourse in Machine Translation*. Lisbon, Portugal, pages 1–16.

Christian Hardmeier, Jörg Tiedemann, and Joakim Nivre. 2013. Latent anaphora resolution for cross-lingual pronoun prediction. In *Proceedings of the 2013 Conference on Empirical Methods in Natural Language Processing*. Seattle, Washington, USA, pages 380–391.

Sepp Hochreiter and Jürgen Schmidhuber. 1997. Long short-term memory. *Neural computation* 9(8):1735–1780.

Mohit Iyyer, Varun Manjunatha, Jordan Boyd-Graber, and Hal Daumé III. 2015. Deep unordered composition rivals syntactic methods for text classification. In *Proceedings of the 53rd Annual Meeting of the Association for Computational Linguistics and the 7th International Joint Conference on Natural Language Processing (Volume 1: Long Papers)*. Beijing, China, pages 1681–1691.

Diederik P. Kingma and Jimmy Ba. 2015. Adam: A method for stochastic optimization. In *Proceedings of the 3rd International Conference on Learning Representations (ICLR)*. San Diego, California, USA.

Eliyahu Kiperwasser and Yoav Goldberg. 2016. Simple and accurate dependency parsing using bidirectional LSTM feature representations. *Transactions of the Association for Computational Linguistics* 4:313–327.

Sharid Loáiciga. 2015. Predicting pronoun translation using syntactic, morphological and contextual features from parallel data. In *Proceedings of the Second Workshop on Discourse in Machine Translation*. Lisbon, Portugal, pages 78–85.

Sharid Loáiciga, Sara Stymne, Preslav Nakov, Christian Hardmeier, Jörg Tiedemann, Mauro Cettolo, and Yannick Versley. 2017. Findings of the 2017 DiscoMT shared task on cross-lingual pronoun prediction. In *Proceedings of the Third Workshop on Discourse in Machine Translation*. Association for Computational Linguistics, Copenhagen, Denmark, DiscoMT-EMNLP17.

Juhani Luotolahti, Jenna Kanerva, and Filip Ginter. 2016. Cross-lingual pronoun prediction with deep recurrent neural networks. In *Proceedings of the First Conference on Machine Translation*. Berlin, Germany, pages 596–601.

Graham Neubig, Chris Dyer, Yoav Goldberg, Austin Matthews, Waleed Ammar, Antonios Anastasopoulos, Miguel Ballesteros, David Chiang, Daniel Clothiaux, Kevin Duh Trevor Cohn, Manaal Faruqui, Cynthia Gan, Dan Garrette, Yangfeng Ji, Lingpeng Kong, Adhiguna Kuncoro, Gaurav Kumar, Chaitanya Malaviya, Paul Michel, Yusuke Oda, Matthew Richardson, Naomi Saphra, Swabha Swayamdipta, and Pengcheng Yin. 2017. DyNet: The dynamic neural network toolkit. *arXiv preprint arXiv:1701.03980* .

Milan Straka, Jan Hajič, and Jana Straková. 2016. UDPipe: Trainable pipeline for processing CoNLL-U files performing tokenization, morphological analysis, POS tagging and parsing. In *Proceedings of the Tenth International Conference on Language Resources and Evaluation (LREC 2016)*. Portorož, Slovenia, pages 4290–4297.

Sara Stymne. 2016. Feature exploration for cross-lingual pronoun prediction. In *Proceedings of the First Conference on Machine Translation*. Berlin, Germany, pages 609–615.

Barret Zoph, Deniz Yuret, Jonathan May, and Kevin Knight. 2016. Transfer learning for low-resource neural machine translation. In *Proceedings of the 2016 Conference on Empirical Methods in Natural Language Processing*. Austin, Texas, USA, pages 1568–1575.

# Neural Machine Translation for Cross-Lingual Pronoun Prediction

**Sebastien Jean***  and  **Stanislas Lauly***  and  **Orhan Firat***  and  **Kyunghyun Cho**
Department of Computer Science
Center for Data Science
New York University
** Both authors contributed equally*

## Abstract

In this paper we present our systems for the DiscoMT 2017 cross-lingual pronoun prediction shared task. For all four language pairs, we trained a standard attention-based neural machine translation system as well as three variants that incorporate information from the preceding source sentence. We show that our systems, which are not specifically designed for pronoun prediction and may be used to generate complete sentence translations, generally achieve competitive results on this task.

## 1 Introduction

Given a source document and its corresponding partial translation, the goal of the DiscoMT 2017 cross-lingual pronoun prediction shared task (Loáiciga et al., 2017) is to correctly replace the missing pronouns, choosing among a small set of candidates. In this paper, we propose and evaluate models on four sub-tasks: En-Fr, En-De, De-En and Es-En.

We consider the use of attention-based neural machine translation systems (Bahdanau et al., 2014) for pronoun prediction and investigate the potential for incorporating discourse-level structure by integrating the preceding source sentence into the models. More specifically, instead of modeling the conditional distribution $p(Y|X)$ over translations given a source sentence, we explore different networks that model $p(Y|X, X_{-1})$, where $X_{-1}$ is the previous source sentence. The proposed larger-context neural machine translation systems are inspired by recent work on larger-context language modeling (Wang and Cho, 2016)

---

*  This work was done during his visit to NYU. Now at Google (orhanf@google.com).

and multi-way, multilingual neural machine translation (Firat et al., 2016).

## 2 Baseline: Attention-based Neural Machine Translation

An attention-based translation system (Bahdanau et al., 2014) is composed of three parts: encoder, decoder, and attention model.

The source sentence $X = (x_1, x_2, \ldots, x_{T_x})$ is encoded into a set of annotation vectors $\{h_1, h_2, \ldots, h_{T_x}\}$. To do so, we use a bidirectional recurrent network (Schuster and Paliwal, 1997) with a gated recurrent unit (GRU, Cho et al., 2014; Hochreiter and Schmidhuber, 1997).

The decoder, composed of a GRU $f$ topped by a one hidden layer MLP $g$, models the conditional probability of the target sentence word $y_i$ knowing the previous words and the source sentence $\mathbf{x}$.

$$p(y_i|y_1, ..., y_{i-1}, \mathbf{x}) = g(y_{i-1}, s_i, c_i) \quad (1)$$

$s_i$ is the RNN hidden state for time $i$, and $c_i$ is a distinct context vector used to predict $y_i$.

$$s_i = f(s_{i-1}, y_{i-1}, c_i) \quad (2)$$

The computation of the context vector $c_i$ depends on the previous decoder hidden state and on the sequence of annotations $(h_1, ..., h_{T_x})$, where each $h_j$ is a representation of the whole source sentence with a focus on the $j^{th}$ word. $c_i$ is a weighted sum of the annotations.

$$c_i = \sum_{j=1}^{T_x} \alpha_{ij} h_j \quad (3)$$

$$\alpha_{ij} = \frac{\exp(e_{ij})}{\sum_{k=1}^{T_x} \exp(e_{ik})} \quad (4)$$



*Proceedings of the Third Workshop on Discourse in Machine Translation*, pages 54–57,
Copenhagen, Denmark, September 8, 2017. ©2017 Association for Computational Linguistics.

$$e_{ij} = a(s_{i-1}, y_{i-1}, h_j) \qquad (5)$$

where $e_{ij}$ is the attention model score, which represents how well the output at time $i$ aligns with the input around time $j$.

# 3 Larger-Context Neural Machine Translation

As the antecedent needed to correctly translate a pronoun may be in a different sentence (inter-sentential anaphora) (Guillou et al., 2016), we added the previous sentence as a auxiliary input to the neural machine translation system, using an additional encoder and attention model. Similarly to the source sentence encoding, we apply a bidirectional recurrent network to generate context annotation vectors $\{h_1^c, \ldots, h_{T_c}^c\}$.

The additional attention model differs slightly from the original one by integrating the current source representation $c_i$ as a new input, so that the context vector depends on the currently attended source words. As such, this attention model takes as input the previous target symbol, the previous decoder hidden state, the context annotation vectors as well as the source vector from the main attention model. That is, the unnormalized alignment scores are computed as

$$e_{ij}^c = a(s_{i-1}, y_{i-1}, h_j, c_i) \qquad (6)$$

Similarly to the source vector $c_i$, the time-dependent context vector $c_i^c$ is also a weighted sum, this time of the context annotation vectors. With this new information, we explored three different approaches.

## 3.1 Simple Context Model (SCM)

For the first approach, we simply use the context representation $c_i^c$ as a additional input to the decoder GRU and the prediction function $g$.

$$s_i = f(s_{i-1}, y_{i-1}, c_i, c_i^c) \qquad (7)$$

$$p(y_i|y_1, \ldots, y_{i-1}, \mathbf{x}, \mathbf{x}^c) = g(y_{i-1}, s_i, c_i, c_i^c) \quad (8)$$

## 3.2 Double-Gated Context Model (DGCM)

Our second approach is very similar to the first with the exception that, for both functions $f$ and $g$, distinct gates ($g_1$ and $g_2$) are applied to the context representation $c_i^c$. Similar context-modulating gates were previously used by (Wang et al., 2017).

$$s_i = f(s_{i-1}, y_{i-1}, c_i, g_1 \odot c_i^c) \qquad (9)$$

$$p(y_i|y_1, \ldots, y_{i-1}, \mathbf{x}, \mathbf{x}^c) = g(y_{i-1}, s_i, c_i, g_2 \odot c_i^c) \qquad (10)$$

Each gate has its own set of parameters and depends on the previous target symbol, the current source representation and the decoder hidden state, at time $i-1$ for $g_1$ and $i$ for $g_2$.

## 3.3 Combined Context Model (CCM)

The last method first combines the source and context representations into a vector $d_i$ through a multi-layer perceptron. As in the second approach, the context is also gated.

$$d_i = \mathbf{W}_3\left(\tanh(\mathbf{W}_1 c_i + \mathbf{W}_2(g_1 \odot c_i^c))\right) \quad (11)$$

$$s_i = f(s_{i-1}, y_{i-1}, d_i) \qquad (12)$$

$$p(y_i|y_1, \ldots, y_{i-1}, \mathbf{x}, \mathbf{x}^c) = g(y_{i-1}, s_i, d_i) \quad (13)$$

# 4 Pronoun prediction task

The DiscoMT 2017 pronoun prediction task serves as a platform to improve pronoun prediction. We are provided source documents and their lemmatized translations for four language pairs: En-Fr, En-De, De-En and Es-En. In each translation, some sentences have one or more pronouns substituted by the placeholder "REPLACE". For each of these tokens, we must select the correct pronoun among a small set of candidates.

There are respectively 8, 5, 9 and 7 target classes for En-Fr, En-De, De-En and Es-En. For example, in the case of En-Fr, the task is concentrated on the translation of "it" and "they". The possible target classes are:

|       | Baseline | SCM  | DGCM | CCM  |
|-------|----------|------|------|------|
| En-Fr | 67.9     | 66.2 | **68.9** | 64.5 |
| En-De | 58.2     | 57.1 | **59.0** | 57.6 |
| De-En | 70.9     | 70.3 | 72.4 | **72.8** |
| Es-En | 69.9     | **77.1** | 70.8 | 72.3 |

Table 1: Validation macro-average recall (in %) for cross-lingual pronoun prediction.

|       | Baseline | SCM  | DGCM | CCM  | Best |
|-------|----------|------|------|------|------|
| En-Fr | 58.1     | 52.2 | 62.3 | 52.1 | 66.9 |
| En-De | 60.9     | 63.2 | 61.3 | 59.5 | 78.4 |
| De-En | 63.3     | 63.8 | 64.8 | 65.5 | 69.2 |
| Es-En | 58.9     | 56.1 | 58.7 | 56.4 | 58.9 |

Table 2: Test macro-average recall (in %) for cross-lingual pronoun prediction. The "Best" column displays the highest score across all primary and contrastive submissions to the DiscoMT 2017 shared task (Loáiciga et al., 2017).

- **ce, elle, elles, il, ils, cela, on, OTHER.**

Although only a subset of the data has context dependencies, it is not difficult to find such instances. The following set of sentences taken from the En-Fr development data is a good example:

- **Context:** *So the idea is that accurate perceptions are fitter perceptions .*

- **Source:** *They give you a survival advantage .*

And here are the source sentence translation with the missing token and the corresponding target:

- **Translation:** *REPLACE vous donner un avantage en terme de survie .*

- **Target:** elles

In this example, "REPLACE" should be the translation of the word "They", which refers to "perceptions" in the previous sentence. This is important because in French, "perceptions" is feminine. Correctly choosing a good pronoun here can only be done confidently with contextual information.

## 5 Experimental settings

To train our models, which are fully differentiable, we use the Adadelta optimizer (Zeiler, 2012). Word embeddings have dimensionality 620, decoder and source encoder RNNs have 1000-dimensional hidden representations, and the context encoder RNN hidden states are of size 620. As the source and context annotations are the concatenation of the forward and backward encoder hidden states, their dimensionality are 2000

and 1240 respectively. The models are regularized with 50% Dropout (Pham et al., 2014) applied to all RNN inputs and on the decoder hidden layer preceding the softmax.

Pronouns are predicted using a modified beam search where the beam is expanded only at the "REPLACE" placeholders, and is otherwise constrained to the reference. The beam size is set to the number of pronoun classes, so that our approach is equivalent to exhaustive search for sentences with a single placeholder. Models for which beam search lead to the highest validation macro-average recall were selected and submitted for the shared task. The baselines were also sent as contrastive submissions.

## 6 Results

Table 1 and 2 respectively present validation and test results across all language pairs for the models described in sections 2 and 3. Amongst the four models we evaluated on the test sets, a different one performs best for each language pair. Nevertheless, the DGCM model is the most consistent, always ranking second or first amongst our systems. Moreover, it beats the baseline on all tasks except Es-En, which it trails by a marginal 0.2%.

Our models, which don't leverage the given part-of-speech tags and external alignments, are generally competitive with the best submissions (Loáiciga et al., 2017). For Es-En, our contrastive submission achieves the best performance. As for En-Fr and De-En, our systems obtain a macro-average recall within 5% of the winners. Finally, the relatively poor performance of our models for En-De is due to their incapacity at correctly predicting the rare pronoun 'er'. Indeed, the recall of 0/8 for that class greatly affects the results.

## 7 Conclusion

In this paper, we have presented our systems for the DiscoMT 2017 cross-lingual pronoun prediction shared task. We have explored various ways of incorporating discourse context into neural machine translation. Even if the DGCM model often achieves better performance than the baseline by taking in account the previous sentence, we believe there is still important progress to be made. In order to improve further, we may need to better understand the impact of context by carefully analyzing the behaviour of our models.

## Acknowledgments

This work was supported by Samsung Electronics ("Larger-Context Neural Machine Translation" and "Next Generation Deep Learning: from pattern recognition to AI"). KC thanks Google (Faculty Award 2016), NVIDIA (NVAIL), Facebook, eBay and TenCent for their generous support.

## References

Dzmitry Bahdanau, Kyunghyun Cho, and Yoshua Bengio. 2014. Neural machine translation by jointly learning to align and translate. *arXiv preprint arXiv:1409.0473* .

Kyunghyun Cho, Bart Van Merriënboer, Caglar Gulcehre, Dzmitry Bahdanau, Fethi Bougares, Holger Schwenk, and Yoshua Bengio. 2014. Learning phrase representations using rnn encoder-decoder for statistical machine translation. *arXiv preprint arXiv:1406.1078* .

Orhan Firat, Kyunghyun Cho, and Yoshua Bengio. 2016. Multi-way, multilingual neural machine translation with a shared attention mechanism. In *NAACL*.

Liane Guillou, Christian Hardmeier, Preslav Nakov, Sara Stymne, Jörg Tiedemann, Yannick Versley, Mauro Cettolo, Bonnie Webber, and Andrei Popescu-Belis. 2016. Findings of the 2016 wmt shared task on cross-lingual pronoun prediction. In *Proceedings of the First Conference on Machine Translation (WMT16), Berlin, Germany. Association for Computational Linguistics*.

Sepp Hochreiter and Jürgen Schmidhuber. 1997. Long short-term memory. *Neural computation* 9(8):1735–1780.

Sharid Loáiciga, Sara Stymne, Preslav Nakov, Christian Hardmeier, Jörg Tiedemann, Mauro Cettolo, and Yannick Versley. 2017. Findings of the 2017 DiscoMT shared task on cross-lingual pronoun prediction. In *Proceedings of the Third Workshop on Discourse in Machine Translation*. Association for Computational Linguistics, Copenhagen, Denmark, DiscoMT-EMNLP17.

Vu Pham, Théodore Bluche, Christopher Kermorvant, and Jérôme Louradour. 2014. Dropout improves recurrent neural networks for handwriting recognition. In *Frontiers in Handwriting Recognition (ICFHR), 2014 14th International Conference on*. IEEE, pages 285–290.

Mike Schuster and Kuldip K Paliwal. 1997. Bidirectional recurrent neural networks. *Signal Processing, IEEE Transactions on* 45(11):2673–2681.

Longyue Wang, Zhaopeng Tu, Andy Way, and Qun Liu. 2017. Exploiting cross-sentence context for neural machine translation. *CoRR* abs/1704.04347. http://arxiv.org/abs/1704.04347.

Tian Wang and Kyunghyun Cho. 2016. Larger-context language modelling. In *ACL*.

Matthew D Zeiler. 2012. Adadelta: an adaptive learning rate method. *arXiv preprint arXiv:1212.5701* .

# Predicting Pronouns with a Convolutional Network and an N-gram Model

**Christian Hardmeier**
Uppsala University
Department of Linguistics and Philology
751 26 Uppsala, Sweden

## Abstract

This paper describes the UU-HARDMEIER system submitted to the DiscoMT 2017 shared task on cross-lingual pronoun prediction. The system is an ensemble of convolutional neural networks combined with a source-aware $n$-gram language model.

## 1 Overview

For the 2017 cross-lingual pronoun prediction shared task, we chose to create a system that could be implemented very quickly while still providing an interesting comparison to the other systems we expect to participate in the shared task. The core components of our system are a convolutional neural network that evaluates the context of the source and target context of the examples. As in our systems from the previous year (Hardmeier, 2016; Loáiciga et al., 2016), we also use a source-aware $n$-gram language model as a complementary component. In contrast to 2016, our neural network classifier does not attempt to model pronominal anaphora explicitly. This change was made to simplify the model and avoid the heavyweight preprocessing that our earlier systems required. Instead, we focused on implementing a more sophisticated system combination method that permits the construction of a larger ensemble of models.

## 2 Convolutional neural network

The neural network architecture of our pronoun prediction model is loosely inspired by the winning system of the WMT 2016 shared task on cross-lingual pronoun prediction (Luotolahti et al., 2016). However, since we expected a large proportion of the participating systems to use recurrent neural networks, we decided to use a simpler convolutional architecture instead. The implementation of the network uses the Keras library (Chollet et al., 2015).

The network independently scans four different input areas for each example: *left source*, *left target*, *right source* and *right target*. All four areas are defined with respect to the position of the element to be predicted, which is a placeholder to be filled on the *target* side aligned to a pronoun on the *source* side. The *left* areas cover the context preceding the pronoun or placeholder, up to the beginning of the previous sentence or at most 50 tokens to the left of the anchoring position, whichever is shorter. The *right* areas cover the context following the pronoun or placeholder, up to the end of the current sentence or at most 50 tokens if the sentence is longer. The context size limit of 50 tokens is large enough to have no effect in most cases, but it ensures that the training efficiency does not suffer from a few overlong sentences. The source language pronoun aligned to the placeholder is included in both the *left* and *right source* context area, whereas the placeholder on the *target* side is excluded from the context areas.

The words of the source and target language are encoded as one-hot vectors using the vocabulary of the IWSLT part of the official training data. Words occurring only once in the IWSLT training set are excluded from the vocabulary and treated as unknown words instead. The part-of-speech tags provided in the training data are ignored. The one-hot vectors are mapped to dense embeddings through an embedding layer with *tanh* activation, whose weights are initialised randomly at training time.

The dense word embeddings form the input of one convolutional layer per input area. The output of the convolutional layers undergo max pooling in a single step over the entire length of the input area. Then the vectors resulting for the four input areas are concatenated together and used as the input of a densely connected layer with softmax activation



*Proceedings of the Third Workshop on Discourse in Machine Translation*, pages 58–62,
Copenhagen, Denmark, September 8, 2017. ©2017 Association for Computational Linguistics.

| | | Network properties | | | | Epochs included | | | |
|---|---|---|---|---|---|---|---|---|---|
| | Training | Weighting | Optimiser | Minibatch | Conv. filters | de-en | en-de | en-fr | es-en |
| A | all | – | Adam | 100 | 100 | 1 | 3 | 3 | – |
| B | IWSLT | + | Adam | 100 | 100 | 15 | 20 | 20 | 20 |
| C | IWSLT | – | Adam | 100 | 100 | – | – | – | 20 |
| D | IWSLT | + | rmsprop | 20 | 50 | – | – | – | 20 |
| E | IWSLT | + | Adam | 20 | 50 | – | – | – | 20 |

Table 1: Properties of the convolutional neural networks included in our submissions

that predicts the class of the example.

We trained the convolutional neural network in different configurations. Five configurations were included in some form in our submissions to the shared task. Unfortunately, we worked under very strong time pressure, and the selection of the included systems and the exploration of the parameter space is not as systematic as we should have wished. We here describe the systems as submitted, without making any specific claims regarding the usefulness of the parameter settings we tested. Also, we did not have time to train the selected systems to convergence. Instead, we saved a snapshot of the network weights after each completed training epoch and ran all these snapshots on the test data. Then we left it to the system combination procedure described in Section 4 to assign weights to all the different snapshots according to their usefulness measured on the development set.

Table 1 shows an overview of the properties distinguishing the five systems used in the submissions and the number of epochs per system included for each language pair (limited by the available training time). Parameters common to all systems are not listed in the table. These include the word embedding in the source and target languages, which were set to 100, and the kernel size in the convolutional layer, which was set to 10.

System A was trained on all training data provided by the organisers, but could only complete a small number of training iterations. The other systems are trained on IWSLT data only. Systems B, D and E use an example weighting scheme that attempts to assign equal weight to all classes in the data regardless of their frequency. Systems A, B, C and E were trained with the Adam optimiser using the default settings in Keras (learning rate 0.001), whilst system D was trained with rmsprop and a learning rate of 0.01. The minibatch sizes were 100 and 20 for different systems, and the number of convolutional filters were 100 and 50.

## 3 Source-aware language model

In our submissions to the WMT 2016 shared task on cross-lingual pronoun prediction (Hardmeier, 2016; Loáiciga et al., 2016), we found that a simple $n$-gram language model extended with access to the identity of the source pronoun achieved quite good results in comparison to our more sophisticated neural network classifier. The information captured by this model seemed to be complementary to that encoded in the neural network, so that additional gains could be realised by combining the two models. This year, we again use a source-aware language model as a component in our work. The following description follows our earlier system description paper (Hardmeier, 2016) and is repeated here for reference.

Our source-aware language model is an $n$-gram model trained on an artificial corpus generated from the target lemmas of the parallel training (Figure 1). Before every REPLACE tag occurring in the data, we insert the source pronoun aligned to the tag (without lowercasing or any other processing). The alignment information attached to the REPLACE tag in the shared task data files is stripped off. In the training data, we instead add the pronoun class to be predicted. The $n$-gram model used for this component is a 6-gram model with modified Kneser-Ney smoothing (Chen and Goodman, 1998) trained with the KenLM toolkit (Heafield, 2011) on the complete set of training data provided for the shared task.

To predict classes for an unseen test set, we first convert it to a format matching that of the training data, but with a uniform, unannotated REPLACE tag used for all classes. We then recover the tag annotated with the correct solution using the `disambig` tool of the SRILM language modelling toolkit (Stolcke et al., 2011). This tool runs the Viterbi algo-

| | |
|---|---|
| *Source:* | **It** 's got these fishing lures on the bottom . |
| *Target lemmas:* | **REPLACE_0** avoir ce leurre de pêche au-dessous . |
| *Solution:* | *ils* |
| *LM training data:* | It **REPLACE_ils** avoir ce leurre de pêche au-dessous . |
| *LM test data:* | It **REPLACE** avoir ce leurre de pêche au-dessous . |

Figure 1: Data for the source-aware language model

rithm to select the most probable mapping of each token from among a set of possible alternatives. The map used for this task trivially maps all tokens to themselves with the exception of the REPLACE tags, which are mapped to the set of annotated RE-PLACE tags found in the training data.

In addition to being included as a component in our primary ensemble systems, we submitted the output of the standalone source-aware language model as a secondary submission for all languages.

## 4   System combination

To combine the neural predictor with the source-aware language model, we linearly interpolated the probabilities assigned to each class by each model. The class finally predicted was the one that scored highest according to the interpolated probability distribution.

The neural network prediction probabilities are obtained trivially as the posterior distribution of the final softmax layer of the convolutional network. For the source-aware language model, we run SRILM's `disambig` tool with the `-posteriors` option, which causes it to output an approximate posterior distribution derived from information collected during the Viterbi decoding pass. For all classes $c$, the probability predicted by the combined model is defined as a convex combination of the probabilities $p_i(c)$ predicted by each model individually:

$$p(c; \lambda) = \sum_i \lambda_i p_i(c) \qquad (1)$$

To estimate the parameter vector $\lambda$, we maximise the log-likelihood of the interpolated model on a development set. The log-likelihood is defined as follows:

$$L(\lambda) = \sum_i \sum_c t_{ic} \log p(c; \lambda) \qquad (2)$$

Here, the index $i$ ranges over the examples in the development set and $c$ ranges over the classes. The indicator variable $t_{ic}$ equals 1 if class $c$ is the correct prediction for example $i$ and 0 otherwise.

The parameter vector $\lambda$ is then obtained as the solution of the following constrained optimisation problem:

Maximise $L(\lambda)$
subject to $\sum_k \lambda_k = 1$ and $\lambda_k \geq 0$ for all $k$.

To solve this problem, we apply the sequential least squares programming (SLSQP) algorithm (Kraft, 1988) as implemented in the SciPy library[1]. The resulting weights are then rounded to 4 decimals and component systems whose weight after rounding equals zero are discarded.

## 5   Results

The results of the official evaluation are shown in Table 2. In this paper, we concentrate on discussing our own systems. For an overview of the shared task results, see the report by Loáiciga et al. (2017). We note that the ensemble system improves over the source-aware n-gram model for all language pairs. The gap in macro-averaged recall exceeds 10 percentage points for German–English and Spanish–English. For English–French, it is about 4 points, and for English–German about 1.5. The results in terms of accuracy show a similar pattern. In Table 3, we find the weights assigned to the individual systems by the system combination procedure. Recall that the ensemble contains multiple instantiations of each of these models (see Table 1); here, the weights are summed over all epochs of a particular model. We observe that the interpolation method assigns appreciable weights to both the neural and the n-gram components in all languages, so that both models make a contribution to the final prediction. The English–German system has the highest language model weight, which partly explains the similar performance of the primary and the contrastive system for this language pair.

---

[1]`http://www.scipy.org/`

|       | Macro-R |        | Accuracy |        |
|-------|---------|--------|----------|--------|
|       | prim.   | contr. | prim.    | contr. |
| de-en | 62.18   | 51.12  | 79.49    | 69.23  |
| en-de | 58.41   | 56.80  | 71.20    | 69.02  |
| en-fr | 62.86   | 58.95  | 73.48    | 71.82  |
| es-en | 52.32   | 42.19  | 54.10    | 46.45  |

Table 2: Official evaluation results for primary (ensemble) and contrastive (n-gram) systems

|    | de-en  | en-de  | en-fr  | es-en  |
|----|--------|--------|--------|--------|
| LM | 0.5437 | 0.7676 | 0.4552 | 0.2931 |
| A  | 0.1886 | 0.0062 | 0.2957 | –      |
| B  | 0.2677 | 0.2262 | 0.2490 | 0.1825 |
| C  | –      | –      | –      | 0.3339 |
| D  | –      | –      | –      | 0.0674 |
| E  | –      | –      | –      | 0.1230 |

Table 3: Weights summed over all epochs for individual systems

Figure 2 shows the development performance of the individual neural networks included in the ensemble for German–English. The size of the dots on the accuracy curve is proportional to the interpolation weight. The figure suggests that system B, which is trained on IWSLT data only, is overfitting the training set and probably needs more regularisation. On the other hand, the performance of system A, trained on the full data set, still improves after 3 epochs, and it is likely that we could have achieved better results with more time for training.

A look at the confusion matrices for the different language pairs (not shown for space reasons) suggests that the convolutional neural networks manage to capture some relevant linguistic information from the context that the n-gram model misses. In particular, the ensemble systems for German–English and English–French are much more successful at distinguishing pronoun classes that require knowledge of the antecedent. In previous work (Hardmeier et al., 2013; Hardmeier, 2014), we used performance on the French pronouns *ils* and *elles* as an indicator of a system's capacity to reason about antecedents. Both pronouns are straightforward translations of the English pronoun *they*, differing in gender only. Our English–French ensemble achieves class F-scores of 76.19% (*elles*) and 83.54% (*ils*) on these classes, as opposed to

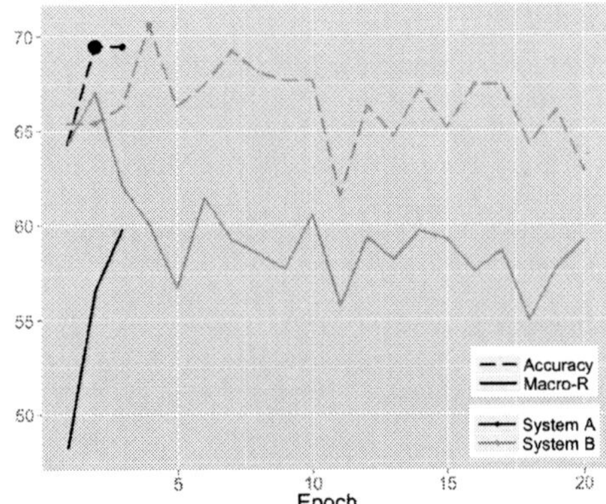


Figure 2: Development set performance of individual snapshots for German–English

35.29% and 79.01% for the n-gram system; this is a large improvement especially for *elles*. The German–English system faces similar difficulties for the pronouns *they* vs. *she* (Hardmeier and Federico, 2010) and likewise improves from 24.00% (*she*) and 56.18% (*they*) to 66.67% and 76.60%. In the other two language pairs, we find no such clear patterns. The predictions for English–German are almost the same in both systems, and Spanish–English improves much more uniformly over all classes.

## 6 Conclusions

The system described in this paper was created to provide an additional point of comparison in the shared task evaluation. It uses a very simple convolutional neural network architecture that can be contrasted with the more sophisticated neural models seen in the previous edition of the shared task. The source-aware *n*-gram model is another approach that achieved reasonable results in the previous evaluation. In comparison with last year, we now apply a better system combination procedure that permits the integration of a large number of systems in the final ensemble.

## Acknowledgements

This work was supported by the Swedish Research Council under grant 2012-916 *Discourse-Oriented Statistical Machine Translation*. Computational resources were provided by CSC – IT Center for Science, Finland, through the Nordic Language Processing Laboratory (NLPL).

## References

Stanley F. Chen and Joshua Goodman. 1998. An empirical study of smoothing techniques for language modeling. Technical report, Computer Science Group, Harvard University, Cambridge (Mass.).

François Chollet et al. 2015. Keras. `https://github.com/fchollet/keras`.

Christian Hardmeier. 2014. *Discourse in Statistical Machine Translation*, volume 15 of *Studia Linguistica Upsaliensia*. Acta Universitatis Upsaliensis, Uppsala.

Christian Hardmeier. 2016. Pronoun prediction with latent anaphora resolution. In *Proceedings of the First Conference on Machine Translation (WMT16)*. Association for Computational Linguistics, Berlin (Germany).

Christian Hardmeier and Marcello Federico. 2010. Modelling pronominal anaphora in statistical machine translation. In *Proceedings of the Seventh International Workshop on Spoken Language Translation (IWSLT)*. Paris (France), pages 283–289.

Christian Hardmeier, Jörg Tiedemann, and Joakim Nivre. 2013. Latent anaphora resolution for cross-lingual pronoun prediction. In *Proceedings of the 2013 Conference on Empirical Methods in Natural Language Processing*. Association for Computational Linguistics, Seattle (Washington, USA), pages 380–391. http://www.aclweb.org/anthology/D13-1037.

Kenneth Heafield. 2011. KenLM: faster and smaller language model queries. In *Proceedings of the Sixth Workshop on Statistical Machine Translation*. Association for Computational Linguistics, Edinburgh (Scotland, UK), pages 187–197. http://www.aclweb.org/anthology/W11-2123.

Dieter Kraft. 1988. A software package for sequential quadratic programming. Technical report, Institut für Dynamik der Flugsysteme, Deutsche Forschungs- und Versuchsanstalt für Luft- und Raumfahrt.

Sharid Loáiciga, Liane Guillou, and Christian Hardmeier. 2016. It-disambiguation and source-aware language models for cross-lingual pronoun prediction. In *Proceedings of the First Conference on Machine Translation (WMT16)*. Association for Computational Linguistics, Berlin (Germany).

Sharid Loáiciga, Sara Stymne, Preslav Nakov, Christian Hardmeier, Jörg Tiedemann, Mauro Cettolo, and Yannick Versley. 2017. Findings of the 2017 DiscoMT shared task on cross-lingual pronoun prediction. In *Proceedings of the 3rd Workshop on Discourse in Machine Translation*.

Juhani Luotolahti, Jenna Kanerva, and Filip Ginter. 2016. Cross-lingual pronoun prediction with deep recurrent neural networks. In *Proceedings of the First Conference on Machine Translation: Volume 2, Shared Task Papers*. Association for Computational Linguistics, pages 596–601. https://doi.org/10.18653/v1/W16-2353.

Andreas Stolcke, Jing Zheng, Wen Wang, and Victor Abrash. 2011. SRILM at sixteen: Update and outlook. In *Proceedings of the IEEE Automatic Speech Recognition and Understanding Workshop*. Waikoloa (Hawaii, USA).

# Cross-Lingual Pronoun Prediction with
# Deep Recurrent Neural Networks v2.0

**Juhani Luotolahti**[1,2] **Jenna Kanerva**[1,2] **and Filip Ginter**[1]
[1]TurkuNLP Group, University of Turku, Finland
[2]University of Turku Graduate School (UTUGS), Turku, Finland
`mjluot@utu.fi` `jmnybl@utu.fi` `figint@utu.fi`

## Abstract

In this paper we present our system in the DiscoMT 2017 Shared Task on Cross-lingual Pronoun Prediction. Our entry builds on our last year's success, our system based on deep recurrent neural networks outperformed all the other systems with a clear margin. This year we investigate whether different pre-trained word embeddings can be used to improve the neural systems, and whether the recently published Gated Convolutions outperform the Gated Recurrent Units used last year.

## 1 Introduction

The DiscoMT 2017 Shared Task on Cross-lingual Pronoun Prediction (Loáiciga et al., 2017) concentrates on the difficult task of translating pronouns between languages. For example different gender marking between languages complicates the translation process. This shared task includes three languages and four translation directions: English-French, English-German, German-English and Spanish-English. In the target language side selected set of pronouns are substituted with `replace` token, and the task is then to predict the missing pronoun. Furthermore, the target side language is not given as running text, but instead in lemma plus part-of-speech tag format, which makes even harder to model the target language. An example of an English-French sentence pair is given in Figure 1.

In this paper we describe the pronoun prediction system of the Turku NLP Group. Our system extends the last year's deep recurrent neural networks based system with word-level embeddings, two layers of Gated Recurrent Units (GRUs) and a softmax layer on top of it to make the final prediction (Luotolahti et al., 2016). This year

*Source: That 's how **they** like to live .*
***Target:** ce|PRON être|VER comme|ADV cela|PRON que|PRON **REPLACE_3** aimer|VER vivre|VER .|.*

Figure 1: An example sentence from the English to French training data, where the REPLACE_3 is a placeholder for the word to be predicted.

we investigate whether pre-trained word embeddings improve the system performance compared to the random initialization used in the previous system. We also study whether the recently published Gated Convolution outperforms Gated Recurrent Units.

The network uses both source and target contexts to make the prediction, and no additional data or tools are used beside the data provided by the organizers. Also our pre-trained word embeddings are trained on the same data.

## 2 System Architecture

As in the previous year, our system is a deep neural network model reading context from both source and target side sentences around the focus pronoun. The most important change are the token-level embeddings, which are now pre-trained before training the full system. The system architecture itself is improved relative to the last year system by filtering from the data aligned pronouns that are too long, as these are alignment errors rather than actual pronouns. We also increase the size of the last dense neural network layer from 320 to 720 units, to address a possible bottleneck caused by excessive data compression. We also experiment with changing the basic network units from Gated Recurrent Units to Gated Convolutions. Otherwise the network and parameters are exactly the same, and are only shortly explained



*Proceedings of the Third Workshop on Discourse in Machine Translation*, pages 63–66,
Copenhagen, Denmark, September 8, 2017. ©2017 Association for Computational Linguistics.

here. More information is provided in Luotolahti et al. (2016).

In both source and target side the context is read separately in left and right directions starting from the focus pronoun[1] or the `replace` token, so that the source side pronoun is always included in both right and left contexts, but the special `replace` token in the target side is not, as it does not provide any useful information. All words in the contexts are embedded and pushed through the layers of either GRU or Gated Convolutions, finally concatenating the vectors, along with the embedding vector for the aligned pronoun, for the last softmax layer, which makes the final prediction.

The systems tested can be divided into three categories, those with pre-trained embeddings, those using GRU as the basic network unit and those using convolutional neural networks as the basic unit. All systems were tested on the dev-set and the best two were chosen for submission. All systems use the same input data, basic structure of the system, and features. The context used by the systems is restricted to a single sentence, as this provided the best results last year and in preliminary experiments we were unable to obtain a consistent gain by expanding the context.

The systems using GRU as the basic network unit are listed in Table 1 as GRU, GRU_dropouts, GRU_Pronoun_Context, Mixed_Context and GRU_Word2Vec. Of these systems, GRU uses randomly initialized embeddings and is essentially our last year's system. GRU_dropouts is identical to the former system, but has dropouts of 0.5 added after every GRU layer to possibly improve generalization of the system. The three latter systems, GRU_Pronoun_Context, GRU_Mixed_Context and GRU_Word2Vec, all have identical architecture to the GRU system, but use pre-trained embeddings. The architecture of these systems is depicted in Figure 2.

Systems GatedConv_1, GatedConv_2 and GatedConv_Mixed_Context use all convolutional neural networks as their basic unit. Of these the last, GatedConv_Mixed_Context, uses the same pre-trained embeddings as the Mixed_Context system. All of these systems use stacked gated convolutional layers as a replacement to stacked GRUs. Gated convolutional networks have lately been demonstrated to offer comparable performance to recurrent neural networks (Dauphin et al., 2016). GatedConv_1 uses two layers of gated linear units and both GatedConv_2 and GatedConv_Mixed_Context use four layers, all convolutional systems use convolution width of 10 and 90 units. For more details on the gated convolutional architectures, refer to Dauphin et al. (2016). The architecture of the network for convolutional systems is identical to the GRU ones, except we have replaced GRU layers with convolutional layers. The convolutional layers are gated, in practice we the output of a gated convolutional layer is an elementwise product between a linear convolutional layer and a convolutional layer with sigmoid activation function, both convolutional layers receiving the same input.

## 2.1 Word Embeddings

Word embeddings are trained on the official training data provided by the organizers having approximately 60 million words per language, which is relatively small for training regular word2vec (Mikolov et al., 2013) style word embeddings. In addition to the regular word2vec embeddings we train two alternative word embedding models with the training task geared towards this particular pronoun prediction task. Firstly, instead of a sliding window of words we define the context for a source word to be all pronouns in the counterpart target sentence. In other words, instead of predicting nearby words, we modify word2vec to predict target sentence pronouns. This way, similar embeddings are given to source-side words which associate with similar pronouns on the target side, which we expect to be a good pre-training strategy for pronoun prediction. This pretraining method we refer to as the *pronoun context*. Secondly, we extend the pronoun context method with the standard skip-gram context, i.e. predicting all target sentence pronouns as well as words nearby in the linear order. Since the shared task training data includes also word alignments, we use a union of skip-gram contexts on the source side and the target side. Therefore, in this *mixed context* method, for every source word, word2vec is used to predict the target sentence pronouns, the source sentence context words, and the target sentence context lemmas.

The word embeddings are trained using

---

[1] As the training data includes word-level alignments between the source and target language, we are able to identify the source language counterpart for the missing pronoun.

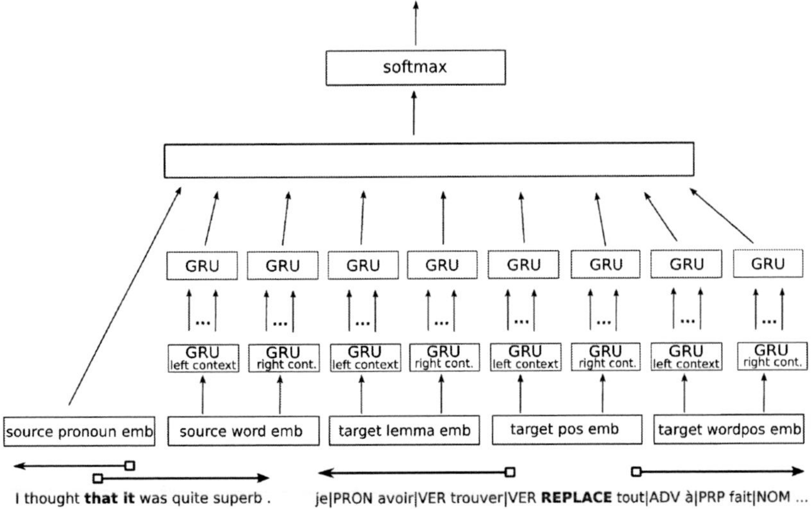



Figure 2: GRU architecture

word2vec[2] and word2vecf[3] softwares by Mikolov et al. (2013) and Levy and Goldberg (2014) respectively, the latter supporting arbitrary contexts for word2vec style embedding learning. All embeddings are trained using the full training data, i.e. also sentences without training examples for the pronoun prediction task and no other data is used. All word embeddings use 90-dimensional vectors, and are trained using the skip-gram architecture with negative sampling and 10 training iterations.

## 2.2 Data and Training

The training data provided by the organizers is based on three different datasets, the Europarl dataset (Koehn, 2005), news commentary corpora (IWSLT15, NCv9), and the TED corpus[4]. We used the whole TED corpus only as development data, and thus our submitted systems and word embeddings are trained on the union of Europarl and news commentary texts, which are randomly shuffled. The total size of training data for each source–target pair is approximately 2.2–2.4 million sentences, having 590K–800K training examples depending on the pair.

Since the main metric in the official evaluation is macro recall, our submission is trained to optimize this metric. This is achieved by weighting the loss of the training examples inversely proportional to the frequencies of the classes, so that misclassifying a rare class is a more serious error than misclassifying a common class. This scheme produces outputs with a higher emphasis on rare classes. This scheme yielded very good results last year, giving more than 4 percent point improvement on average.

Exactly the same system architecture is used for all four language pairs, and no language-dependent optimization was carried out. This makes our system fully language-agnostic. The only difference is the number of epochs used in training, set for each language pair separately using the prediction performance on the development set.

## 3 Results

Table 1 shows our system variants evaluated on the test data. In general, the recurrent systems seem to be performing better than the convolutional systems. However, since due to time restrictions we were unable to perform a specialized hyper-parameter search on any of the systems, only tentative conclusions can be made. Further, all systems seem to generally benefit from the pre-trained input vectors, with the excpeption of plain word2vec. Pre-trained embeddings with context which includes pronoun information perform better than plain word2vec pre-training and random initialization. Adding dropouts also improved performance on the test set, which was not

---

[2]`https://github.com/tmikolov/word2vec`
[3]`https://github.com/BIU-NLP/word2vecf`
[4]`http://www.ted.com`

| | En-De | De-En | En-Fr | Es-En | Average | Rank |
|---|---|---|---|---|---|---|
| GRU | 52.22 | 56.79 | 53.65 | 45.51 | 52.22 | 7 |
| GRU_dropouts | 49.44 | 64.25 | 56.05 | 54.63 | 56.09 | 5 |
| GRU_Pronoun_Context | 61.66 | 69.21 | 64.74 | 58.78 | 63.60 | 2 |
| GRU_Mixed_Context | **68.95** | 68.88 | **66.89** | **58.82** | **65.89** | 1 |
| GRU_Word2Vec | 42.91 | 45.98 | 48.49 | 49.67 | 46.76 | 8 |
| GatedConv_1 | 43.57 | 59.22 | 60.37 | 52.29 | 53.86 | 6 |
| GatedConv_2 | 45.77 | 69.35 | 58.02 | 52.4 | 56.39 | 4 |
| GatedConv_Mixed_Context | 46.64 | **68.91** | 61.53 | 58.78 | 58.97 | 3 |

Table 1: Test set results of the variants of the system tested against the test sets.

visible in the development set results.

It is to be noted that the systems performed worse on the test data than the development data, indicating overfitting to the development data, but their relative strength remained roughly the same with all top three systems utilizing embedding pretraining based on the task, with the only exception being that system with dropouts performed better than without, which is fitting because dropouts should reduce overfitting. Also, surprisingly word2vec embedding initialization performed worse than random initialization.

Compared to systems submitted for the task, our system performed fairly well. For language pairs German − English and English − French our systems, when measured with macro recall, the official task metric, our system received the best scores among the submitted systems, and for language pair Spanish - English second best scores by 0.05 percent points. This is in contrast to language pair English - German in which our system received second best score, but the difference to the winning system is almost 10 percent points.

## 4   Conclusions

In this paper we presented our improved system for cross-lingual pronoun prediction shared task. We included pre-trained word embeddings as well as evaluated the performance of Gated Convolutions compared to Gated Recurrent Units as basic units of our deep network. On the development set, we found that the Gated Recurrent Units outperform the Gated Convolution and that pretraining the embeddings in a task-specific fashion outperforms the vanilla word2vec method.

Our system is openly available at `https://github.com/TurkuNLP/smt-pronouns`.

## Acknowledgments

This work was supported by the Kone Foundation and the Finnish Academy. Computational resources were provided by CSC – IT Center for Science, Finland.

## References

Yann N Dauphin, Angela Fan, Michael Auli, and David Grangier. 2016. Language modeling with gated convolutional networks. *arXiv preprint arXiv:1612.08083* .

Philipp Koehn. 2005. Europarl: A parallel corpus for statistical machine translation. In *MT summit*. volume 5, pages 79–86.

Omer Levy and Yoav Goldberg. 2014. Dependency-based word embeddings. In *Proceedings of ACL*.

Sharid Loáiciga, Sara Stymne, Preslav Nakov, Christian Hardmeier, Jörg Tiedemann, Mauro Cettolo, and Yannick Versley. 2017. Findings of the 2017 DiscoMT shared task on cross-lingual pronoun prediction. In *Proceedings of the Third Workshop on Discourse in Machine Translation*. Association for Computational Linguistics, Copenhagen, Denmark, DiscoMT-EMNLP17.

Juhani Luotolahti, Jenna Kanerva, and Filip Ginter. 2016. Cross-lingual pronoun prediction with deep recurrent neural networks. In *Proceedings of the First Conference on Machine Translation*. Association for Computational Linguistics, pages 596–601. http://www.aclweb.org/anthology/W/W16/W16-2353.pdf.

Tomas Mikolov, Kai Chen, Greg Corrado, and Jeffrey Dean. 2013. Efficient estimation of word representations in vector space. In *Proceedings of ICLR*.

# Combining the output of two coreference resolution systems for two source languages to improve annotation projection

**Yulia Grishina**
Applied Computational Linguistics
FSP Cognitive Science
University of Potsdam
grishina@uni-potsdam.de

## Abstract

Although parallel coreference corpora can to a high degree support the development of SMT systems, there are no large-scale parallel datasets available due to the complexity of the annotation task and the variability in annotation schemes. In this study, we exploit an annotation projection method to combine the output of two coreference resolution systems for two different source languages (English, German) in order to create an annotated corpus for a third language (Russian). We show that our technique is superior to projecting annotations from a single source language, and we provide an in-depth analysis of the projected annotations in order to assess the perspectives of our approach.

## 1 Introduction

Most of the recent work on exploiting coreference relations in Machine Translation focused on improving the translation of anaphoric pronouns (Le Nagard and Koehn, 2010; Hardmeier and Federico, 2010; Guillou, 2012; Novák et al., 2015; Guillou and Webber, 2015), disregarding other types of coreference relations, one of the reasons being the lack of annotated parallel corpora as well as the variability in the annotated data. However, this could be alleviated by exploiting annotation projection across parallel corpora to create more linguistically annotated resources for new languages. More importantly, applying annotation projection using several source languages would support the creation of corpora less biased towards the peculiarities of a single source annotation scheme.

In our study, we aim at exploring the usability of annotation projection for the transfer of automatically produced coreference chains. In particular, our idea is that using several source annotations produced by different systems could improve the performance of the projection method. Our approach to the annotation projection builds upon the approach recently introduced by (Grishina and Stede, 2017), who experimented with projecting manually annotated coreference chains from two source languages to the target language. However, our goal is slightly different: We are interested in developing a fully automatic pipeline, which would support the automatic creation of parallel annotated corpora in new languages. Therefore, in contrast to (Grishina and Stede, 2017), we use automatic source annotations produced by two state-of-the-art coreference systems, and we combine the output of our projection method for two source languages (English and German) to obtain target annotations for a third language (Russian). Through performing the error analysis of the projected annotations, we investigate the most common projection errors and assess the benefits and drawbacks of our method.

The paper is organized as follows: Section 2 presents an overview of the related work and Section 3 describes the experimental setup. In Section 4, we give a detailed error analysis and discuss the results of our experiment. The conclusions and the avenues for future research are presented in Section 5.

## 2 Related work

Annotation projection is a method that allows for automatically transferring annotations from a well-studied (source) language to a low-resource (target) language in a parallel corpus in order to automatically obtain annotated data. It was first introduced in the work of (Yarowsky et al., 2001)



*Proceedings of the Third Workshop on Discourse in Machine Translation*, pages 67–72,
Copenhagen, Denmark, September 8, 2017. ©2017 Association for Computational Linguistics.

|          |  News  |       | Stories |       |  Total |        |
|----------|--------|-------|---------|-------|--------|--------|
|          | EN     | DE    | EN      | DE    | EN     | DE     |
| Markables | 486   | 621   | 429     | 414   | 915    | 1035   |
| Chains    | 125   | 200   | 57      | 68    | 182    | 268    |

Table 1: Number of markables and coreference chains in the automatic annotations

|               | MUC  |      |      | $B^3$ |      |      | CEAF$_m$ |      |      | Avg. |      |      |
|---------------|------|------|------|-------|------|------|----------|------|------|------|------|------|
|               | P    | R    | F1   | P     | R    | F1   | P        | R    | F1   | P    | R    | F1   |
| berkeley (EN) | 49.5 | 41.4 | 45.0 | 38.9  | 27.8 | 32.1 | 45.9     | 40.4 | 42.9 | 44.7 | 36.5 | 40.0 |
| CorZu (DE)    | 66.9 | 59.2 | 62.5 | 59.2  | 41.3 | 46.6 | 52.4     | 52.8 | 52.3 | 59.5 | 51.1 | 53.8 |

Table 2: Evaluation of the automatic source annotations

and then extensively exploited for different kinds of linguistic tasks, including coreference resolution. Specifically, several studies used annotation projection to acquire annotated data, such as (Postolache et al., 2006; Rahman and Ng, 2012; Martins, 2015; Grishina and Stede, 2015).

Thereafter, (Grishina and Stede, 2017) proposed a multi-source method for annotation projection: They used a manually annotated trilingual coreference corpus and two source languages (English-German, English-Russian) to transfer annotations to the target language (Russian and German, respectively). Although their approach showed promising results, it was based on transferring manually produced annotations, which are typically not available for other languages and, more importantly, can not be acquired large-scale due to the complexity of the annotation task.

## 3  Annotation projection experiment

In our experiment, we propose a fully automatic projection setup: First, we perform coreference resolution on the source language data and then we implement the single- and multi-source approaches to transfer the automatically produced annotations. We use the English-German-Russian unannotated corpus of (Grishina and Stede, 2017) as the basis for our experiment, which contains texts in two genres – newswire texts (229 sentences per language) and short stories (184 sentences per language). Furthermore, we use manual annotations present in the corpus as the gold standard for our evaluation. It should be noted that the manual annotations were performed according to the parallel coreference annotation guidelines of (Grishina and Stede, 2016) that are in general compatible with the annotation of the the OntoNotes corpus (Hovy et al., 2006) and are therefore suitable for our evaluation.

### 3.1  Coreference resolution on the source language data

Since the main goal of this experiment is to assess the quality of the projection of automatic annotations, first we need to automatically label the source language data. For the English side of the corpus, we chose the Berkeley Entity Resolution system (Durrett and Klein, 2014), which was trained on the English part of the OntoNotes corpus (Hovy et al., 2006) and achieves the average F1 of 61.71 on the OntoNotes dataset (Durrett and Klein, 2014). For the German side of the corpus, we use the state-of-the-art CorZu system (Tuggener, 2016) to obtain the source annotations, which achieves the average of 66.9 F1 on the German part of the SemEval 2010 dataset (Klenner and Tuggener, 2011).

Corpus statistics for the English and German datasets are presented in Table 1. Interestingly, CorZu was able to resolve slightly more markables and coreference chains in total than Berkeley (1035 vs. 915, 268 vs. 182 respectively). In particular, the numbers of found markables and chains in English and German diverge for the newswire texts, which further supports the claim that this part of the corpus contains more complex coreference relations than the short stories[1].

To estimate the quality of the automatically produced annotations, we evaluate the resulting dataset against the manually annotated English and German parts of the corpus (Table 2). As one can see from this table, CorZu and Berkeley do not perform equally good on our dataset: the average F1 of 53.8 for German as compared to the average F1 of 40.0 for English.

---

[1] As already stated in (Grishina and Stede, 2017), the newswire texts contain a larger percentage of complex noun phrases than the short stories.

|  | MUC | | | $B^3$ | | | $CEAF_m$ | | | Avg. | | |
|---|---|---|---|---|---|---|---|---|---|---|---|---|
|  | P | R | F1 | P | R | F1 | P | R | F1 | P | R | F1 |
| en-ru | 51.7 | 32.6 | 39.8 | 40.6 | 19.6 | 26.0 | 45.7 | 31.3 | 37.0 | 46.0 | 27.8 | 34.3 |
| de-ru | 55.5 | 23.6 | 32.8 | 42.1 | 13.0 | 19.1 | 43.0 | 25.3 | 31.6 | 46.9 | 20.6 | 27.8 |
| en,de-ru |  |  |  |  |  |  |  |  |  |  |  |  |
| Setting 1 | 58.5 | 33.6 | 42.5 | 43.9 | 19.8 | 26.9 | 55.7 | 30.3 | 39.1 | 52.7 | 27.9 | **36.2** |
| Setting 2 | 85.2 | 14.9 | 24.7 | 76.8 | 7.8 | 13.8 | 75.8 | 17.1 | 27.6 | **79.3** | 13.3 | 22.0 |
| Setting 3 | 49.4 | 36.1 | 41.5 | 35.9 | 22.1 | 26.7 | 38.3 | 35.2 | 36.5 | 41.2 | **31.1** | 34.9 |

Table 3: Projection results from English and German into Russian

## 3.2 Annotation projection strategies

For our experiment, we implement a direct projection method for coreference as described in (Grishina and Stede, 2015). Our method works as follows: For each markable on the source side, we automatically select all the corresponding tokens on the target side aligned to it, and we then take the span between the first and the last word as the new target markable, which has the same coreference chain number as the source one. Since the corpus was already sentence- and word-aligned[2], we use the available alignments to transfer the annotations.

Thereafter, we re-implement the multi-source approach as described in (Grishina and Stede, 2017). In particular, they (a) looked at disjoint chains coming from different sources and (b) used the notion of chain overlap to measure the similarity between two coreference chains that contain some identical mentions[3]. In our experiment, we apply the following strategies from (Grishina and Stede, 2017):

1. Setting 1 ('add'): disjoint chains from one source language are added to all the chains projected from the other source language;

2. Setting 2 ('unify-intersect'): the intersection of mentions for overlapping chains is selected.

3. Setting 3 ('unify-concatenate'): chains that overlap are treated as one chain starting from a certain percentage of overlap.

For both single- and multi-source approaches, we deliberately rely solely on word alignment information to project the annotations, in order to keep our approach easily transferable to other languages.

<hr>

[2]Sentence alignment was performed using HunAlign (Varga et al., 2007); word alignments were computed with GIZA++ (Och and Ney, 2003) on a parallel newswire corpus (Grishina and Stede, 2015).

[3]Computed as Dice coefficient.

## 3.3 Results

To evaluate the projection results, we computed the standard coreference metrics – MUC (Vilain et al., 1995), B-cubed (Bagga and Baldwin, 1998) and CEAF (Luo, 2005) – and their average for each of the approaches (Table 3). As one can see from the table, the quality of projections from English to Russian outperforms the quality of projections from German to Russian by 6.5 points F1. Moreover, while Precision number are quite similar, projections from English exhibit higher Recall numbers.

As for the multi-source settings, we were able to achieve the highest F1 of 36.2 by combining disjoint chains (Setting 1), which is 1.9 point higher than the best single-source projection scores and constitutes almost 62% of the quality of the projection of gold standard annotations reported in (Grishina and Stede, 2017). We were able to achieve the highest Precision scores by intersecting the overlapping chains (Setting 2) and the highest Recall by concatenating them (Setting 3).

Finally, we evaluate the annotations coming from English and German against each other, in order to estimate their comparability and the percentage of overlap. Interestingly, we achieve 52.0 F1, with Precision being slightly higher than Recall (53.9 vs. 50.2), which shows the dissimilarity between the two projections.

## 4 Error analysis and discussion

Analyzing the errors coming from each of the source languages, we first looked at the percentage of transferred mentions (Table 4): Using our method we were able to automatically transfer 82.7% of all the source markable from English and only 57.6% of all the source markables from German; similarly, the percentage of the transferred chains is lower for German than for English. Interestingly, while CorZu performs better on the source dataset than Berkeley, the results for the annotations projected from a single source are the opposite: Annotation projection from English to Russian performs better than from German to Russian. Our hypothesis is that the reason for the lower percentage of transferred annotations is the lower quality of word alignments for German-Russian as compared to English-Russian. Furthermore, since the original language of the texts was English, we presume that the German and Russian translations are closer to English and less similar to each other.

|  | English | | German | |
|---|---|---|---|---|
|  | # | % | # | % |
| Markables | 757 | 82.7 | 596 | 57.6 |
| Chains | 182 | 100.0 | 227 | 84.7 |

Table 4: Transferred chains and markables

Since we do not have access to any gold alignment data, we estimate the quality of the word alignments by computing the number of unaligned tokens. Not surprisingly, we see a higher percentage of unaligned words for German-Russian than for English-Russian: 17.03% vs. 14.96% respectively, which supports our hypothesis regarding the difference in the alignment quality for the two pairs. Furthermore, we computed the distribution of unaligned words: The highest percentage of unaligned tokens disregarding punctuation marks are prepositions; pronouns constitute only 3% and 5% of all unaligned words for the alignments between English-Russian and German-Russian respectively. However, these numbers do not constitute more than 5% of the overall number of pronouns in the corpus.

Following the work of (Grishina and Stede, 2017), we analyse the projection accuracy for common nouns ('Nc'), named entities ('Np') and pronouns ('P') separately[4]: Table 5 shows the percentage of correctly projected markables of each type out of all the projected markables of this type. Our results conform to the results of (Grishina and Stede, 2017): For both languages, pronouns exhibit the highest projection quality, while common and proper nouns are projected slightly less accurately, which is probably due to the fact that pronouns typically consist of single tokens and are better aligned than multi-token common and proper names. Overall, for all the markables, the projection accuracy for English-Russian is around

---



10% better than projection accuracy for German-Russian.

|  | en-ru | de-ru |
|---|---|---|
| Nc | 64.5 | 60.7 |
| Np | 70.5 | 66.6 |
| P | 83.6 | 76.5 |
| All | 65.1 | 55.6 |

Table 5: Projection accuracy for common nouns, proper nouns and pronouns (%)

Moreover, we compare the projected annotations across the two genres. Interestingly, the results for the two languages vary: While the average coreference scores for English-Russian are quite comparable (news: 34.2 F1, stories: 33.3 F1), the scores for German-Russian differ considerably (news: 30.8 F1, stories: 20.8 F1). We attribute this difference to the quality of the source annotations and the performance of the source coreference resolvers on different genres of texts.

## 5  Summary and outlook

In this study, we assessed the applicability of annotation projection in a scenario where we have access to two coreference resolvers in two source languages, the output of which is projected to a third language in a low-resource setting. Our results have shown that projection from two source languages is able to reach 62% of the quality of the projection of manual annotations and improves the projection scores by 1.9 F1. Moreover, using the output of two completely different coreference resolution systems, we observed the similar tendencies as while projecting gold standard annotations: Projection from English to Russian achieves higher scores than projection from German to Russian, and pronouns have the highest projection accuracy.

Another important finding is that better source annotations does not necessarily result in better projection scores, which can be explained by the different quality of word alignments for both language pairs. Having investigated this issue, we conclude that alignments between German and Russian contain more unaligned units than the alignments between English and Russian. Our next steps include examining the alignment quality in more detail, which would require establishing a gold standard set of alignments (for at least noun phrases).

---

[4]Using the automatic POS annotations already present in the corpus and provided by TreeTagger (Schmid, 2013).

Overall, we envision our future work in exploiting more than two source annotations as well as multiple coreference resolution systems for a single source language to improve the source coreference annotations. Specifically, we plan on applying our method on other language pairs and datasets, in order to explore its generalizabililty for a wider range of languages. Furthermore, we are interested in exploiting our approach as a first step to create coreference annotated corpora in new languages by providing automatically projected target coreference chains to human annotators for a subsequent validation.

# References


Amit Bagga and Breck Baldwin. 1998. Entity-based cross-document coreferencing using the vector space model. In *Proceedings of the 17th international conference on Computational linguistics-Volume 1*. Association for Computational Linguistics, pages 79–85.

Greg Durrett and Dan Klein. 2014. A joint model for entity analysis: Coreference, typing, and linking. In *Transactions of the Association for Computational Linguistics*.

Yulia Grishina and Manfred Stede. 2015. Knowledge-lean projection of coreference chains across languages. In *Proceedings of the 8th Workshop on Building and Using Comparable Corpora, Beijing, China*. Association for Computational Linguistics, page 14.

Yulia Grishina and Manfred Stede. 2016. *Parallel coreference annotation guidelines*. University of Potsdam.

Yulia Grishina and Manfred Stede. 2017. Multi-source annotation projection of coreference chains: Assessing strategies and testing opportunities. In *Second Workshop on Coreference Resolution Beyond OntoNotes*. Association for Computational Linguistics, page 41.

Liane Guillou. 2012. Improving pronoun translation for statistical machine translation. In *Proceedings of the Student Research Workshop at the 13th Conference of the European Chapter of the Association for Computational Linguistics*. Association for Computational Linguistics, pages 1–10.

Liane Guillou and Bonnie Webber. 2015. Analysing ParCor and its translations by state-of-the-art SMT systems. In *Proceedings of the Second Workshop on Discourse in Machine Translation*. Association for Computational Linguistics, page 24.

Christian Hardmeier and Marcello Federico. 2010. Modelling pronominal anaphora in statistical machine translation. In *IWSLT (International Workshop on Spoken Language Translation); Paris, France; December 2nd and 3rd, 2010.*. pages 283–289.

Eduard Hovy, Mitchell Marcus, Martha Palmer, Lance Ramshaw, and Ralph Weischedel. 2006. OntoNotes: the 90% solution. In *Proceedings of the Human language technology conference of the NAACL, Companion Volume: Short Papers*. Association for Computational Linguistics, pages 57–60.

Manfred Klenner and Don Tuggener. 2011. An incremental entity-mention model for coreference resolution with restrictive antecedent accessibility. In *Proceedings of the international conference on Recent Advances in Natural Language Processing*. pages 178–185.

Ronan Le Nagard and Philipp Koehn. 2010. Aiding pronoun translation with co-reference resolution. In *Proceedings of the Joint Fifth Workshop on Statistical Machine Translation and Metrics (MATR)*. Association for Computational Linguistics, pages 252–261.

Xiaoqiang Luo. 2005. On coreference resolution performance metrics. In *Proceedings of the conference on Human Language Technology and Empirical Methods in Natural Language Processing*. Association for Computational Linguistics, pages 25–32.

André Martins. 2015. Transferring coreference resolvers with posterior regularization. In *Proceedings of the 53rd Annual Meeting of the Association for Computational Linguistics*. volume 1, pages 1427–1437.

Michal Novák, Dieke Oele, and Gertjan van Noord. 2015. Comparison of coreference resolvers for deep syntax translation. In *Proceedings of the Second Workshop on Discourse in Machine Translation*. Association for Computational Linguistics, page 17.

Franz Josef Och and Hermann Ney. 2003. A systematic comparison of various statistical alignment models. *Computational Linguistics* 29(1):19–51.

Oana Postolache, Dan Cristea, and Constantin Orasan. 2006. Transferring coreference chains through word alignment. In *Proceedings of 5th international conference on Language Resources and Evaluation (LREC)*.

Altaf Rahman and Vincent Ng. 2012. Translation-based projection for multilingual coreference resolution. In *Proceedings of the 2012 Conference of the North American Chapter of the Association for Computational Linguistics: Human Language Technologies*. Association for Computational Linguistics, pages 720–730.

Helmut Schmid. 2013. Probabilistic part-of speech tagging using decision trees. In *New methods in language processing*. Routledge, page 154.

Don Tuggener. 2016. *Incremental Coreference Resolution for German*. Ph.D. thesis, University of Zurich.

Dániel Varga, Péter Halácsy, András Kornai, Viktor Nagy, László Németh, and Viktor Trón. 2007. Parallel corpora for medium density languages. *Amsterdam Studies in the Theory and History of Linguistic Science Series 4* 292:247.

Marc Vilain, John Burger, John Aberdeen, Dennis Connolly, and Lynette Hirschman. 1995. A model-theoretic coreference scoring scheme. In *Proceedings of the 6th conference on Message understanding*. Association for Computational Linguistics, pages 45–52.

David Yarowsky, Grace Ngai, and Richard Wicentowski. 2001. Inducing multilingual text analysis tools via robust projection across aligned corpora. In *Proceedings of the first international conference on Human language technology research*. Association for Computational Linguistics, pages 1–8.

# Discovery of Discourse-Related Language Contrasts through Alignment Discrepancies in English-German Translation


**Ekaterina Lapshinova-Koltunski**
Saarland University
`e.lapshinova`
`@mx.uni-saarland.de`

**Christian Hardmeier**
Uppsala University
`christian.hardmeier`
`@lingfil.uu.se`



## Abstract

In this paper, we analyse alignment discrepancies for discourse structures in English-German parallel data – sentence pairs, in which discourse structures in target or source texts have no alignment in the corresponding parallel sentences. The discourse-related structures are designed in form of linguistic patterns based on the information delivered by automatic part-of-speech and dependency annotation. In addition to alignment errors (existing structures left unaligned), these alignment discrepancies can be caused by language contrasts or through the phenomena of explicitation and implicitation in the translation process. We propose a new approach including new type of resources for corpus-based language contrast analysis and apply it to study and classify the contrasts found in our English-German parallel corpus. As unaligned discourse structures may also result in the loss of discourse information in the MT training data, we hope to deliver information in support of discourse-aware machine translation (MT).


## 1 Introduction

All human languages provide means to create coherence and cohesion in texts, but the precise structures used to achieve this vary even across closely related languages. In this paper, we introduce an automatic method to extract examples of cross-linguistically divergent discourse structures from a corpus of parallel text, creating a new type of resource that is useful for the discovery and description of discourse-related language contrasts. This type of analysis is useful from the point of view of contrastive linguistics, and it can also provide researchers interested in discourse-level machine translation (MT) with a collection of data to guide their intuitions about how text-level phenomena are affected in translation. Our method is strongly data-driven; it enables a bottom-up approach to linguistic analysis that starts from individual occurrences of cross-linguistic correspondences without being constrained by existing linguistic assumptions and theoretical frameworks.

The data source in our analysis is a sentence- and word-aligned parallel corpus, the same type of resource that is typically used for training MT systems. We begin by defining a set of surface patterns that identify the discourse structures of interest and permit their automatic extraction. We then use the word alignments to establish correspondences between the languages. We particularly focus on those cases where there is a relevant pattern in one language, but the word aligner is unable to find a corresponding structure in the other. Such *alignment discrepancies* can simply be due to alignment errors, but they can also stem from systematic language contrasts (Grishina and Stede, 2015, p. 19–20) or from the phenomena of explicitation and implicitation in the translation process.

Our general goal is to explore these alignment discrepancies and analyse their causes. We use a corpus of English-German translations that we automatically annotate for part-of-speech and dependency information. Alignment discrepancies are detected with the help of sentence and word alignment of the annotated structures. Thus we do not use any manually annotated resources, and linguistic knowledge involved is rather of shallow character. Specific cases of extracted discrepancies represented through linguistic patterns are then manually analysed. We concentrate on English-to-German translations, as although these




*Proceedings of the Third Workshop on Discourse in Machine Translation*, pages 73–81,
Copenhagen, Denmark, September 8, 2017. ©2017 Association for Computational Linguistics.

two languages are typologically close, this language pair is still among those that are hard for machine translation.

This paper is structured as follows: in the following section (Section 2), we define the phenomenon under analysis and explain the problem. Section 3 provides information on related works. In Section 4, we describe the data, methods and procedures applied for our analysis. Section 5 presents the results. In Section 6, we discuss the outcome of the study and outline the ideas for future work.

## 2  Defining the Problem

In this paper, we focus on the analysis of English-German parallel data – aligned sentence pairs, in which discourse-related structures in target or source texts have no alignment in the corresponding parallel sentences. The discourse-related structures we consider are defined as potential elements of coreference chains that can be either personal or demonstrative pronouns. These structures are designed in form of linguistic patterns based on the information delivered by automatic part-of-speech and dependency annotation and include both bare pronouns, as *she* and *it* or *this* and *that*, and determiners modifying nouns – parts of full nominal phrases, as *this system* and *the system* in (1).

(1)  *..all these chemicals ultimately boost the activity of the brain's <u>reward system</u>... goosing <u>this system</u> makes us feel good... But new research indicates that chronic drug use induces changes in the structure and function of <u>the system</u>.*

As these are parts of coreference chains, they contribute to the overall coherence and hence carry part of the discourse information in both the source and the target language.

Linguistic means expressing coreference exist in both languages. However, the choice between referring expressions is governed by language-specific constraints. For instance, pronouns and adjectives in German are subject to grammatical gender agreement, whereas in English, only person pronouns have this marking and adjectives (for instance, in nominal ellipsis) are unmarked. Such differences in the realisation give rise to transformation patterns in translation, for instance *he – der* in (2), which can be obtained from parallel data on the basis of word-level alignment.

(2)  *Then we take this piece of paper and give it to a <u>fellow student</u> and <u>he</u> must make us a drawing out of it.  – Dann nehmen wir dieses Blatt Papier und geben es <u>einem Kommilitonen</u> und <u>der</u> muss uns daraus eine Zeichnung machen.*

However, in some cases, these differences may cause alignment discrepancies. For instance, German pronominal adverbs like *damit* in example (3) can function as a referring expression (*damit* refers to an event expressed through the whole preceding clause, but can also establish a conjunctive relation). English does not have a direct equivalent for this form. So, the English translation example from a parallel corpus does not preserve this coreference chain.

(3)  *Die demographischen Kurven verraten, dass der Sozialstaat von den Jüngeren nicht mehr zu finanzieren ist. <u>Damit</u> versinkt das Land nicht in einer beinah unvergleichlichen Krise, wie manchmal behauptet wird. – The demographic curves reveal that the welfare state can no longer be financed by the younger members of society. This does not mean that the country is descending into an unparalleled crisis <u>...</u>*

This would result in an alignment discrepancy attributed to language contrasts.

At the same time, alignment discrepancies can also be attributed to the translation process and the phenomenon of explicitation based on the Explicitation Hypothesis, formulated in its most prominent form by Blum-Kulka (1986), who assumes elements in the target text are expressed more explicitly than in the source text. For example, the full nominal phrase *die Aufgabe (the task)* in the German translation in (4) is lexically more explicit than the demonstrative *that*. Its counterpart is called implicitation.

(4)  *You want your employees to do what you ask them to do, and if they've done <u>that</u>, then they can do extra. – Sie erwarten von Ihren Angestellten, dass sie tun worum Sie sie gebeten haben, wenn sie <u>die Aufgabe</u> ausgeführt haben, können sie <u>Zusätzliches</u> tun.*

In a parallel corpus of English-German translations, we use automatic word alignment to extract transformation patterns. Those sentence pairs which contain a discourse structure in either the source or the target sentence and for which no transformation patterns could be extracted are defined as alignment discrepancies.

## 3  Related Work

The method that we use to extract transformation patterns is similar to coreference annotation projection applied by Postolache et al. (2006) and by Grishina & Stede (2015). Both studies use data manually annotated for coreference relations. In our approach, we use automatic annotations only that allow us to define candidate referring expressions – linguistic expressions that are potential members of a coreference chain (not resolved by a human annotator).

Postolache et al. (2006) mark patterns containing heads of the resulting referring expression in the target language aligned with heads of the source referring expressions. Although they mention the situations when the source head is not aligned with any target word or no words of the source referring expressions are aligned with any target words, they do not consider these cases of alignment discrepancies in their analysis.

Grishina & Stede (2015) apply a direct projection algorithm on parallel data to automatically produce coreference annotations for two target languages without exploiting any linguistic knowledge of the languages. However, they describe a number of projection problems, when a referring expression is present in both source and target text but is not projected correctly. They analyse non-equivalences in translation from a linguistic point of view but could not find enough evidence to characterise them as systematic, as the dataset they use is very limited. However, the cases that they describe can be attributed to language contrasts or the effects of translation process. In our study, we use more data creating a resource that can be used for further systematic description of alignment discrepancies and their sources. We suggest that these sources can be classified into three categories: (1) alignment errors; (2) language contrasts and (3) translation process. A number of studies (Kunz and Steiner, 2012; Kunz and Lapshinova-Koltunski, 2015; Novak and Nedoluzhko, 2015) have shown that although the coreference relation is shared across all languages, they may differ considerably in the range of referring expressions.

The phenomenon of explicitation in translation is often understood to occur when a translation explicitly realises meanings that were implicit in its source text. In terms of discourse phenomena, this would mean that a source text does not contain linguistic markers that trigger some discourse relations, whereas its translation does, as was analysed by Meyer & Webber (2013) or by Becher (2011b), including also the opposite process of implicitation.

In other studies, explicitation is seen if a translated text realises meanings with more explicit means than the source text does. In relation to coreference, some referring expressions can be more explicit than the others, as in example (4) in Section 2 above. For instance, Becher (2011a, p. 98) presents a scale for the explicitness of various referring expressions for the language pair English-German.

Most of these studies start from the description of the expressions existing in the language systems they compare, and analyse the distributions of these categories with corpus-based methods. This can be defined as a top-down procedure – starting from what is given (in theories and grammars) and looking for the contrasts in a huge number of language examples represented in corpus data. In our approach, we perform in a different way – we start with the corpus data and try to detect patterns revealing language contrasts or the phenomena of explicitation/implicitation that we define in form of alignment discrepancies.

## 4  Resources, Tools and Methods

### 4.1  Data

Our corpus data consists of talks given at the TED conference[1]. It is taken from the training set of the IWSLT 2015 MT evaluation campaign[2], which in turn uses texts downloaded from the TED web site.

We need to mention that the translations of TED talks are rather subtitle than translations, and consequently, there exist some genre-/register specific transformations in this parallel data. However, the transformations in the TED talks are also interesting, especially because the latter have been frequently used as training data for MT.

---

[1] http://www.ted.com
[2] https://wit3.fbk.eu/mt.php?release=
2015-01

We automatically annotated the corpus data using a pipeline of standard tools. The texts in both languages were preprocessed with Penn Treebank tokeniser and Punkt sentence splitter with the language-specific sentence splitting models bundled with NLTK (Bird et al., 2009). Then, the corpus was tagged with the Marmot tagger (Mueller et al., 2013) for the part-of-speech information and parsed for dependency information with the MATE tools (Bohnet, 2010). The tagger and parser were trained on version 1.0 of the Universal Dependency treebank (Nivre et al., 2015).

Word alignment was performed in both direction with *mgiza*[3] and models 1-HMM-3-4, using the training scripts bundled with the Moses machine translation software[4] and default settings. The alignments were symmetrised with the grow-diag-final-and heuristic (Koehn et al., 2003).

|         | sentences | tokens    |
|---------|-----------|-----------|
| **English** | 214,889   | 3,940,079 |
| **German**  | 227,649   | 3,678,503 |

Table 1: Corpus size

The total number of parallel segments amounts to 194,370 (see details in Table 1).

### 4.2 Pattern extraction

Using the part-of-speech and dependency annotations, we compiled lists of discourse-related structures defined in terms of lexico-grammatical patterns (combination of part-of-speech tags and grammatical functions that were produced by the parser) for both English and German texts. While the discourse structures we study may be composed of multiple words, we find that they can often be identified reliably with patterns anchored to single words. We select pronouns and demonstratives (which also include definite articles) only (corresponding to the part-of-speech tags 'DET' and 'PRON').

Then, we extracted parallel patterns from the above described data using the word-level alignment. The patterns are based on $1 : N$ word alignments linking the word identified by our pattern (for instance *which DET-nsubj* in example (5)) to 1 or more words in the other language (*dies PRON-dobj* in example (5)). If a word has multiple alignment links, multiple output records were

generated, one for each aligned target language word.

(5)   `which DET-nsubj → dies PRON-dobj`
*Educational researcher Benjamin Bloom, in 1984, posed what's called the 2 sigma problem, <u>which</u> he observed by studying three populations. – 1984 veröffentlichte der Bildungsforscher Benjamin Bloom etwas, das '2-Sigma-Problem' heißt. Er beobachtete <u>dies</u> bei drei Populationen.*

The resulting data also contains sentence pairs for which no corresponding structure was found in either the source or the target language. These are the cases of alignment discrepancies in discourse-related structures that we select for our analysis. We count the occurrences of the alignment discrepancy patterns with the aim to answer the following questions: (1) Which are the most frequent ones in English? (2) Which are the most frequent ones in German?

In our corpus, English is always the source and German is the target, but we can search discourse-related patterns in the English sources and see what are the corresponding structures in the German translations and which structures are missing. And in the same way, we can search in the German translations and analyse the aligned English sources. This allows us to discover which discourse phenomena 'get lost' in the translation data due to the missing alignment. We can also measure the amount of these discrepancies – perform quantitative analysis, and analyse the underlying causes of these discrepancies in a qualitative analysis. These might include: (1) language contrasts that include both differences in language system and differences of idiomatic character, e.g. collocation use; (2) translation process phenomena such as explicitation – when a German translated sentence contains a discourse pattern which was not aligned to any discourse structure in the corresponding English source sentence, and implicitation – when the English original sentence contains a marked discourse pattern which was not aligned to any discourse structure in the corresponding translated sentence in German; (3) other possible causes, including errors.

---

[3] `https://github.com/moses-smt/mgiza`
[4] `http://www.statmt.org/moses/`

# 5 Analyses and Results

## 5.1 General observations

On the total, we extract 26 patterns (types) of discourse structures marked in the German translations, for which no English alignment was automatically assigned (explicitation candidates). The total number of unaligned cases is around 11% in both language settings.

In the English source sentences, there were 14 discourse patterns, for which the alignment in the corresponding German translations is missing (implicitation candidates). The total number of occurring cases (measured by tokens) is also higher for German (69,851) than for English (57,608), which on the one hand, may be interpreted as an evidence for more explicitation than implicitation phenomena in translation. And on the other hand, it may indicate that German has more discourse-related structures that differ from those available in English.

In Table 2, we provide an overview of the 10 most frequent discourse-related structures that were found in the German translation data, for which no corresponding discourse structures were aligned in the English sources.

| freq.abs | pattern | example |
|---|---|---|
| 29868 | DET-det | *der Fall* |
| 18026 | PRON-nsubj | *er, sie* |
| 10986 | PRON-dobj | *ihn, sie* |
| 3525 | PRON-nmod | *sein, ihr* |
| 3383 | PRON-det | *diese, einige* |
| 1481 | PRON-nsubjpass | *das, dieses* |
| 1439 | PRON-iobj | *ihm, ihr* |
| 530 | PRON-dep | *daran, dafür* |
| 297 | PRON-neg | *kein* |
| 48 | PRON-appos | *etwas, alles* |

Table 2: Patterns in German with no alignment in the corresponding English data

| freq.abs | pattern | example |
|---|---|---|
| 23145 | DET-det | *the things* |
| 19030 | PRON-nsubj | *he, they* |
| 6798 | PRON-nmod | *his, their* |
| 4341 | PRON-dobj | *him, them* |
| 1764 | DET-nsubj | *this, that* |
| 990 | DET-nmod | *which, that* |
| 650 | DET-dobj | *this, that* |
| 516 | PRON-iobj | *him, them* |
| 253 | DET-neg | *no* |
| 54 | PRON-conj | *what* |

Table 3: Patterns in the English sentences with no alignment in the corresponding German translations

| pattern | EN | DE |
|---|---|---|
| DET-det | 23145 | 29868 |
| DET-dobj | 650 | 24 |
| DET-nmod | 950 | 18 |
| DET-nsubj | 1764 | 44 |
| PRON-det | 14 | 3383 |
| PRON-dobj | 4341 | 10986 |
| PRON-iobj | 516 | 1439 |
| PRON-nmod | 6798 | 3525 |
| PRON-nsubj | 19030 | 18026 |

Table 4: Patterns shared by English and German

Table 3 presents an overview of the 10 most frequent discourse-related structures in the English sources, for which no alignment was found in the corresponding translations into German.

DET-det is the most frequent structure in both languages, followed by PRON-subj and PRON-nmod or PRON-dobj (the ranking of the latter two is different in English and German). Further (less frequent) discourse-related structures vary across languages, with English showing preferences for demonstratives (DET) and German – for personal pronouns (that also include relatives in the universal part-of-speech tagset). If the full lists (with 24 and 14 patterns) is considered, we see that PRON and DET are more evenly distributed (53% PRON vs. 47% DET) in English than in German (57% PRON vs. 43% DET).

It is interesting that eight out of the most frequent structures in the 'English' list are shared (occur in both lists). We outline all the shared patterns (nine in total) along with their frequencies in both English and German in Table 4.

## 5.2 Observations on particular patterns

In the following, we perform a manual qualitative analysis of the most frequent patterns (DET-det and PRON-nsubj) that are shared by both languages. The information on their categorisation frequencies is derived automatically on the basis of extracted patterns containing word information. For instance, structures like der-DET-det[5] are defined as cases of the definite article use, and the structures like der-PRON-nsubj represent relative pronouns. This manual analysis provides us with the information on possible causes of alignment discrepancies. However, at this stage, we do not provide the information on the distribution of these causes in our data.

---

[5] *der* is one of the forms of the German definite article

**DET-det** Most cases (ca. 96%) concern the German translations containing definite articles that may trigger a coreference relation between the noun phrase that contains this article and another noun phrase or a clause, as *die Aufgabe* in example (4) in Section 2 above, and for which no alignment was found in the English sources.

Manual analysis of the data sample shows that the discrepancies are often caused by the variation in article use in the expression of generic reference in both languages: in German, generic meaning is expressed with a definite noun, whereas in the English source, it is expressed with a bare noun (often in plural), see examples *people/die Leute, conversations/die...Unterhaltung, technology/die Technologie* in (6).

(6)    a.    *You know, it's just like the hail goes out and* <u>*people*</u> *are ready to help. – Es ist einfach so, jemand ruft um Hilfe, und* <u>*die Leute*</u> *stehen zur Hilfe bereit.*

        b.    *And we use conversations with each other to learn how to have* <u>*conversations*</u> *with ourselves. – Wir benutzen* <u>*die gegenseitige Unterhaltung*</u>*, um zu lernen, wie wir Gespräche untereinander führen.*

        c.    *We turn to* <u>*technology*</u> *to help us feel connected in ways we can comfortably control. – Wir wenden uns* <u>*der Technologie*</u> *zu, um uns auf Arten und Weisen verbunden zu fühlen, die wir bequem kontrollieren können.*

Many studies have claimed that there is variation in article use in the expression of generic reference in German (Krifka et al., 1995; Oosterhof, 2004), especially in relation to plural generics. German plural generics can be used both as definite nominal phrases and as bare nouns, whereas definite plurals in English cannot be interpreted generically. However, Barton et al. (2015) provide the only empirical analysis known to us, but concentrate on plural generics only. We believe that our approach creates a good foundation (and resource) for a more detailed quantitative analysis of such cases.

In other cases, the discrepancy between definite constructions in German has a rather idiomatic character, as in example (7).

(7)    *But in the process, we* <u>*set ourselves up*</u> *to be isolated. – Aber dabei* <u>*fallen*</u> *wir der Isolation direkt* <u>*vor die Füße*</u>*.*

Some individual sentence pairs revealed the phenomena of explicitation, for instance, *der Fall* ('the case') in example (8) is used in German translation to explicate the information given through the ellipsis of the clause *but it's not cheesy* in English.

(8)    *You would expect it to be cheesy, but* <u>*it*</u> *'s not. – Man könnte annehmen, dass so etwas kitschig ist, aber dem ist nicht* <u>*der Fall*</u>*.*

Most cases of the DET-det structure in the English sources missing alignment in the corresponding German translations are also definite noun phrases (ca. 85%). Manual analysis of a sample reveals that most of these cases are alignment errors. This means that the German translation also contains the corresponding definite nominal phrase which was not automatically aligned to the English article.

The phenomenon of implicitation was represented by individual cases that we observed in the data, e.g. in (9), where the English source is more explicit than the corresponding translation.

(9)    *Secondly, there had to be an acceptance that we were not going to be able to use all of this vacant land* <u>*in the way that we had before*</u> *and maybe for some time to come. – Zweitens musste es eine Übereinkunft geben, dass wir das gesamte brachliegende Land nicht* <u>*wie vorher*</u> *nutzen können würden, vielleicht für längere Zeit nicht.*

**PRON-nsubj** In the German translations, many PRON-subj structures with no alignment in the corresponding English sources are represented by personal pronouns (ca. 54% out of all cases). Around 46% of these pronouns are 1st and 2nd person pronouns that are used for speaker and addressee reference. In many cases, both the source and the target sentence contain this reference type that was not automatically aligned and thus, an error occurred. Addressee and speaker reference is very common in our dataset, as this is one of the specific features of the register under analysis – public talks by experts (mostly addressed to laypeople).

The remaining structures are 3rd person pronouns, among which we observe some interesting cases, for instances, differences in the expression of impersonal meaning in English and German, as seen in example (10).

(10)  a.  *A reaction to the medication <u>the clinic</u> gave me for my depression left me suicidal. – Die Medikamente, die <u>sie</u> mir <u>in der Ambulanz</u> gegen meine Depressionen gaben, führten bei mir zu Selbstmordgedanken.*

      b.  *People <u>say</u>, "I'll tell you what's wrong with having a conversation... – <u>sagen sie</u>, "Ich sage dir, was verkehrt daran ist...*

They are followed relative pronouns (ca. 31% out of all cases) that introduce a relative clause in the German translations. However, their English sources do not contain any relative clauses and the information is expressed in a different construction, as illustrated in example (11).

(11)  a.  *A <u>polar bear swimming</u> in the Arctic, by Paul Nicklen. – Ein Eisbär, der in der Arktis schwimmt, aufgenommen von Paul Nicklen.*

      b.  *Across the generations, I see that <u>people can't get enough</u> of each other... – Über alle Generationen hinweg sehe ich Menschen, die nicht genug voneinander bekommen...*

The English sentence in example (11-a) contains a non-finite *ing*-clause. This clause type has direct equivalents in form of present participle in German *schwimmend* ("swimming"). However, the English *ing*-form is used much more widely than the German present participle (Durrell, 2011, p.281–285). In particular, participial clauses are restricted to formal written registers in German and can sound stilted and they are used much less frequently than clauses with *ing*-forms in English (Durrell, 2011, p.281–285). To our knowledge, there are no corpus-based studies confirming this quantitatively. Königs (2011) provides a number of examples as possibilities of translation equivalents for English *ing*-clauses. However, statistical evidence is missing. We believe that our dataset can be used as a resource for this kind of empirical evidence.

Explicitation examples related to this structure include various way of the source reformulation, as in example (12). Here, a nominal phrase was reformulated into a nominal phrase with a clause containing the exophoric pronoun *es*.

(12)  *Clouds are <u>the most egalitarian of nature's displays</u>, because we all have a good, fantastic view of the sky. – Wolken sind die größten Gleichmacher, <u>wenn es um die Schönheit der Natur geht</u>, weil wir alle einen gleich guten Blick auf den Himmel haben.*

50% of the PRON-nsubj structures in the English sources that were not aligned to any structures in German include speaker and addressee references. This discrepancy is a clear indicator of the contrasts in pragmatics and style of speeches in English and German and goes in hand with what was stated by House (2014) who provides several dimensions of such contrasts, e.g. addressee (English) vs. content (German) orientation in texts.

(13)  a.  *If <u>you</u> have fluid with no wall to surround it and keep pressure up, <u>you</u> have a puddle. – Eine Flüssigkeit ohne eine Wand, die sie umgibt und den Druck aufrechterhält, ist eine Pfütze.*

      b.  *And if <u>you</u> go there, <u>you</u> say, "Hey, everybody's really healthy." Und wenn <u>man</u> dorthin geht und sagt: "Hey, jeder ist kerngesund."*

In example (13-a), the English *you* does not have any correspondences in the German translation, whereas *you* in example (13-b) is transferred to *man* ("one").

The other 50% of discrepancy cases include the third person pronouns, with *it* being most frequent among other forms (43% out of all 3rd person pronouns and 21% of all the PRON-nsubj structures).

These cases also reveal language contrasts such as differences between certain syntactic constructions in English in German. For instance, the German coordinated clause with a negation *an manchen Tagen nicht* in (14-a) does not require a repetition of the subject, whereas the English clause does.

In example (14-b), *it* introduces a cleft sentence construction. These are frequent in English but used much less frequently in German, where the topic can be shifted into initial position before the verb (Durrell, 2011, p. 455).

(14)   a.  *Some days it goes up and some days it doesn't go up. – An manchen Tagen geht er hoch und an manchen Tagen nicht.*

       b.  *And so it was that day that we decided we needed to build a crisis text hotline. – Und an diesem Tag beschlossen wir, dass wir eine Krisen-SMS-Hotline einrichten mussten.*

## 6 Discussion and Future Work

To our knowledge, this paper is the first attempt to quantitatively describe alignment discrepancies between English-German discourse-related phenomena from a language contrastive perspective. This approach is novel and can be characterised as data-driven, as we use "bottom-up" procedures instead of theory-driven ones that start from the grammar-based contrasts and then use data to find quantitative evidence. This is a new approach of contrast discovery.

Although we concentrated on a limited number of patterns only and described some particular causes of the discrepancies, we were able to obtain interesting observations, e.g. those on the article use with generics or the use of non-finite constructions and their alternatives in German in English. Although these cases are described in traditional grammars, corpus data shows a different behaviour, especially when spoken data is concerned.

We were not able to provide much evidence for systematic translation-process-driven discrepancies. However, we could see that they are also present in our data. We believe that a more detailed quantitative and qualitative analysis of discrepancy sources would provide more corpus evidence for the variation across the two languages under analysis. Our approach, as well as the parallel dataset created allows for such an analysis.

Moreover, the information on systematic discrepancies could serve the task of alignment improvement. For instance, we observed a great number of cases when a pronoun does not have or need a corresponding element in the parallel sentence. These cases are important for MT model development. Naive models for pronouns often lead to overgeneration of such elements in the tar-

get language. Having the information on such cases, we could think of ways of integrating them into the models to avoid the overgeneration.

Our future work will include a more detailed analysis of discrepancy sources. For language contrasts, we will investigate further patterns that are less frequent but not less important. It would be also interesting to look into the patterns that occur either in the English or in the German sentences only. Besides, we will extend our analysis on explicitation using Klaudy's classification of various types of explicitations as a starting point (Klaudy, 2008). Then, we will define a scale for coreferential explicitness based on Kunz's reduced scale of Accessibility (Kunz, 2010, p. 76) and existing analyses of connective explicitation (Denturck, 2012; Zufferey and Cartoni, 2014).

## Acknowledgements

Christian Hardmeier was supported by the Swedish Research Council under project 2012-916 *Discourse-Oriented Statistical Machine Translation*. We used computing resources on the Abel cluster, owned by the University of Oslo and the Norwegian metacenter for High Performance Computing (NOTUR), provided through the Nordic Language Processing Laboratory (NLPL).

## References

Dagmar Barton, Nadine Kolb, and Tanja Kupisch. 2015. Definite article use with generic reference in german: an empirical study. *Zeitschrift für Sprachwissenschaft* 34:147–173. https://doi.org/10.1515/zfs-2015-0009.

Viktor Becher. 2011a. *Explicitation and implicitation in translation. A corpus-based study of English-German and German-English translations of business texts.* Ph.D. thesis, Universität Hamburg.

Viktor Becher. 2011b. When and why do translators add connectives? a corpus-based study. *Target* 23.

Steven Bird, Edward Loper, and Ewan Klein. 2009. *Natural Language Processing with Python.* O'Reilly Media.

Shoshana Blum-Kulka. 1986. Shifts of cohesion and coherence in translation. In Juliane House and Shoshana Blum-Kulka, editors, *Interlingual and intercultural communication*, Gunter Narr, Tübingen, pages 17–35.

Bernd Bohnet. 2010. Top accuracy and fast dependency parsing is not a contradiction. In *Proceedings of the 23rd International Conference* on *Computational Linguistics (Coling 2010)*. Coling 2010 Organizing Committee, pages 89–97. http://aclweb.org/anthology/C10-1011.

Kathelijne Denturck. 2012. Explicitation vs. implicitation: a bidirectional corpus-based analysis of causal connectives in french and dutch translations. *ACROSS LANGUAGES AND CULTURES* 13(2):211–227. http://dx.doi.org/10.1556/Acr.13.2012.2.5.

Martin Durrell. 2011. *Hammer's German Grammar and Usage*. Routledge, London and New York, 5 edition.

Yulia Grishina and Manfred Stede. 2015. Knowledge-lean projection of coreference chains across languages. In *Proceedings of the 8th Workshop on Building and Using Comparable Corpora, Beijing, China*. page 14.

Juliane House. 2014. *Translation Quality Assessment. Past and Present*. Routledge.

Kinga Klaudy. 2008. Explicitation. In Mona Baker and Gabriela Saldanha, editors, *Routledge Encyclopedia of Translation Studies*, Routledge, London & New York, pages 104–108. 2 edition.

Philipp Koehn, Franz Josef Och, and Daniel Marcu. 2003. Statistical phrase-based translation. In *Proceedings of the 2003 Conference of the North American Chapter of the Association for Computational Linguistics on Human Language Technology*. Edmonton (Canada), pages 48–54.

Karin Königs. 2011. *Übersetzen Englisch - Deutsch. Lernen mit System*. Oldenbourg Verlag, Oldenbourg, 3 edition. Vollstäädig überarbeitete Auflage.

Manfred Krifka, Francis J. Pelletier, Gregory N. Carlson, Alice ter Meulen, Gennaro Chierchia, and Godehard Link. 1995. Genericity: An introduction. In Gregory N. Carlson and Francis J. Pelletier, editors, *The generic book*, University of Chicago Press, Chicago, IL, pages 1–124.

K.A. Kunz. 2010. *Variation in English and German Nominal Coreference: A Study of Political Essays*. Saarbrücker Beiträge zur Sprach- und Translationswissenschaft. Peter Lang. https://books.google.de/books?id=F_jmEbmeGnoC.

Kerstin Kunz and Ekaterina Lapshinova-Koltunski. 2015. Cross-linguistic analysis of discourse variation across registers. *Special Issue of Nordic Journal of English Studies* 14(1):258–288.

Kerstin Kunz and Erich Steiner. 2012. Towards a comparison of cohesive reference in english and german: System and text. In M. Taboada, S. Doval Suárez, and E. González Álvarez, editors, *Contrastive Discourse Analysis. Functional and Corpus Perspectives*, Equinox, London.

Thomas Meyer and Bonnie Webber. 2013. Implicitation of discourse connectives in (machine) translation. In *Proceedings of the Workshop on Discourse in Machine Translation*. Association for Computational Linguistics, Sofia, Bulgaria, pages 19–26. http://www.aclweb.org/anthology/W13-3303.

Thomas Mueller, Helmut Schmid, and Hinrich Schütze. 2013. Efficient higher-order CRFs for morphological tagging. In *Proceedings of the 2013 Conference on Empirical Methods in Natural Language Processing*. Association for Computational Linguistics, Seattle, Washington, USA, pages 322–332. http://www.aclweb.org/anthology/D13-1032.

Joakim Nivre, Cristina Bosco, Jinho Choi, Marie-Catherine de Marneffe, Timothy Dozat, Richárd Farkas, Jennifer Foster, Filip Ginter, Yoav Goldberg, Jan Hajič, Jenna Kanerva, Veronika Laippala, Alessandro Lenci, Teresa Lynn, Christopher Manning, Ryan McDonald, Anna Missilä, Simonetta Montemagni, Slav Petrov, Sampo Pyysalo, Natalia Silveira, Maria Simi, Aaron Smith, Reut Tsarfaty, Veronika Vincze, and Daniel Zeman. 2015. Universal dependencies 1.0. LINDAT/CLARIN digital library at the Institute of Formal and Applied Linguistics, Charles University. http://hdl.handle.net/11234/1-1464.

Michael Novak and Anna Nedoluzhko. 2015. Correspondences between czech and english coreferential expressions. *Discours [En ligne]* 16. http://discours.revues.org/9058.

Albert Oosterhof. 2004. In Fred Karlsson, editor, *Proceedings of the 20 th Scandinavian Conference of Linguistics*. University of Helsinki, Helsinki, page 1–22.

Oana Postolache, Dan Cristea, and Constantin Orasan. 2006. Tranferring coreference chains through word alignment. In *Proceedings of the 5th International Conference on Language Resources and Evaluation*.

Sandrine Zufferey and Bruno Cartoni. 2014. A multifactorial analysis of explicitation in translation. *Target* 26(3):361–384.

# Neural Machine Translation with Extended Context

**Jörg Tiedemann** and **Yves Scherrer**
Department of Modern Languages
University of Helsinki

## Abstract

We investigate the use of extended context in attention-based neural machine translation. We base our experiments on translated movie subtitles and discuss the effect of increasing the segments beyond single translation units. We study the use of extended source language context as well as bilingual context extensions. The models learn to distinguish between information from different segments and are surprisingly robust with respect to translation quality. In this pilot study, we observe interesting cross-sentential attention patterns that improve textual coherence in translation at least in some selected cases.

## 1 Introduction

Typical models of machine translation handle sentences in isolation and discard any information beyond sentence boundaries. Efforts in making statistical MT aware of discourse-level phenomena appeared to be difficult (Hardmeier, 2012; Carpuat and Simard, 2012; Hardmeier et al., 2013a). Various studies have been published that consider textual coherence, document-wide translation consistency, the proper handling of referential elements such as pronominal anaphora and other discourse-level phenomena (Guillou, 2012; Russo et al., 2012; Voigt and Jurafsky, 2012; Xiong et al., 2013a; Ben et al., 2013; Xiong and Zhang, 2013; Xiong et al., 2013b; Loaiciga et al., 2014). The typical approach in the literature focuses on the development of task-specific components that are often tested as standalone modules that need to be integrated with MT decoders (Hardmeier et al., 2013b). Modest improvements could, for example, be shown for the translation of pronouns (Le Nagard and Koehn, 2010; Hardmeier and Fed-

erico, 2010; Hardmeier, 2014) and the generation of appropriate discourse connectives (Meyer et al., 2012). Textual coherence is also often tackled in terms of translation consistency for domain-specific terminology based on the one-translation-per-discourse principle (Carpuat, 2009; Tiedemann, 2010; Ma et al., 2011; Ture et al., 2012).

Overall, none of the ideas lead to significant improvements of translation quality. Besides, the development of task- and problem-specific models that work independently from the general translation task is not very satisfactory. However, the recent success of neural machine translation opens new possibilities for tackling discourse-related phenomena in a more generic way. In this paper, we present a pilot study that looks at simple ideas for extending the context in the framework of standard attention-based encoder-decoder models. The purpose of the paper is to identify the capabilities of NMT to discover cross-sentential dependencies without explicit annotation or guidance. In contrast to related work that modifies the neural MT model by an additional context encoder an a separate attention mechanism (Jean et al., 2017), we keep the standard setup and just modify the input and output segments. We run a series of experiments with different context windows and discuss the effect of additional information on translation and attention.

## 2 Attention-Based NMT

Encoder-decoder models with attention have been proposed by Bahdanau et al. (2014) and have become the de-facto standard in neural machine translation. The model is based on recurrent neural network layers that encode a given sentence in the source language into a distributed vector representation that will be decoded into the target language by another recurrent network. The attention

82

*Proceedings of the Third Workshop on Discourse in Machine Translation*, pages 82–92,
Copenhagen, Denmark, September 8, 2017. ©2017 Association for Computational Linguistics.

model makes use of the entire encoding sequence, and the attention weights specify the proportions with which information from different positions is combined. This is a very powerful mechanism that makes it possible to handle arbitrarily long sequences without limiting the capacity of the internal representation. Previous work has shown that NMT models can successfully learn attention distributions that explain intuitively plausible connections between source and target language. This framework is very well suited for the study we conduct in this paper as we emphasise the capabilities of NMT to pick up contextual dependencies from wider context across sentence boundaries.

In our work, we rely on the freely available Helsinki NMT system (HNMT) (Östling et al., 2017)[1] that implements a hybrid bidirectional encoder with character-level backoff (Luong and Manning, 2016) using recurrent LSTM units (Hochreiter and Schmidhuber, 1997). The system also features layer normalisation (Ba et al., 2016), variational dropout (Gal and Ghahramani, 2016), coverage penalties (Wu et al., 2016), beam search decoding and straightforward model ensembling. The backbone is Theano, which enables efficient GPU-based training and decoding with mini-batches.

## 3 Data Sets

In our experiments, we focus on the translation of movie subtitles and in particular on the translation from German to English. The choice of languages is rather arbitrary and mainly due to better comprehension for our qualitative inspections. There are relevant discourse phenomena that need to be considered for English and German, for example, referential pronouns with grammatical agreement requirements. The choice of movie subtitles has several reasons: First of all, large quantities of training data are available, a necessary prerequisite for neural MT. Secondly, subtitles expose significant discourse relations and cross-sentential dependencies. Referential elements are common, as subtitles usually represent coherent stories with narrative structures with dialogues and natural interactions. Proper translation in this context typically requires more than just the text but also information from the plot and the audiovisual context. However, as those types of information are not available, we hope that extended context at least helps to incorporate more knowledge about the situation and in consequence leads to better translations, also stylistically. The final advantage of subtitles is the size of the translation units. Sentences (and sentence fragments) are typically much shorter compared to other genres such as newspaper texts or other edited written material. Utterances are even shortened substantially for space limitations. This property supports our experiments in which we want to include context beyond sentence boundaries. Similar to statistical MT, neural MT also struggles most with long sequences and, therefore, it is important to keep the segments short. On average there are about 8 tokens per language in each aligned translation unit (which may cover one or more sentences or sentence fragments).

In particular, we use the publicly available OpenSubtitles2016 corpus (Lison and Tiedemann, 2016) for German and English[2] and reserve 400 randomly selected movies for development and testing purposes. In total, there are 16,910 movies and TV series in the collection. We tokenized and truecased the data sets using standard tools from the Moses toolbox (Koehn et al., 2007). The final corpus comprises 13.9 million translation units with about 107 million tokens in German and 115 million tokens in English. The training data includes 13.5 million training instances and we selected the 5,000 first translation units of the test set for automatic evaluation. Note that we trust the alignment and do not correct any possible alignment errors in the data.

## 4 Extended Context Models

We propose to simply extend the context when training models (and translating data). This does not lead to any changes in the model itself, and we let the training procedures discover what kind of information is needed for the translation. We evaluate two models that extend context in different ways:

**Extended source:** Include context from the previous sentences in the source language to improve the encoder part of the network.

**Extended translation units:** Increase the segments to be translated. Larger segments in

---

[1] https://github.com/robertostling/hnmt

[2] http://opus.lingfil.uu.se/ OpenSubtitles2016.php

SOURCE | TARGET

cc_sieh cc_, cc_Bob cc_! **-Wo sind sie ?**    - Where are they ?
cc_-Wo cc_sind cc_sie cc_? **siehst du sie ?**    do you see them ?
cc_siehst cc_du cc_sie cc_? **-Ja .**    - Yes .

Figure 1: Example of data with extended source language context.

SOURCE | TARGET

sieh , Bob ! _BREAK_ -Wo sind sie ?    look , Bob ! _BREAK_ - Where are they ?
-Wo sind sie ? _BREAK_ siehst du sie ?    - Where are they ? _BREAK_ do you see them ?
siehst du sie ? _BREAK_ -Ja .    do you see them ? _BREAK_ - Yes .

Figure 2: Example of data with extended translation units.

the source language have to be translated into corresponding units in the target language.

**Model 2+1 (extended source):** In order to keep the segments as short as possible, we will limit ourselves to one contextual unit. Hence, in the first setup, we add the source language sentence(s) from the previous translation unit to the sentence to be translated and mark all tokens (BPE segments in our case) with a special prefix ($cc_-$) to indicate that they come from contextual information. We also test a second model without prefix-marked context words but additional sentence-break tokens between the source language units (similar to model 2+2 below). In that case, we do not make a difference between contextual words and sentence-internal words, which makes it possible to treat intra-sentential anaphora in the same way as cross-sentential ones. We run through the training data with a sliding window, adding the contextual history to each sentence in the corpus. Note that we have to make sure that each movie starts without context. Figure 1 shows a few examples from our test set with the prefix-markup described above.

The task now consists in learning the influence of specific context word sequences on the translation of the focus sentence. An example is the ambiguous pronoun "sie" that could be a feminine singular or a plural third person pronoun. The use of grammatical gender in German also makes it possible to refer to an inanimate antecedent. Discourse-level information is needed to make correct decisions. The question is whether our model can actually pick this up and whether attention patterns can show the relevant connections.

**Model 2+2 (extended translation units):** In the second setup, we simply add the previous translation unit to extend context in both source and target during training. With this model, the decoder also has to generate more content but is probably less likely to confuse information from different positions as it simply translates larger units. Another advantage is that target-language-specific dependencies like grammatical agreement between referential expressions may be captured if they cannot be determined by the source language alone. As above, we run through the training data with a sliding window and create extended training examples, marking the boundaries between the segments with a special token _BREAK_. Figure 2 shows the example from the test data.

The NMT models that we train rely on subword-units. We apply standard byte-pair encoding (BPE) (Sennrich et al., 2016) for splitting words into segments. For the extended source context models, we set a vocabulary size of 30,000 when training BPE codes and apply a vocabulary size of 60,000 when training the models (context words double the vocabulary because of their $cc_-$ prefix). For the 2+2 model, we train BPE codes from both languages together (with a size of 60,000) and we set a vocabulary threshold of 50 when applying BPE to the data.

## 5 Experiments and Results

We train attention-based models using the Helsinki NMT system with similar parameters but different training data to see the effect of contextual information. Our baseline system involves a standard setup where the training examples come from the aligned parallel subtitle corpus (1 source translation unit and 1 target translation unit). This will be the reference in our evaluations and discussions. In all cases, we translate the test set of 5,000 sentences with an ensemble model consisting of the final four savepoint models after running roughly the same number of training iterations with similar amounts of training instances seen by the model. Savepoint averaging slightly alleviates the problem that each model will differ due to the stochastic nature of the training procedures, making a direct comparison of the outcomes difficult especially if the observed differences are small.

Automatic evaluation metrics are problematic, in particular for assessing discourse-related phenomena. However, it is important to verify that the context-models are on-par with the baseline. Table 1 shows the BLEU scores and also the alternative character-level chrF3 measure for all systems (2+1 in its two variants with and without prefix markup). The 2+2 model is evaluated on the last segment in the generated output and ignores all other parts before.

| in % | BLEU | chrF3 | (precision) | (recall) |
|---|---|---|---|---|
| baseline | 27.1 | 42.9 | **54.7** | 41.9 |
| 2+1 (prefix) | 26.5 | 42.7 | 51.2 | 41.9 |
| 2+1 (break) | **27.5** | **43.3** | 52.8 | **42.5** |
| 2+2 | 26.5 | **43.3** | 54.4 | 42.3 |

Table 1: Automatic evaluation: BLEU and chrF3 (including precision and recall).

The table shows that all models are quite similar to each other, with a slightly higher BLEU score for the 2+1 system with sentence breaks. The chrF3 score is also slightly higher for both, the 2+1 and 2+2 systems with sentence breaks, due to a higher recall. The differences are small but the results already show that the system is capable of handling larger units without harming the performance and additional improvements are possible. Let us know look at some details to study the effects of contextual information on translation output.

## 5.1 2+1: Extended Source Language Context

The most difficult part for the model in the 2+1 setup is to learn to ignore most of the contextual information when generating the target language output. In other words, the attention model needs to learn to focus on words and word sequences that are relevant to the translation process. It is interesting to see that the system is actually able to do that and produce adequate translations even though a lot of extra information is given in the source. There is certainly some confusion in the beginning of the training process but the model figures out surprisingly quickly what kind of information to consider and what information to discard.

It is interesting to see, of course, how much of the contextual information is still used and where. For this, we looked at the distribution of attention in the whole data set, for individual sentences and for individual target words. The total proportion of attention that goes to the contextual history is about 7.1%. This is small – as expected – but certainly not negligible. When sorting by contextual attention, some sentences actually show quite high proportions of attention going to the previous context. They mainly refer to translations that include information from the previous history or rather creative translations that are less faithful to the original source. An example is given below (context in parentheses):

| input | (Danke , Mr. Vadas .) **Mr. Kralik , kommen Sie bitte ins Büro . ich möchte Sie sprechen .** |
|---|---|
| transl. | Mr. Kralik , please come to the office , I want to talk to you . |
| input | (Mr. Kralik , kommen Sie bitte ins Büro . ich möchte Sie sprechen .) **ja .** |
| transl. | Yes , I want to speak to you . |

The second sentence to be translated (*"ja ."*) is filled with a repetition from the contextual history. The part *"I want to speak to you"* is indeed mostly linked to the German *"ich möchte Sie sprechen"* from the history. Such repetitions may feel quite natural (for example, if the speaker is the same and would like to stress the previous request) and one is tempted to say that the model picks this possibility up from the data where such examples occur. However, such cases seem to occur especially in connection with multiple sentences in the source context. The following translation illustrates another interesting case with two context sentences. Figure 3 shows the attention pattern in which the model replaced the referential *"Sie"* from the source sentence by *"my lady"* from the previous context.

Similarly, the following example shows again how information from the context is merged with the current sentence to be translated:

| input | (Pirovitch .) **- Hm ? - Wollen Sie was Nettes hören ?** |
|---|---|
| transl. | - You want to hear something nice ? |
| input | (- Hm ? - Wollen Sie was Nettes hören ?) **Was denn ?** |
| transl. | - What do you want to hear ? |

The attention heatmap in Figure 4 nicely illustrates how the translation picks up from the conversation history. Once again, this kind of mix could be possible if the speaker stays the same but,

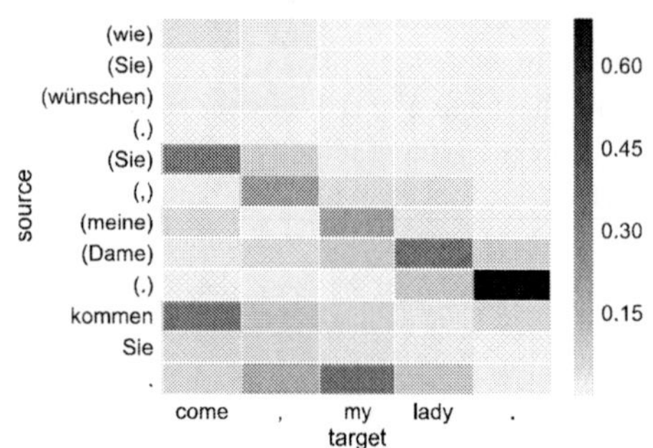

Figure 3: Attention with extended source context. Words from the contextual history are in parentheses.

probably, this is not the case and the translation is altered in such a way that it becomes incorrect in this context. These observations suggest that additional information such as speaker identities or dialog turns will be necessary to handle such cases correctly.

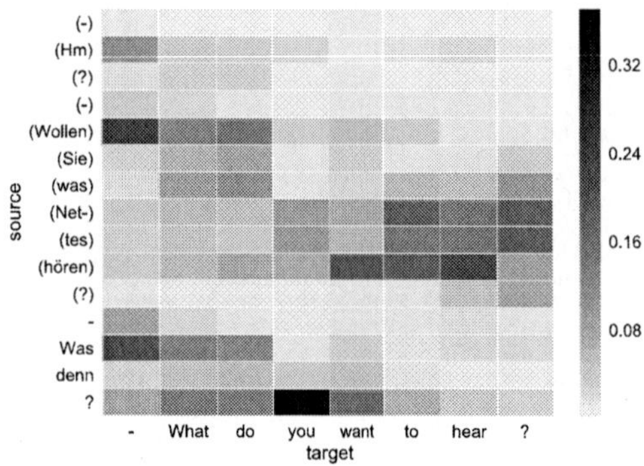

Figure 4: Another example for attention with extended source context.

The examples above constitute rather anecdotal evidence and systematic patterns are difficult to extract. We leave it to future work to study various cases in more detail and to inspect certain properties in connection with specific discourse phenomena. In this paper, we inspect instead the distribution of attention for individual target words to see what word types depend most on contextual history. For this, we counted the overall attention of each word type in our test set and computed the proportion of external attention on average. The list of the top ten words (after lowercasing) with frequency above four is given in Table 2. Those

words receive considerably larger external attention (17-26%) than the average (4.9%).

| word | freq | external | internal | prop.% | ∅ pos. |
|---|---|---|---|---|---|
| yeah | 35 | 0.224 | 0.622 | 26.5 | 3.71 |
| yes | 182 | 0.212 | 0.601 | 26.1 | 4.22 |
| wake | 6 | 0.239 | 0.684 | 25.8 | 6.67 |
| anywhere | 6 | 0.223 | 0.655 | 25.4 | 7.67 |
| course | 35 | 0.191 | 0.631 | 23.2 | 3.17 |
| oh | 61 | 0.199 | 0.712 | 21.9 | 2.08 |
| saying | 5 | 0.177 | 0.690 | 20.5 | 5.20 |
| tired | 9 | 0.174 | 0.774 | 18.3 | 5.67 |
| latham | 5 | 0.169 | 0.796 | 17.5 | 7.80 |
| really | 13 | 0.161 | 0.763 | 17.4 | 2.77 |
| *average* | — | 0.045 | 0.891 | 4.9 | — |
| (36) she | 98 | 0.124 | 0.837 | 12.9 | 3.70 |
| (62) he | 232 | 0.103 | 0.851 | 10.8 | 4.04 |
| (79) it | 533 | 0.089 | 0.807 | 10.0 | 4.81 |
| (83) they | 135 | 0.095 | 0.871 | 9.9 | 4.17 |
| (97) you | 1349 | 0.084 | 0.828 | 9.2 | 4.28 |

Table 2: Word types with the highest external attention and the rank of some cross-lingually ambiguous pronouns in the list sorted by the proportion (*prop.*) of external attention. *∅ pos.* gives the average token position of the target word.

Unfortunately, there is no straightforward interpretation of the words that receive substantial attention from the extended contextual history, but several response particles such as "yes", "yeah", "oh", which glue together interactive dialogues, are in the list. Furthermore, we can see that the words with significant cross-sentential attention does not consist of sentence-initial words only. The token position varies quite a lot. We also list the values of pronouns with significant cross-lingual ambiguity and their rank in the list sorted by the proportion of external attention. The third-person pronouns "he", "she" and "it" put significant attention (over 10%) on the previous sentence(s).

Some words are simply not easy to link to particular source language words and, therefore, their attention may be spread all over the place. Therefore, we also computed the proportion of external attention at specific positions in the input by considering only the highest internal and the highest external attention for each target word in each sentence. The list of words with the highest external attention according to that measure are listed in Table 3.

The list is quite similar to the previous one, but one notes that the pronouns all advance in the rankings, suggesting a more focused attention of these entities. This is an interesting observation, and we will leave further investigations to future

| word | freq | external | internal | prop.% | ∅ pos. |
|---|---|---|---|---|---|
| yeah | 35 | 0.135 | 0.242 | 35.9 | 3.71 |
| wake | 6 | 0.179 | 0.326 | 35.4 | 6.67 |
| yes | 182 | 0.091 | 0.259 | 26.1 | 4.22 |
| tired | 9 | 0.113 | 0.364 | 23.7 | 5.67 |
| oh | 61 | 0.086 | 0.288 | 23.1 | 2.08 |
| anywhere | 6 | 0.094 | 0.326 | 22.4 | 7.67 |
| dover | 6 | 0.119 | 0.426 | 21.9 | 5.83 |
| course | 35 | 0.069 | 0.271 | 20.3 | 3.17 |
| speak | 15 | 0.072 | 0.305 | 19.1 | 4.67 |
| sure | 29 | 0.065 | 0.284 | 18.7 | 3.59 |
| *average* | — | 0.021 | 0.441 | 4.5 | — |
| (20) she | 98 | 0.062 | 0.343 | 15.3 | 3.70 |
| (50) he | 232 | 0.048 | 0.355 | 11.9 | 4.04 |
| (64) it | 533 | 0.040 | 0.332 | 10.8 | 4.81 |
| (72) you | 1349 | 0.038 | 0.327 | 10.4 | 4.28 |
| (79) they | 135 | 0.040 | 0.356 | 10.1 | 4.17 |

Table 3: Word types with the highest average of external attention peaks.

work.

## 5.2  2+2: Larger Translation Units

Let us turn now to the second model that works with larger translation units. Here, the neural network produces a translation of the entire extended input. This includes the generation of segment break symbols and attention for the entire sequence. Again, the question arises whether the model learns to look at information outside of the aligned segment. External context is not marked with specific prefixes anymore and token representations are completely shared in the model. Theoretically, the model can now swap, shuffle or merge information that comes from different segments. Random inspection does not yield many such cases, but we do see a number of cases where translations include information from previous parts or where the segment break is placed in a different position than in the reference translation. Often, this is actually due to alignment errors in the reference data, such that the translation system is penalised without reason in our automatic evaluation. Table 4 shows scores of the extended context translations and we can now see a slight improvement in BLEU and chrF3. Note that each translation hypothesis and each reference now refers to two segments with break tokens between them removed. Hence, the scores do not match the ones in Table 1.

Figure 5 illustrates an example with a large proportion of cross-segmental attention. In this case, the model summarises part of segment one with segment two into one translation, and the attention goes mainly to segment one.

| in % | BLEU | chrF3 | (precision) | (recall) |
|---|---|---|---|---|
| baseline* | 27.25 | 44.14 | 55.61 | 43.15 |
| 2+2* | 27.41 | 44.54 | 55.51 | 43.58 |

Table 4: BLEU and chrF3 on extended context segments (sliding window). Individual segments are simply concatenated in the baseline system where necessary.

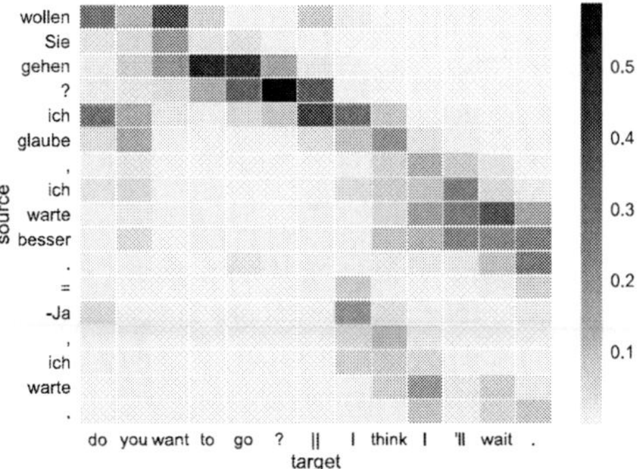


Figure 5: Attention with multiple sentences and large cross-segment attention. The double bars refer to segment breaks.

This looks quite acceptable from the point of view of coherence. Looking at the reference used for automatic evaluation, we can actually see a misalignment in the data where *"do you want to go ?"* should have been aligned to *"wollen Sie gehen ?"*:

| |
|---|
| I don 't care what you 've started . do you want to go ? |
| mir ist egal , was sie angefangen haben . |
| no , I think I 'd better wait . |
| wollen Sie gehen ? ich glaube , ich warte besser . |
| - Yes , I 'll wait . |
| -Ja , ich warte . |

It is also interesting to see that the generation of the segment break symbol uses information from segment-initial tokens and punctuations such as question marks. This also follows the intuitions about the decision whether a segment is complete or not.

We also computed word-type-specific attention again. However, the list of words that put significant focus on other segments looks quite different from the previous model. The top-ten list is shown in Table 5.

We also computed the average attention peak and the proportion of such attention to other segments. The words with highest values are shown in Table 6. Again, we can see response particles

| word | freq | external | internal | prop.% | ∅ pos. |
|---|---|---|---|---|---|
| exactly | 5 | 0.190 | 0.644 | 22.8 | 2.20 |
| shelf | 5 | 0.202 | 0.692 | 22.6 | 8.40 |
| upstairs | 5 | 0.186 | 0.757 | 19.7 | 7.60 |
| unbelievable | 7 | 0.151 | 0.641 | 19.1 | 2.86 |
| yeah | 91 | 0.144 | 0.667 | 17.8 | 1.95 |
| hardly | 5 | 0.155 | 0.740 | 17.4 | 2.20 |
| cares | 5 | 0.144 | 0.755 | 16.0 | 2.60 |
| horns | 8 | 0.134 | 0.713 | 15.8 | 5.25 |
| fossils | 7 | 0.137 | 0.744 | 15.5 | 3.57 |
| -what | 10 | 0.121 | 0.660 | 15.5 | 1.00 |
| *average* | — | 0.028 | 0.880 | 3.1 | — |

Table 5: Word types with the highest cross-segmental attention (excluding attention on sentence break symbols)).

but also some additional adverbials that can have connective functions. Pronouns appear quite low in the ranked list and, therefore, we leave them out in the presentation here.

| word | freq | external | internal | prop.% | ∅ pos. |
|---|---|---|---|---|---|
| -the | 5 | 0.436 | 0.541 | 44.6 | 1.00 |
| -what | 10 | 0.358 | 0.519 | 40.9 | 1.00 |
| exactly | 5 | 0.171 | 0.266 | 39.2 | 2.20 |
| -aye | 12 | 0.345 | 0.550 | 38.5 | 1.00 |
| -yes | 7 | 0.281 | 0.472 | 37.3 | 1.00 |
| apparently | 7 | 0.308 | 0.536 | 36.5 | 1.00 |
| hardly | 5 | 0.178 | 0.321 | 35.7 | 2.20 |
| anyway | 9 | 0.241 | 0.443 | 35.2 | 1.00 |
| ah | 6 | 0.217 | 0.407 | 34.8 | 1.00 |
| ahoy | 6 | 0.304 | 0.590 | 34.0 | 1.00 |
| *average* | — | 0.043 | 0.440 | 8.9 | — |

Table 6: Word types with the highest average of cross-segmental attention peaks.

Cross-segmental attention peaks are dominated by tokens with relatively low overall frequency, some of which arise from tokenization errors (e.g. the words starting with a hyphen, typically from sentence-initial positions). Therefore, we propose another type of evaluation, less sensitive to overall frequency: we only count occurrences of target words whose external attention is higher than the internal attention, and normalize them by the total occurrence count of the target word. We discard words which have majoritarily external attention in four or less cases. Results are shown in Table 7.

In addition to the known response particles and punctuation signs, we also see pronouns and demonstrative particles (such as *here, what, that*) ranked prominently. However, the absolute numbers are small and only permit tentative conclusions. This analysis also allows us to see the direction of cross-segmental attention. Items that tend to occur at the beginning of the sentence show

| word | proportion | freq ext peak | freq |
|---|---|---|---|
| yeah | 0.077 | 7 | 91 |
| oh | 0.069 | 7 | 101 |
| yes | 0.054 | 11 | 204 |
| thank | 0.049 | 7 | 144 |
| no | 0.025 | 8 | 320 |
| - | 0.023 | 44 | 1890 |
| good | 0.018 | 5 | 284 |
| here | 0.017 | 6 | 346 |
| ? | 0.016 | 29 | 1812 |
| ... | 0.016 | 5 | 316 |
| . | 0.014 | 104 | 7645 |
| what | 0.012 | 6 | 486 |
| you | 0.009 | 23 | 2458 |
| that | 0.008 | 6 | 725 |
| 's | 0.008 | 9 | 1102 |
| it | 0.005 | 5 | 914 |
| , | 0.004 | 16 | 3561 |
| i | 0.004 | 10 | 2372 |

Table 7: Word types with the highest proportion of cross-segmental attention peaks, with absolute frequencies of cross-segmental attention peak and overall absolute word frequencies.

attention towards the previous sentence, whereas items that occur at the end of a sentence (such as punctuation signs, but also the *'s* token) show attention towards the following sentence.

We also inspected some translations and their attention distributions in order to study the effect of larger translation units on translation quality. One example is the translation in Figure 6.

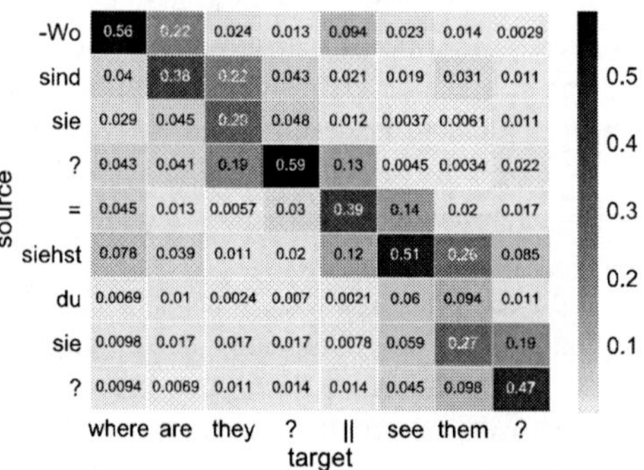



Figure 6: Attention patterns with referential pronouns in extended context.

The example illustrates how the model works when deciding translations of ambiguous words like the German pronoun "sie". First, when generating "they", the model looks at the verb for agreement constraints and the representation around the plural inflection "sind" of the German equivalent of "are" receives significant attention. Even more interesting is the translation of "siehst du sie?", which in isolation is translated to (the intuitively most likely translation) "do you see **her** ?" by our baseline model. In the extended model, the translation changes to "them", which agrees with the context and is coherent here. Why the auxiliary verb and the subject pronoun are left out is another question but that could be due to the colloquial style of the training data. In any case, the figure shows that "them" also looks at "sind" in the previous sentence with a weight (0.031) that is significantly larger than for other positions in the previous sentence. This amount seems to contribute to the change to plural, which is, of course, satisfactory in this case. Target language context will certainly also contribute to this effect but even the 2+1 model produces "them" in this particular example without the additional target context but the same information from the source.

However, sometimes the extended model is worse than the baseline with respect to pronoun translation. An example is shown below. In this case, the context window is too small and does not cover the important reference (*der Sonnenaufgang/the sunrise*), which appears two sentences before the anaphoric pronoun (*er/it*). But whether an even larger context model would pick this up correctly is not certain.

| |
|---|
| context 2: hast du je den Sonnenaufgang in China gesehen? |
| reference: ever notice the sunrise in China ? |
| context 1: solltest du . |
| reference: you should . |
| source: er ist wunderschön . |
| reference: it 's beautiful . |
| baseline: it 's beautiful . |
| extended: he 's beautiful . |

Some translations also become more idiomatic due to the additional context. Empirical evidence is difficult to give but here are three examples that illustrate small changes that make sense:

| |
|---|
| source: los , Fenner ! |
| reference: go ahead , Fenner ! |
| baseline: go , Fenner ! |
| extended: come on , Fenner ! |
| source: was Sie nicht sagen ! |
| reference: you don 't say ! |
| baseline: what you don 't say ! |
| extended: you don 't say ! |
| source: ganz meiner Meinung . |
| reference: that 's what I say . |
| baseline: my opinion . |
| extended: I agree . |

### 5.3  Manual Evaluation

The example of Figure 6 raises the question whether the extended model is able to reliably and systematically disambiguate pronominal translations. In order to answer this question, we extracted all occurrences of the ambiguous pronoun *sie/Sie* from our test set (1143 occurrences in 1018 sentences, i.e. in every fifth sentence of the test set) and manually evaluated about half of them (565 occurrences in 516 sentences), comparing the output of the baseline system with the one of the 2+2 system. We distinguish four categories on the basis of the reference translation: polite imperative *Sie*, other occurrences of the polite pronoun *Sie*, feminine singular *sie* and plural *sie*. Figure 8 lists the results.

| Word category | Occurrences | Baseline | 2+2 |
|---|---|---|---|
| Polite imperative | 101 | 98.0% | 97.0% |
| Polite other | 301 | 94.4% | 95.0% |
| Feminine singular | 77 | 85.7% | 85.7% |
| Plural | 86 | 69.8% | 79.1% |
| All | 565 | 90.1% | 91.7% |

Table 8: Percentages of correct translations of the pronoun *sie/Sie*.

The table shows that polite forms are most frequent in the corpus and also rather easy to translate thanks to capitalisation. In the case of imperatives, they simply are deleted (e.g., *Kommen Sie!* becomes *Come!*), whereas in other contexts they are consistently translated to *you*. The remaining errors are mainly due to entire segments that are left untranslated, or to erroneous lowercasing of sentence-initial positions during preprocessing.

Distinguishing singular from plural readings is harder: a non-polite form *sie* can be translated as *she* or *it* in its singular reading (depending on the grammatical gender of the antecedent), or as *they* or *them* in its plural reading (depending on case). The figures show that the extended model is better at correctly predicting *they* (and *them*), but that correctly predicting *she* or *it* is equally hard with or without context. While the superiority of the 2+2 model cannot be established numerically (none of the reported figures are statistically significant, according to $\chi^2$ tests at $p = 0.05$), there are examples that show corrected output:

| |
|---|
| context: du bist nur ein Junge und das sind böse Männer . |
| reference: you 're only a boy , they 're vicious men . |
| source: such sie , Max . |
| reference: get ' em , Max . |
| baseline: find her , Max . |
| 2+2: find them , Max . |
| context: Sie verstecken sich wie die Ratten im Müll . |
| reference: they hide out like rats in the garbage . |
| source: wenn du sie finden willst , musst du ebenso im Müll wühlen wie sie . |
| reference: so if you 're gonna get ' em , you 'll have to wallow in that garbage right with them . |
| baseline: if you want to find her , you 'll have to wallow in the trash like her . |
| 2+2: if you want to find them , you have to dig through the garbage as well as them . |

The decision of translating feminine singular pronouns as *sie* or *it* is also improved in some cases by the 2+2 model:

| |
|---|
| context: mehr bedeutet dir die Sache nicht ? |
| reference: is that all my story meant to you ? |
| source: was sonst könnte sie mir bedeuten ? |
| reference: what else could it mean to me ? |
| baseline: what else could she mean to me ? |
| 2+2: what else could it mean to me ? |
| context 2: kennst du die alte Mine hier ? |
| reference: know the old mine around here ? |
| context 1: - Davon gibt ' s hier viele . |
| reference: - There 's a lot of them here . |
| source: - Sie gehört einem gewissen Sand . |
| reference: - It 's worked by a man named Sand . |
| baseline: - She owns a certain sand . |
| 2+2: - It belongs to a certain sand . |

However, there is currently not much evidence that these improvements are due to cross-segmental attention. It remains to be investigated if this also holds for the 2+1 model and variants thereof.

## 6 Conclusions and Future Work

In this paper, we present two simple models that use larger context in neural MT, one that adds source language history to the input and one that concatenates subsequent segments in the training data. We discuss the effect on translation and the attention model in particular. We can show that neural MT is indeed capable of translating with wider context and that it also learns to distinguish information coming from different segments or discourse history. We run experiments on German-English subtitle data and we can find various examples in which referential expressions across sentence boundaries can be handled properly. The current study is our first attempt to model discourse-aware neural MT and the outcome is already encouraging. However, evidence so far is rather anecdotal but in the future, we plan to run more systematic experiments with detailed analyses and evaluations. We will look at different windows and other ways of encoding discourse history. We will also study specific discourse phenomena in more depth trying to find out whether NMT learns to handle them in a linguistically plausible way. Finally, this research also intends to provide insights into the development of discourse-aware coverage models for NMT. Indeed, explicit models of coverage have been shown to reduce the amount of overtranslation and undertranslation, whereas our translation models with extended context settings are targeted to make use of overtranslation and undertranslation to some extent. Our experiments will hopefully contribute to a better understanding of the attention and coverage dynamics in discourse-aware NMT.

## Acknowledgments

We wish to thank the anonymous reviewers for their detailed reviews. We would also like to acknowledge the Finnish IT Center for Science (CSC) for providing computational resources and NVIDIA for their support by means of their GPU grant.

## References

Jimmy Lei Ba, Jamie Ryan Kiros, and Geoffrey E. Hinton. 2016. Layer normalization. *ArXiv e-prints* .

Dzmitry Bahdanau, Kyunghyun Cho, and Yoshua Bengio. 2014. Neural machine translation by jointly learning to align and translate. *CoRR* abs/1409.0473.

Guosheng Ben, Deyi Xiong, Zhiyang Teng, Yajuan Lü, and Qun Liu. 2013. Bilingual lexical cohesion trigger model for document-level machine translation. In *Proceedings of the 51st Annual Meeting of the Association for Computational Linguistics (Volume 2: Short Papers)*. Association for Computational Linguistics, Sofia (Bulgaria), pages 382–386. http://www.aclweb.org/anthology/P13-2068.

Marine Carpuat. 2009. One translation per discourse. In *Proceedings of the Workshop on Semantic Evaluations: Recent Achievements and Future Directions (SEW-2009)*. Association for Computational Linguistics, Boulder (Colorado, USA), pages 19–27. http://www.aclweb.org/anthology/W09-2404.

Marine Carpuat and Michel Simard. 2012. The trouble with SMT consistency. In *Proceedings of the Seventh Workshop on Statistical Machine Translation*. Association for Computational

Linguistics, Montréal (Canada), pages 442–449. http://www.aclweb.org/anthology/W12-3156.

Yarin Gal and Zoubin Ghahramani. 2016. A theoretically grounded application of dropout in recurrent neural networks. In *Advances in Neural Information Processing Systems 29 (NIPS)*.

Liane Guillou. 2012. Improving pronoun translation for statistical machine translation. In *Proceedings of the Student Research Workshop at the 13th Conference of the European Chapter of the Association for Computational Linguistics*. Association for Computational Linguistics, Avignon (France), pages 1–10. http://www.aclweb.org/anthology/E12-3001.

Christian Hardmeier. 2012. Discourse in statistical machine translation: A survey and a case study. *Discours* 11.

Christian Hardmeier. 2014. *Discourse in Statistical Machine Translation*, volume 15 of *Studia Linguistica Upsaliensia*. Acta Universitatis Upsaliensis, Uppsala.

Christian Hardmeier and Marcello Federico. 2010. Modelling pronominal anaphora in statistical machine translation. In *Proceedings of the Seventh International Workshop on Spoken Language Translation (IWSLT)*. Paris (France), pages 283–289.

Christian Hardmeier, Sara Stymne, Jörg Tiedemann, and Joakim Nivre. 2013a. Docent: A document-level decoder for phrase-based statistical machine translation. In *Proceedings of the 51st Annual Meeting of the Association for Computational Linguistics: System Demonstrations*. Association for Computational Linguistics, Sofia (Bulgaria), pages 193–198. http://www.aclweb.org/anthology/P13-4033.

Christian Hardmeier, Jörg Tiedemann, and Joakim Nivre. 2013b. Latent anaphora resolution for cross-lingual pronoun prediction. In *Proceedings of the 2013 Conference on Empirical Methods in Natural Language Processing*. Association for Computational Linguistics, Seattle (Washington, USA), pages 380–391. http://www.aclweb.org/anthology/D13-1037.

Sepp Hochreiter and Jürgen Schmidhuber. 1997. Long short-term memory. *Neural Computation* 9(8):1735–1780. https://doi.org/10.1162/neco.1997.9.8.1735.

Sebastien Jean, Stanislas Lauly, Orhan Firat, and Kyunghyun Cho. 2017. Does Neural Machine Translation Benefit from Larger Context? *ArXiv e-prints, 1704.05135* https://arxiv.org/abs/1704.05135.

Philipp Koehn, Hieu Hoang, Alexandra Birch, Chris Callison-Burch, Marcello Federico, Nicola Bertoldi, Brooke Cowan, Wade Shen, Christine Moran, Richard Zens, Christopher J. Dyer, Ondřej Bojar, Alexandra Constantin, and Evan Herbst. 2007. Moses: Open Source Toolkit for Statistical Machine Translation. In *Proceedings of ACL*. pages 177–180.

Ronan Le Nagard and Philipp Koehn. 2010. Aiding pronoun translation with co-reference resolution. In *Proceedings of the Joint Fifth Workshop on Statistical Machine Translation and MetricsMATR*. Association for Computational Linguistics, Uppsala (Sweden), pages 252–261.

Pierre Lison and Jörg Tiedemann. 2016. Opensubtitles2015: Extracting large parallel corpora from movie and tv subtitles. In *Proceedings of the 10th International Conference on Language Resources and Evaluation (LREC-2016)*.

Sharid Loaiciga, Thomas Meyer, and Andrei Popescu-Belis. 2014. English-french verb phrase alignment in europarl for tense translation modeling. In Nicoletta Calzolari, Khalid Choukri, Thierry Declerck, Hrafn Loftsson, Bente Maegaard, Joseph Mariani, Asuncion Moreno, Jan Odijk, and Stelios Piperidis, editors, *Proceedings of the Ninth International Conference on Language Resources and Evaluation (LREC'14)*. European Language Resources Association (ELRA), Reykjavik, Iceland, pages 674–681. ACL Anthology Identifier: L14-1205. http://www.lrec-conf.org/proceedings/lrec2014/pdf/205_Paper.pdf.

Minh-Thang Luong and Christopher D. Manning. 2016. Achieving open vocabulary neural machine translation with hybrid word-character models. In *Proceedings of the 54th Annual Meeting of the Association for Computational Linguistics (Volume 1: Long Papers)*. Association for Computational Linguistics, Berlin, Germany, pages 1054–1063.

Yanjun Ma, Yifan He, Andy Way, and Josef van Genabith. 2011. Consistent translation using discriminative learning – A translation memory-inspired approach. In *Proceedings of the 49th Annual Meeting of the Association for Computational Linguistics: Human Language Technologies*. Association for Computational Linguistics, Portland (Oregon, USA), pages 1239–1248. http://www.aclweb.org/anthology/P11-1124.

Thomas Meyer, Andrei Popescu-Belis, Najeh Hajlaoui, and Andrea Gesmundo. 2012. Machine translation of labeled discourse connectives. In *Proceedings of the Tenth Biennial Conference of the Association for Machine Translation in the Americas (AMTA)*. San Diego (California, USA).

Robert Östling, Yves Scherrer, Jörg Tiedemann, Gongbo Tang, and Tommi Nieminen. 2017. The Helsinki neural machine translation system. In *Proceedings of the Second Conference on Machine Translation*. Association for Computational Linguistics, Copenhagen, Denmark.

Lorenza Russo, Sharid Loáiciga, and Asheesh Gulati. 2012. Improving machine translation of null subjects in Italian and Spanish. In *Proceedings of the Student Research Workshop at the 13th Conference of the European Chapter of the Association for*

*Computational Linguistics*. Association for Computational Linguistics, Avignon (France), pages 81–89. http://www.aclweb.org/anthology/E12-3010.

Rico Sennrich, Barry Haddow, and Alexandra Birch. 2016. Neural machine translation of rare words with subword units. In *Proceedings of the 54th Annual Meeting of the Association for Computational Linguistics (Volume 1: Long Papers)*. Association for Computational Linguistics, Berlin, Germany, pages 1715–1725. http://www.aclweb.org/anthology/P16-1162.

Jörg Tiedemann. 2010. Context adaptation in statistical machine translation using models with exponentially decaying cache. In *Proceedings of the ACL 2010 Workshop on Domain Adaptation for Natural Language Processing (DANLP)*. Association for Computational Linguistics, Uppsala (Sweden), pages 8–15. http://www.aclweb.org/anthology/W10-2602.

Ferhan Ture, Douglas W. Oard, and Philip Resnik. 2012. Encouraging consistent translation choices. In *Proceedings of the 2012 Conference of the North American Chapter of the Association for Computational Linguistics: Human Language Technologies*. Association for Computational Linguistics, Montréal (Canada), pages 417–426. http://www.aclweb.org/anthology/N12-1046.

Rob Voigt and Dan Jurafsky. 2012. Towards a literary machine translation: The role of referential cohesion. In *Proceedings of the NAACL-HLT 2012 Workshop on Computational Linguistics for Literature*. Association for Computational Linguistics, Montréal (Canada), pages 18–25. http://www.aclweb.org/anthology/W12-2503.

Yonghui Wu, Mike Schuster, Zhifeng Chen, Quoc V. Le, Mohammad Norouzi, Wolfgang Macherey, Maxim Krikun, Yuan Cao, Qin Gao, Klaus Macherey, Jeff Klingner, Apurva Shah, Melvin Johnson, Xiaobing Liu, Lukasz Kaiser, Stephan Gouws, Yoshikiyo Kato, Taku Kudo, Hideto Kazawa, Keith Stevens, George Kurian, Nishant Patil, Wei Wang, Cliff Young, Jason Smith, Jason Riesa, Alex Rudnick, Oriol Vinyals, Greg Corrado, Macduff Hughes, and Jeffrey Dean. 2016. Google's neural machine translation system: Bridging the gap between human and machine translation. *CoRR* abs/1609.08144. http://arxiv.org/abs/1609.08144.

Deyi Xiong, Yang Ding, Min Zhang, and Chew Lim Tan. 2013a. Lexical chain based cohesion models for document-level statistical machine translation. In *Proceedings of the 2013 Conference on Empirical Methods in Natural Language Processing*. Association for Computational Linguistics, Seattle (Washington, USA), pages 1563–1573. http://www.aclweb.org/anthology/D13-1163.

Deyi Xiong, Ben Guosheng, Min Zhang, Yajuan Lü, and Qun Liu. 2013b. Modeling lexical cohesion for document-level machine translation. In *Proceedings of the Twenty-Third International Joint Conference on Artificial Intelligence*. AAAI Press, Beijing (China), pages 2183–2189.

Deyi Xiong and Min Zhang. 2013. A topic-based coherence model for statistical machine translation. In *Proceedings of the Twenty-Seventh AAAI Conference on Artificial Intelligence*. Bellevue (Washington, USA), pages 977–983.

# Translating Implicit Discourse Connectives Based on Crosslingual Annotation and Alignment


**Hongzheng Li[1], Philippe Langlais[2], Yaohong Jin[3]**

[1] Institute of Chinese Information Processing, Beijing Normal University, Beijing, 100875, China

[2] RALI Lab, University of Montreal, Montreal, QC H3T 1N8, Canada

[3] Beijing Ultrapower Software Co., Ltd., Beijing, 100107, China

lihongzheng@mail.bnu.edu.cn, felipe@iro.umontreal.ca, jinyaohong@hotmail.com



## Abstract

Implicit discourse connectives and relations are distributed more widely in Chinese texts, when translating into English, such connectives are usually translated explicitly. Towards Chinese-English MT, in this paper we describe cross-lingual annotation and alignment of discourse connectives in a parallel corpus, describing related surveys and findings. We then conduct some evaluation experiments to testify the translation of implicit connectives and whether representing implicit connectives explicitly in source language can improve the final translation performance significantly. Preliminary results show it has little improvement by just inserting explicit connectives for implicit relations.


## 1 Introduction

Discourse relations refer to various relations between elementary discourse units(EDUs) in discourse structures, these relations are usually expressed explicitly or implicitly by certain surface words known as discourse connectives(DCs).

Distribution of DCs varies between different languages. Let's just take Chinese and English for example. According to previous surveys, explicit and implicit DCs account for 22% and 76% respectively in the Chinese Discourse Treebank(CDTB) (Zhou and Xue, 2015), while they account for 45% and 40% in the Penn Discourse Treebank (PDTB) (Prasad et al., 2008), indicating that there are more implicit DCs in Chinese, correspondingly, discourse relations are usually implicit.

DCs should have some impacts on the translation performance and quality. As Chinese tends to use more implicit DCs, such DCs will be expressed explicitly when necessary in Chinese-English translation. Here is an example sentence show the implicit relation.

天气预报　说 今天 会 下雨，
weather report say today will rain
"Weather report says it will rain today,"
我们 决定 不 在 公园 举办 演唱会。
We decide not in park hold concert
"We decide not to hold the concert in the park."

There is no explicit DC between the two Chinese sub-sentences in the simple example, and the implicit discourse relation is CAUSAL. While translating into English, it is better to add an explicit DC such as "so/thus" before the second sub-sentence to express the relation, which will also make the translation more fluent and more acceptable.

In this paper, based on bilingual corpus, we first present cross-lingual annotation of DCs on both cross-sentence and within-sentence levels, and describe some related findings, then make a further survey on how to translate implicit DCs in Chinese-English discourse-level MT, and whether translation of DCs will have some impacts on final MT outputs.

The rest of the paper are organized as follows: section2 introduce some related works. Section 3 present annotation and findings of DCs in the bilingual parallel corpus. Section4 discuss some preliminary experiment results and analysis. And last section follow the conclusion.

## 2 Related Work

Discourse related issues have become increasingly popular in Natural Language Processing in recent




*Proceedings of the Third Workshop on Discourse in Machine Translation*, pages 93–98,
Copenhagen, Denmark, September 8, 2017. ©2017 Association for Computational Linguistics.

years, especially the release of some famous discourse treebanks including PDTB, CDTB and RST (Mann and Thompson, 1986) corpus has promoted the research greatly.

Some research (Li et al. 2014, Rutherford and Xue, 2014) has done on monolingual annotation and analysis of Chinese DCs. Li et al. (2014a) and Yung et al. (2015a, 2015b) also present some cross-lingual discourse relation analysis. But they just analyze within sentences instead of cross-sentences.

In the field of MT, some previous works have been mainly focus on DCs in European language pairs (Becher, 2011; Zufferey and Cartoni, 2014) such as English, French and German, including but not limited to disambiguating DCs in translation (Meyer et al., 2011; Meyer and Popescu-Belis, 2012), labeled and implicit DCs translation (Meyer and Webber, 2013).

As for Chinese discourse relations and translation, Tu et al. (2013) employ a RST-based discourse parsing approaches in SMT, in their following work (Tu et al. 2014), they also present a tree-string model on Chinese complex sentences, integrating discourse relations into MT, gaining some improvement on translation performance. Li et al. (2014b) argues the influence of discourse factors in translation.

## 3  Cross-lingual Annotations of DCs

In order to investigate the DCs in the translation, we first manually align DCs in Chinese and English in the bilingual corpus, News-commentary corpus [1] downloaded from OPUS [2] (Tiedemann, 2012), then further annotate them with essential information on both the source and target sides.

The reasons why we choose news-commentary corpus lie in two sides: first, each line in the corpus usually includes several consecutive sentences, and each sentence is further composed of several sub-sentences(clauses), which provide rich cross-sentence and within-sentence discourse-level information. Second, sentences in each line are neither too long nor too short, which are suitable to train the MT models.

In this part, we will describe the annotation scheme and some corresponding findings.

---

[1] http://opus.lingfil.uu.se/News-Commentary.php
[2] http://opus.lingfil.uu.se/

### 3.1  Annotation Principles

As mentioned above, we will analyze the DCs on both cross-sentence and within-sentence levels, we decide to annotate the corpus in a top-down way. That is, we first annotate DCs between cross-sentences, and then within the sentences. Note that, if there exist sentences end with only full stop marks and have no commas or other punctuations, these sentences will not be annotated. Because they have no sub-sentences, and have no corresponding discourse relations within the sentence.

Here is an example:

a.　瑞典　　本月　　担任 欧盟 轮值 主席
Sweden this month as EU rotating presidency
有助于 推动 这项 计划。
help promote this plan

b.　但是 此时 正值 欧盟 东部　　邻国
but now is EU eastern neighbor countries
面临 严重 挑战　　的 时刻，因此 很多
face severe challenges DE time, so many
伙伴国　　　都 遭受了　　金融
partner countries all encounter financial
和 经济危机　　　的 沉重 打击。
and economic crisis DE severe hitting.

(Sweden's assumption of the EU Presidency this month should help these efforts. However, it comes at a time when the Union's eastern neighborhood faces severe challenges, and the financial and economic crisis hitting many of the partner countries hard.)

The example has two consecutive sentences *a* and *b*, we first need to indicate the DC and relation between them. Next, we will continue to analyze in *b*. As sentence *a* has no sub-sentences, we don't need to analyze on it.

Based on the principle, we first randomly extract 5,000 cross-sentence pairs from the corpus by using systematic sampling approach, and then extract possible sentences from the pairs.

Note that, as quite preliminary research, all current annotation is done by the first author of the paper alone, who is a PhD student majored in Linguistics and Computational Linguistics. As a result, unlike many previous works on corpus annotation, we don't conduct consistency experiments between different annotators to justify the performance of annotation until now. But we try to guarantee the annotation quality as much as possible. In the future, we will expand the annotation size, asking other annotators to work together on the corpus and minimize the inconsistence during the annotation.

## 3.2 Annotation Labels

Inspired by (Yung, et al., 2015b), in our annotation scheme, we design several following labels. Most labels will be annotated on both cross/within-sentence levels on bilingual sides.

**Nature of relations**. Indicating the relations belong to explicit (E) or implicit (I) relations.

**Explicit DCs**. Annotating explicit DCs(EDCs) appeared in the sentences. On Chinese side, we try to find out all the possible DCs as much as possible. As for English, the DCs are annotated based on the 100 distinct types of explicit connectives in PDTB.

**Implicit DCs(IDCs)**. If there are no explicit connectives in the sentences, proper DCs are inserted according to the discourse relations. If insertion is not grammatical, the DC is labelled as 'redundant'.

**AltLex**. This label is only for English side, referring relations a discourse relation that cannot be isolated from context as an explicit DCs.

**Semantic types of discourse relations**. Considering the expression features of Chinese, based on the 8 senses of relations defined in CDTB, we also add 5 other relation types on Chinese side (shown in following table). As on English side, we adapt 4 top-level discourse senses defined in PDTB, namely Expansion(EXP), Contingency (CON), Comparison (COM) and Temporal(TEM).

| *Causation* | *Purpose* |
|---|---|
| *Conditional* | *Temporal* |
| *Conjunction* | *Progression* |
| *Contrast* | *Expansion* |
| hypothetical | concession |
| example | explanation |
| successive | |

Table 1: Relation types in Chinese. In which first 8 italic relations are defined in CDTB, and last 5 are newly added.

| | Cross-sent (a, b) | | Within-sent (b) | |
|---|---|---|---|---|
| | Zh | En | Zh | En |
| Nature | E | E | E | E |
| EDC | 但是 | however | 但，因此 | However, and |
| IDC | / | / | / | / |

| types | Con-trast | Com | Conjunction, Cause | Exp, Con |
|---|---|---|---|---|

Table 2: An annotation example

According to the scheme, annotation of the above example in section 3.1 is shown in above table.

## 3.3 Annotation Statistics

Through the annotation, we annotate 5,000 cross-sentences and 8163 sentences, finally getting 5000 pairs of cross-sentence and 9308 within-sentence relations.

| | Cross-sentence | | | within-sentence | | |
|---|---|---|---|---|---|---|
| | Exp. | Imp. | Alt. | Exp. | Imp. | Alt. |
| ZH | 1163 (23%) | 3837 (77%) | / | 2513 (27%) | 6795 (73%) | / |
| EN | 1094 (22%) | 3622 (72%) | 284 (6%) | 4128 (44%) | 4458 (48%) | 742 (8%) |

Table 3: Bilingual distribution of explicit and implicit relations

| ZH \ EN | Exp. | Imp. | Alt. | Total |
|---|---|---|---|---|
| Exp. | 947 (81%) | 118 (10%) | 88 (9%) | 1163 |
| Imp. | 147 (4%) | 3494 (91%) | 196 (5%) | 3837 |
| Total | 1094 | 3622 | 284 | 5000 |

Table 4: Cross-sentence DCs Alignment matrix

| ZH \ EN | Exp. | Imp. | Alt. | Total |
|---|---|---|---|---|
| Exp. | 1884 (75%) | 351 (14%) | 278 (11%) | 2513 |
| Imp. | 2244 (33%) | 4107 (60%) | 464 (7%) | 6795 |
| Total | 4128 | 4458 | 742 | 9308 |

Table 5: Within-sentence DCs Alignment matrix

Table3 shows on cross-sentence level, there exist more implicit DCs both in Chinese and English. The discourse relation "Consecutive" occupies highest frequency. While on within-sentence level there are still more implicit DCs than explicit ones in Chinese, but in English, their proportions are similar. The bilingual distribution of DCs in news-commentary corpus once again prove the similar findings in CDTB and PDTB before. We can also conclude that discourse relation types are more various within sentences, on the other hand, relations between sentences seem not so close, sentences are often independent with each other.

From the DC alignment matrixes in Table4 and 5, most explicit Chinese DCs usually have corresponding explicit DC translations. As for implicit DCs, although most of them map to implicit DCs on English side, there are still about 30% of them are aligned to explicit ones, indicating the important status and common usage of explicit DCs in English discourse structures.

We also find a quite prominent and interesting phenomenon that, a range of implicit discourse relations in Chinese, such as *Temporal, Conjunction, Coordination* and *Causation*, all can be mapped to the simple explicit DC "and" in English, with a rather high frequency. Just as similar conclusion shown in Appendix A of the PDTB 2.0 Annotation Manual[3], as one of top ten polysemous DCs, "and" can represent more than 15 senses in 3000 sentences in PDTB.

## 4 Preliminary Experiments & Analysis

We conduct MT automatic evaluation experiments on the annotated Chinese sentences with inserted implicit DCs to testify the translation performance before and after representing implicit DCs with explicit ones. Evaluation metrics include BLEU (Papineni et al., 2002) and METEOR (Lavie and Agarwal, 2007) scores, calculated by the Asiya toolkit[4] (Giménez and Màrquez, 2010).

### 4.1 Experimental Setting

With Moses decoder (Koehn et al., 2007), we train a phrase-based SMT model on another different version of News-Commentary corpus[5] provided respectively by OPUS (69,206 sentence pairs) and WMT2017 Shared Task[6] (235,724 pairs), and the model is tuned by MERT (Och, 2003) with the development sets (2002 pairs) provided by WMT2017. GIZA++ (Och and Ney, 2003) is used for automatic word alignment and a 5-gram language model is trained on English Gigaword (Parker et al., 2011). 1500 sentences randomly chosen from the annotated corpus in section3 are used as test sets.

[3] https://www.seas.upenn.edu/~pdtb/PDTBAPI/pdtb-annotation-manual.pdf
[4] http://nlp.lsi.upc.edu/asiya/
[5] http://opus.lingfil.uu.se/News-Commentary11.php
[6] http://www.statmt.org/wmt17/translation-task.html

The training data is not annotated with any discourse information, and thus the translation models are not trained with any discourse markups. But as the training data include both explicit and implicit DCs, it is suitable for the experiments.

### 4.2 Experimental Results and Analysis

|  | BLEU | METEOR |
|---|---|---|
| Before inserting implicit DCs | 21.41 | 34.57 |
| After inserting implicit DCs | 21.43 | 34.56 |

Table 6: Evaluation scores of MT outputs

Table 6 shows the scores for SMT outputs of the test sets without/with inserting implicit DCs for source language. The scores indicate that adding explicit DCs for implicit DCs in Chinese seems have little improvement and impacts on translation performance.

We guess one reason resulting in the scores is that, although DCs appear frequently in English, they usually occupy a very small portion of total word counts in the MT outputs and may not very sensitive to BLEU. As (Meyer et al., 2012) also argues that translation of DCs can actually be improved while BLEU scores remain similar.

After manually analyzing some sentences of the outputs, it is observed that after inserting explicit DCs for implicit relations, most of them are indeed translated and aligned to the source side, just as the examples shown in following table7, stating that our preprocessing for the implicit DCs can be identified by the decoder. But, if we compare the translated DCs with those in reference, some of them are different, thus the n-gram based BLEU evaluation will not able to capture the information, which support our guess.

**Source:** 作为货币联盟，金融一体化在欧元区非常牢固，[implicit = Causation, added DC = *因此*] 这使得欧洲央行成了了不二之选。

**Ref:** Given that financial integration is particularly strong within the monetary union, putting the ECB in charge was an obvious choice.

**MT:** As a monetary union, financial integration in the euro area is very strong, *so* it makes the ECB has become the best choice.

---

**Source:** 这些国家需要采取措施助贫民摆脱贫困陷阱，[Implicit = Coordination, added DC = *并且*] 给他们现实的机会改善其经济福利。

**Ref:** These economies need measures that help to keep the poor out of poverty traps, and that give them realistic opportunities to improve their economic well-being.

**MT:** These countries need to take measures to help the poor get rid of poverty traps **and** give them real opportunities to improve their economic well-being.

Table 7: Some examples of MT outputs

## 5 Conclusion

In this paper, we cross-lingually annotate and align DCs from both the cross-sentence and within-sentence levels on a Chinese-English parallel corpus. Based on the annotation, we present some statistics and basic findings on DCs, which have some accordance with previous survey.

We also conduct some preliminary MT evaluation experiments to testify the impacts on translation performance resulted from expressing implicit DCs explicitly. Although the results temporarily indicate no significant improvement of MT outputs, preprocessing DCs for MT indeed has some positive effects, we still believe that DCs are one of useful factors that cannot be ignored for discourse-level MT.

In the future, we need to consider other possible discourse-related information and integrate them into MT, on the other hand, it is also worthy considering more on the issue that how to evaluate discourse-MT outputs properly, after all, BLEU scores alone may not enough.

### Acknowledgments

We would like to sincerely thank all the reviewers for their constructive and helpful suggestions on this paper. The work is supported by China Scholarship Council (Grant No. 201606040144).

### References


Viktor Becher. 2011. When and why do translators add connectives? a corpus-based study. *Target*, 23(1): 26 –47..

Alon Lavie and Abhaya Agarwal. 2007. METEOR: An Automatic Metric for MT Evaluation with High Levels of Correlation with Human Judgments. In: *Proceedings of the ACL 2007 Workshop on Statistical Machine Translation*, pages228-231.

Junyi Jessy Li, Marine Carpuat, and Ani Nenkova. 2014a. Cross-lingual discourse relation analysis: A corpus study and a semi-supervised classification system. In: *Proceedings of the International Conference on Computational Linguistics*, pages577-587.

Junyi Jessy Li, Marine Carpuat, and Ani Nenkova. 2014b. Assessing the discourse factors that influence the quality of machine translation. In: *Proceedings of the Annual Meeting of the Association for Computational Linguistics*, pages283-288.

Yancui Li, Wenhi Feng, Jing Sun, Fang Kong, and Guodong Zhou. 2014. Building Chinese discourse corpus with connective-driven dependency tree structure. In: *Proceedings of the Conference on Empirical Methods on Natural Language Processing*, pages2105–2114.

William C Mann and Sandra A Thompson. 1986. Rhetorical structure theory: Description and construction of text structures. *Natural language generation: New results in artificial intelligence, psychology, and linguistics*, 279-300.

Thomas Meyer, Andrei Popescu-Belis, Sandrine Zufferey et al. 2011. Multilingual annotation and disambiguation of discourse connectives for machine translation. In: *Proceedings of the Annual Meeting of the Special Interest Group on Discourse and Dialogue*, pages194-203.

Thomas Meyer and Andrei Popescu-Belis. 2012. Using sense-labeled discourse connectives for statistical machine translation. In: *Proceedings of the Workshop on Hybrid Approaches to Machine Translation*, pages 129-138.

Thomas Meyer and Bonnie Webber. 2013. Implicitation of discourse connectives in (machine) translation. In: *Proceedings of the Discourse in Machine Translation Workshop*.

Jörg Tiedemann, 2012. Parallel Data, Tools and Interfaces in OPUS. In: *Proceedings of the 8th International Conference on Language Resources and Evaluation (LREC 2012)*, pages 2214-2218.

Philipp Koehn, Hieu Hoang, Alexandra Birch et al. 2007. Moses: Open source toolkit for statistical machine translation. In *Proceedings of the Annual Meeting of the Association for Computational Linguistics*, pages177-180.

Franz Josef Och and Hermann Ney. 2003. A systematic comparison of various statistical alignment models. *Computational Linguistics*, 29(1), 19-51.

Franz Josef Och. 2003. Minimum error rate training in statistical machine translation. In: *Proceedings of the Annual Meeting of the Association for Computational Linguistics*, pages 160-167.

Robert Parker, David Graff, Junbo Kong, Ke Chen, and Kazuaki Maeda. 2011. English Gigaword fifth edition ldc2011t07. *Linguistic Data Consortium*.

Kishore Papineni, Salim Roukos, Todd Ward, and WeiJing Zhu. 2002. BLEU: A Method for Automatic Evaluation of Machine Translation. In: *Proceedings of 40th Annual Meeting of the ACL*, pages 311–318.

Attapol Rutherford and Nianwen Xue. 2014. Discovering implicit discourse relations through brown cluster pair representation and coreference patterns. In: *Proceedings of the Conference of the European Chapter of the Association for Computational Linguistics*, pages645–654.

Mei Tu, Yu Zhou, and Chengqing Zong. 2013. A novel translation framework based on rhetorical structure theory. In: *Proceedings of the Annual Meeting of the Association for Computational Linguistics*, pages 370-374.

Mei Tu, Yu Zhou, and Chengqing Zong. 2014. Enhancing grammatical cohesion: Generating transitional expressions for smt. In: *Proceedings of the Annual Meeting of the Association for Computational Linguistics*, pages 850-860.

Frances Yung, Kevin Duh, and Yuji Matsumoto. 2015a. Sequential annotation and chunking of Chinese discourse structure. In: *Proceedings of The SIGHAN Workshop on Chinese Language Processing*, pages1-6.

Frances Yung, Kevin Duh, and Yuji Matsumoto. 2015b. Crosslingual Annotation and Analysis of Implicit Discourse Connectives for Machine Translation. In: *Proceedings of the Second Workshop on Discourse in Machine Translation (DiscoMT)*, pages 142–152.

Sandrine Zufferey and Bruno Cartoni. 2014. A multifactorial analysis of explicitation in translation. *Target*, 26(3):361 –384.

Yuping Zhou and Nianwen Xue. 2015. The Chinese Discourse TreeBank: a Chinese corpus annotated with discourse relations. *Language Resources and Evaluation*, 49(2):397-431.

# Lexical Chains meet Word Embeddings in Document-level Statistical Machine Translation

**Laura Mascarell**

Institute of Computational Linguistics, University of Zürich

`mascarell@cl.uzh.ch`

## Abstract

The phrase-based Statistical Machine Translation (SMT) approach deals with sentences in isolation, making it difficult to consider discourse context in translation. This poses a challenge for ambiguous words that need discourse knowledge to be correctly translated. We propose a method that benefits from the semantic similarity in lexical chains to improve SMT output by integrating it in a document-level decoder. We focus on word embeddings to deal with the lexical chains, contrary to the traditional approach that uses lexical resources. Experimental results on German→English show that our method produces correct translations in up to 88% of the changes, improving the translation in 36%-48% of them over the baseline.

## 1 Introduction

Current phrase-based Statistical Machine Translation (SMT) systems translate sentences in a document independently (Koehn et al., 2003), ignoring document context. This sentence-level approach causes wrong translations when discourse knowledge is needed. Therefore, many methods that integrate discourse features have been proposed to improve lexical choice.

Documents are a set of sentences that function as a unit. When we translate at document-level we take into account document properties that help to improve the quality of the translation, not only locally, but also in the context of the document. Coherence and cohesion are terms that describe properties of texts. Coherence concerns the semantic meaningfulness of the text, whereas cohesion has to do with relating the sentences through reference, ellipsis, substitution, conjunction, and the use of semantically-similar words. Often, these words are related sequentially in the document, defining the topic of the text segment that they cover. These sequences of words are lexical chains, and they have been successfully used in research areas such as information retrieval (Stairmand, 1996; Rinaldi, 2009) and document summarization (Barzilay and Elhadad, 1997; Pourvali and Abadeh, 2012). However, they have received little attention in Machine Translation (MT).

Galley and McKeown (2003) introduce a method to detect lexical chains using WordNet (Miller, 1995). The method first builds a representation of all words in the document and all their senses, creating semantic links such as synonym, hypernym, hyponym, and sibling between them. It then uses the semantic links to disambiguate each word and builds the lexical chains accordingly.

The performance of the method is evaluated on a sense disambiguation task. Indeed, lexical chains help to disambiguate the sense of polysemic words by looking at the words in the chain. Despite the problems of word senses (Kilgarriff, 1997, 2006; Hanks, 2000), it shows the potential that lexical chains have to improve the lexical choice of words with multiple translations in MT.

In this paper, we present a method that uses word embeddings instead of lexical resources to detect the lexical chains in the source and also to maintain their semantic similarity on the target side. We focus on the German→English translation and integrate our model into the document-level SMT decoder Docent (Hardmeier et al., 2013). We perform a manual evaluation of the output, which shows that our method improves the translation over the baseline, with a tendency to consistently translate the words in the chain. Furthermore, experimental results reveal that the use of word embeddings in lexical chain detection outperforms lexical resources on the translation task.



*Proceedings of the Third Workshop on Discourse in Machine Translation*, pages 99–109,
Copenhagen, Denmark, September 8, 2017. ©2017 Association for Computational Linguistics.

## 2 Related Work

The one-sense-per-discourse hypothesis (Gale et al., 1992) is applied in MT, revealing lexical choice errors when words in a document are inconsistently translated (Carpuat, 2009). As a consequence, several approaches improve lexical choice by enforcing consistency throughout the document. Tiedemann (2010) and Gong et al. (2011) use cache-models for this purpose, and Xiao et al. (2011) apply a three-steps procedure that consist of identifying the ambiguous words in a document, obtaining a set of consistent translation for each of them, and generating a new translation of the document, where the identified words are translated consistently. Pu et al. (2017) also study consistency in translation and train classifiers on syntactic and semantic features to predict how to consistently translate pairs of nouns in a document. More specifically, Mascarell et al. (2014) and Pu et al. (2015) benefit from text dependencies to improve the translation of words that refer back to compounds.

Guillou (2013) analyses *when* (i.e. genre) and *where* (i.e. part-of-speech) lexical consistency is desirable. The results suggest that nouns should be encouraged to be translated consistently throughout the document, across all genres. Additionally, consistent translation of verbs and adjectives is beneficial for technical and public information documents, respectively.

Garcia et al. (2017) implement a feature for the document-level decoder Docent that uses word embeddings to translate repeated words consistently. The manual evaluation reveals that 60% of the time the output improves over the baseline and 20% of the time is equivalent or equal.

Word embeddings have also been proposed for Word Sense Disambiguation (WSD) (Iacobacci et al., 2016). Previously, other approaches were introduced to utilise embeddings for supervised (Zhong and Ng, 2010; Rothe and Schütze, 2015; Taghipour and Ng, 2015) and knowledge-based WSD (Chen et al., 2014).

Other approaches focus on including topic modelling and topic distributions for disambiguation (Hasler et al., 2014). Xiong and Zhang (2013) translate the coherence chain of the source document and use it to produce a coherent translation.

Xiong et al. (2013) are the first to explore the benefits of using lexical chains in MT. They introduce lexical chain based cohesion models in a hierarchical phrase-based SMT system (Chiang, 2005) trained on Chinese→English. To do so, they first use Galley and McKeown (2003)'s method to detect the lexical chains in the source and next generate the target lexical chains that are used by their cohesion models. To generate these target lexical chains, they train MaxEnt classifiers — one per unique source chain word — that predict the translation of each word given the previous and the next word in the chain and the immediate surrounding context. This machine learning approach results in limitations concerning chain words from the test set that are infrequent or even missing in the training data. Later, Xiong and Zhang (2014) integrate a sense-based translation model also using MaxEnt classifiers.

## 3 A Lexical Chain Model for SMT

This section describes the proposed method to improve the quality of translation in SMT utilising lexical chains. The method works as follows: it first detects the lexical chains in the source document (Section 3.1) and feeds them into the Lexical Chain Translation Model (LCTM), which is integrated into the document-level decoder Docent (Hardmeier et al., 2013). The model then gets their counterpart in the target through word alignment and computes the LCTM score that contributes to the overall translation score in the SMT system (Section 3.2). The reminder of this section describes the method in more detail.

### 3.1 Detecting Source Lexical Chains

Our automatic method to detect and build lexical chains from a document is inspired by the approach proposed by Morris and Hirst (1991). Their approach consists of manually detecting those lexical chains using a thesaurus to find the similarity between words. Our method implements the manual algorithm, detecting and building the lexical chains automatically.

Instead of using a thesaurus, we use word embeddings to compute the semantic similarity. Word embeddings are representations of words in a vector-space, which are commonly exploited to compute similarity between words (Mikolov et al., 2013) (See discussion in Section 3.3).

The method works as follows. It processes sentences in a given document sequentially. For each content word $c$ (i.e. nouns, verbs, and adjectives) in every sentence, it checks whether $c$ is semanti-

ihr nächstes *smartphone* wird zwei *betriebssysteme* beherrschen.
Die amerikaner rechnen für die zukunft mit einem *handy*, auf dem der *benutzer* durch drücken einer einzigen taste zwischen verschiedenen *betriebssystemen* *umschalten* kann.
Die vorgelegten Pläne sehen vielversprechend aus.

Lexical Chain$_1$: {*umschalten* ("switch"), *betriebssystemen* ("operating system"), *benutzer* ("user"), *betriebssysteme* ("operating system")}
Lexical Chain$_2$: {*handy* ("cell phone"), *smartphone* ("smart phone")}

Figure 1: Output of our lexical chain detection method on three sentences from newstest2010.

cally related to the previous content words *c'* in a span of five sentences, as suggested by Morris and Hirst (1991). If *c* and *c'* are semantically related, we proceed as follows:

- If *c* and *c'* do not belong to any chain, we create a new chain consisting of *c* and *c'*.

- If *c'* is in a chain $ch_i$, we append *c* to $ch_i$.

- If *c* and *c'* belong to two different chains, we then merge both chains.

The detected lexical chains preserve the semantic link between related content words, creating also one-transitive links. That is, $c_i$ links to $c_{i+l}$ by transitivity if $c_i$ links to $c_{i+k}$ and $c_{i+k}$ to $c_{i+l}$, where $i<k<l$ (Morris and Hirst, 1991).

Every link to a word in the lexical chain gives context to disambiguate the word itself. Therefore, the more links are created, the better. One-transitive links are safe to consider, because they are still semantically related as indicated by Morris and Hirst (1991), but further than that leads to errors. As an example, they point to the following lexical chain: {*cow, sheep, wool, scarf, boots, hat, snow*}. Here, we observe that while consecutive words in the chain like *wool* and *scarf* are semantically related, *cow* and *snow* are not. Figure 1 shows the lexical chains detected with our method on three sentences extracted from the document `idnes.cz/2009/12/11/76504` in newstest2010.[1]

## 3.2 The Lexical Chain Translation Model

In order to improve translation quality utilising lexical chains, we develop a model that favours document translations where the words in the target lexical chain are semantically related. The target lexical chains are the corresponding counterpart of the source lexical chains detected, and they

are obtained by the LCTM through word alignment.

### 3.2.1 Integration into Docent

The LCTM is integrated as an additional feature function in the document-level decoder Docent as a standard SMT model:

$$f(s,t) = \sum_k \lambda_k h_k(s,t), \qquad (1)$$

where $h_k$ are feature functions scores and $\lambda_k$ their corresponding weight, obtained with the MERT optimisation technique (Och, 2003).

To understand how the model is integrated into Docent, we summarise how Docent works. Docent implements a search procedure based on local search. At every stage of the search, the decoder randomly applies a state operation such as `change-phrase-translation` (replaces the translation of a phrase with another from the phrase table), `swap-phrases` (exchanges phrases), `move-phrases` (randomly moves phrases in the sentence), and `resegment` (changes the segmentation of the source phrase). The search algorithm accepts then a new state (i.e. a new translation of the document), when its document score computed by Equation 1 is higher than the last accepted. To compute the document score, it considers the score obtained from each feature function. The initial translation of the whole document is either randomly generated or a translation from Moses (Koehn et al., 2007).

The LCTM is implemented as one of the feature functions in Docent, and therefore it contributes to the overall document score. Consider the example in Figure 2. This example shows two hypothetical Docent states when applying the state operation `change-phrase-translation` on the German word *Preis* (English "price" or "award") from *Diesen Preis haben heute … davongetragen*.

---

[1] `http://www.statmt.org/wmt16/translation-task.html`

State $q$: This *award* was received today by ...
State $r$: This *price* was received today by ...

Chain: {*Nobelpreis, Preis, Preisträger*}

Figure 2: Translation output of two different Docent states after applying the operation `change-phrase-translation`. Each state considers a different translation candidate of the German word *Preis*.

Since *Preis* is linked to *Nobelpreis* ("Nobel Prize") and *Preisträger* ("prize winner") in the source lexical chain, the semantic similarity of its counterpart lexical chain in the target is higher when *Preis* is translated into *award*. This leads to a higher LCTM score that contributes to a higher document score. The State $q$ is then preferred by the decoder. Note that in this case, the language model also increases in State $q$. That is because *received* has a higher probability together with *award* than with *price*.

### 3.2.2 Computation of the Model Score

Each lexical chain is a chain of words connected by their semantic similarity, which is also computed using word embeddings. We define the model score as the mean of the semantic similarity scores of each target lexical chain in a document translation. To compute the semantic similarity $sim_i$ of a lexical chain $ch_i$, we average the semantic similarity of all links in $ch_i$ as in the following Equation

$$sim_i = \frac{1}{m} \sum_{j=1}^{m} SemLink_{ij}, \qquad (2)$$

where every link is comprised of two words, and its semantic similarity *SemLink* is the cosine similarity between their embeddings. In the experiments, we use German in the source, which is a language rich in compounds. These compounds have multiword equivalents in English and can be detected as part of a lexical chain (e.g. *Nordwand* is translated into the English *north face*). To deal with such cases, $sim_i$ is the maximum similarity score obtained from each content word in the translation of a compound and the rest of the words in the lexical chain.

Every lexical chain has a different relevance in the computation of the LCTM score, which depends on three factors introduced by Morris and Hirst (1991): length ($\lambda$), repetition ($\beta$), and density ($\rho$). The later is defined as the ratio of words in the lexical chain to all words in the fragment of text that it covers. Accordingly, the longer, the denser the lexical chain is and the more repetition it has, the higher its weight is in the computation of the overall model score. These factors have not been addressed in the literature when dealing with lexical chains. Morris and Hirst (1991) define the strength of lexical chains, but they do not use it in their experiments.

To compute the length, density, and repetition of every lexical chain (i.e. $\lambda_{ch_i}$, $\rho_{ch_i}$ and $\beta_{ch_i}$) we proceed as follows. Let *rel* be the total number of semantic relations in a lexical chain $ch_i$, *rep* the total number of repetitions, and *span* the number of words in the fragment of the document between the head and the tail of $ch_i$. $\rho_{ch_i}$ and $\beta_{ch_i}$ are then computed by the following two Equations

$$\rho_{ch_i} = \frac{rel}{span}, \qquad (3)$$

$$\beta_{ch_i} = \frac{rep}{span}. \qquad (4)$$

Finally, the length $\lambda_{ch_i}$ is the ratio of *rel* to the number of relations of the longest lexical chain detected. The longest lexical chain gets therefore the highest length value (i.e. 1.0) among all lexical chains in the document.

After computing all factor values for each lexical chain, the model computes the weight for each of them. The weight of a chain $w_{ch_i}$ is then the average of $\rho_{ch_i}$, $\lambda_{ch_i}$ and $\beta_{ch_i}$, where $\rho_{ch_i}$, $\lambda_{ch_i}$, $\beta_{ch_i}$, and $w_{ch_i}$ are all values between 0 and 1.[2]

Finally, the overall LCTM score is computed by

$$LCTM = \frac{1}{n} \sum_{i=1}^{n} w_{chi} \cdot \frac{1}{m_i} \sum_{j=1}^{m_i} SemLink_{ij}. \quad (5)$$

### 3.3 Computation of Semantic Similarity

Dictionaries have been described in the literature to deal not only with lexical chains (Galley and McKeown, 2003), but with any task related to semantics such as WSD. However, it is unrealistic to assume that the fine-grained classification of

---

[2]We evaluated the impact of length, density, and repetition on translation by allowing tunable weights (0.0, 0.5, or 1.0) to each parameter and computing $w_{ch_i}$ as the weighted average. The translation differences between the configurations were small, and the best performance was obtained when all of them had the maximum weight (1.0).

senses in dictionaries is adequate for any NLP application (Kilgarriff, 2006). Even the classification itself has been questioned in terms of cognitive validity (Kilgarriff, 1997, 2006; Hanks, 2000).

As Firth (1957) stated "You shall know a word by the company it keeps". That is, words that are used and occur in the same contexts tend to have similar meanings. Essentially, word embeddings are vector representations of words in a vector space that are learned based on the immediate context in which they occur. Our method uses word embeddings as a means to compute semantic similarity between words independently of dictionary senses to detect the lexical chains in the source and to compute the LCTM score.

The coverage and the quality of the lexical chains are the most important factors in our approach to improve translation. Words that are not in any lexical chain are not considered for improvement at the decoding stage by our LCTM. Word embeddings detect words as semantically related when they occur in similar context, even if they do not have a hypernym, hyponym or sibling relation. Halliday and Hasan (2014) define the words that do not have a traditional sense relation, but belong to the notion of lexical cohesion as *collocations*. The lexical chain detection method includes them in the same lexical chain, since they also help to disambiguate the translation of a word. For example, the word *climber* can be related to *mountain* with word embeddings, but not with Galley and McKeown (2003)'s approach.

The main problem of word embeddings arises from words with multiple senses that are not disambiguated in the training phase. That is, each word has only one vector representation, including those polysemic words. For example, consider the English word *play*, which appears in different contexts such as to perform on a musical instrument, to take part in a sport or game, and to interpret a role. The word embedding then represents all senses together. Consequently, the semantic similarity between *play* and *guitar* is low, because the similarity is computed between *guitar* and all the senses of *play* together.

Word senses need to be disambiguated in the training phase to generate distinct vector representations for each sense. We therefore employ a method introduced by Thater et al. (2011), which uses the syntactic information to build *contextual-*

| | Training | Tuning | LM |
|---|---|---|---|
| Lines | 400K | 5K | 570K |
| Tokens | $\sim$ 11M | $\sim$ 125K | $\sim$ 15M |

Table 1: Total of segments per language pair from Europarl and News Commentary used to train the German→English phrase-based SMT system.

*ized* embeddings.[3] Consider again the word *play*, which appears in the sentences *we play the piano*, *we play the guitar*, *we play tennis*, *they play football*, and *they play Hamlet*. Following the approach proposed by Thater et al. (2011), we extract all the syntactic relations such as subject or object and group sentences in the same context by computing the semantic similarity between the context words (e.g. *piano* and *guitar*). As a result, we obtain (1) *we play the piano, we play the guitar*; (2) *we play tennis, they play football*; and (3) *they play Hamlet*. Lastly, we build the corresponding word embeddings *play_piano* for play the piano and the guitar, *play_tennis* for play tennis and football, and *play_Hamlet*.

Finally, to compute the semantic similarity of two words, our method computes the cosine similarity between their vector representation. The closer to 1.0 the resulting value is, the more similar they are. We set a threshold of 0.45 to distinguish between similar and non-similar words. This threshold is manually picked by looking at how different values impact on the resulting lexical chains. A lower threshold introduces too many words that are mostly related by their part-of-speech. A higher threshold results in semantically strong lexical chains, but it misses out on words that are also related.

## 4 Task Setup

We conducted several experiments to prove the efficacy of the lexical chain detection and LCTM in SMT. Lexical chains are difficult to evaluate in isolation, and therefore their quality is usually evaluated on the basis of the application for which they are used. Thus, we assess the performance of the method on the German→English translation task.

We then compare it to the algorithm presented by Galley and McKeown (2003), which uses external resources instead of word embeddings to build

---

[3]Any method that disambiguates the word senses and computes their word embeddings accordingly could be used.

the lexical chains. To build the lexical chains following Galley and McKeown (2003)'s method, we use GermaNet (Hamp and Feldweg, 1997) as external resource on the German side. The detected lexical chains are automatically annotated in the MMAX format[4] and then fed into Docent.

The data comes from the shared WMT'16 translation task.[5] We build a German→English phrase-based SMT system with Moses using standard settings (Koehn et al., 2003), 5-gram language model KenLM (Heafield, 2011) and GIZA++ (Och and Ney, 2003). The system is trained on Europarl, a parallel corpus of the proceedings of the European Parliament and News Commentary in equal parts (see Table 1). We use the first 17 documents of newstest2011 (554 segments), newstest2012 (684 segments), and newstest2013 (1,053 segments) for testing and newstest2010 (375 segments) as a development set of the LCTM and LCTM$_{base}$.

The method uses word embeddings to detect the source lexical chains. We therefore train a skip-gram 300-dimensional model in German using the *word2vec* tool.[6] The texts come mainly from SdeWaC (Faaß and Eckart, 2013) ($\sim$768M words) and Common Crawls ($\sim$775M words). The rest of the data is from Europarl ($\sim$47M words) and News Commentary ($\sim$6M words). The LCTM model also needs to compute the similarity of the words in the target lexical chains. For this purpose, we employ a skip-gram 300-dimensional model trained on English Google News ($\sim$100 billion words).[6]

## 5  Experimental Results

In this section, we present the results obtained through the combination of lexical chain detection (using word embeddings and GermaNet) and the LCTM. The LCTM takes into account the relevance (i.e. strength) of every lexical chain to compute the overall score. We also perform a third experiment that ignores this fact to assess its impact in the translation quality. To do so, we develop a model that behaves like the LCTM, except that it assigns the maximum strength value (i.e. 1.0) to all lexical chains. We refer to this new model in the following as LCTM$_{base}$.

The baseline BLEU scores (Papineni et al., 2002) of the test sets newstest2010, newstest2011,

| Chain | *politik* → *politischer* |
|---|---|
| Input | ich bin ein neuling in der prager **politik** |
| Ref. | i'm a novice in prague ***politics*** |
| Base. | i am a newcomer in the prague ***policy*** |
| LC | i am a newcomer in the prague ***politics*** |

| Chain | *erklärt* → ***meint*** → *meint* |
|---|---|
| Input | "hier geht niemand vor gericht", **meint** ... |
| Ref. | "nobody will sue them here," ***said*** ... |
| Base. | "here is no one in court", ... |
| LC | "here is no one in court", ***says*** ... |

| Chain | *rakete* → ***rakete*** → *motor* |
|---|---|
| Input | ...technische schäden an der **rakete** |
| Ref. | ...technical damage to the ***missile*** |
| Base. | ...technical damage to the ***rocket*** |
| LC | ...technical damage to the ***missile*** |

| Chain | *erhöht* → ***lohn*** → *lohnerhöhungen* |
|---|---|
| Input | ...mehr als sie für **lohn** spenden. |
| Ref. | ...more than it spends on ***salaries***. |
| Base. | ...more than they for ***wage*** donations. |
| LC | ...more than they for ***pay*** donations. |

Figure 3: In these examples, the method produces a correct translation of the ambiguous word *Politik*, forces the translation of the German verb *meint*, and generates another good translation of *Rakete*. In the last example, the presented method incorrectly translates *lohn* into *pay*, despite the context given by the lexical chain: *ehöht* ("increase") and *lohnerhöhungen* ("wage increases").

and newstest2013 are 12.44, 12.18, and 17.64, respectively. The results of the experiments show between 20 to 30 translation changes in every test set due to lexical chains. We observe that the translation changes are often correct although they do not use the same terms as in the reference. Therefore, the fluctuations in BLEU scores are small ($\pm 0.1$), and so BLEU does not provide sufficient insight into the performance.

We then perform a manual evaluation to assess the results of the experiments. The annotation is carried out by two annotators who judge the quality of the translation changes due to the lexical chains. Specifically, the annotators obtain for each translation change the source sentence, the baseline (i.e. the translation ignoring lexical chains), the translation produced by the method we want to evaluate, and the reference. They then anno-

---

[4]http://mmax2.sourceforge.net
[5]http://www.statmt.org/wmt16/translation-task.html
[6]https://code.google.com/p/word2vec

|                                | newstest2011 | | | newstest2012 | | | newstest2013 | | |
| --- | --- | --- | --- | --- | --- | --- | --- | --- | --- |
|                                | $+$ | $-$ | $++$ | $+$ | $-$ | $++$ | $+$ | $-$ | $++$ |
| Word Emb. & LCTM (1)           | 0.81 | 0.19 | 0.48 | 0.88 | 0.12 | 0.36 | 0.83 | 0.17 | 0.39 |
| GermaNet & LCTM (2)            | 0.71 | 0.29 | 0.38 | 0.62 | 0.38 | 0.31 | 0.65 | 0.35 | 0.35 |
| Word Emb. & LCTM$_{base}$ (3)  | 0.64 | 0.36 | 0.22 | 0.67 | 0.33 | 0.18 | 0.61 | 0.39 | 0.16 |

Table 2: Manual evaluation results of the presented method (1) compared to using GermaNet for lexical chain detection (2). The analysis shows the percentage of correct (+), wrong translations (-), and the improvement over the baseline (++). There are a total of 20 to 30 translation changes in every test set due to the lexical chains. We observe that the method (1) outperforms the approach that uses GermaNet (2). It also performs better than the method that ignores length, density, and repetition for the computation of the strength of each lexical chain in the overall score (3).

tate whether the word that changes due to lexical chains is better than the one produced by the baseline, equally good or worse. The Cohen's Kappa coefficient of inter-rater agreement between the two annotators is 0.77 (Cohen, 1960). We then compute from the annotations the percentage of incorrect and good translations and the improvement over the baseline.

Table 2 shows the results of the manual evaluation. We observe that the combination of lexical chain detection using word embeddings with our LCTM performs best. In particular, 81%-88% of the changes are correct translations, and among them, 36%-48% are improvements over the baseline. Only 12%-19% of the changes are incorrect. With GermaNet to detect lexical chains, the correctness decreases between 10% and 26%. Word embeddings may work better than lexical resources as they capture contextual information from the text, without relying on whether is defined in a resource. In those cases, where the resource does not provide a relation for two given words such as in idiomatic or metaphoric uses, the lexical chain cannot benefit from them.

The parameters length, density, and repetition have an impact on translation when using them to compute the strength of each lexical chain in the overall LCTM score. We see that the correctness of the translation output decreases approximately by 20% in all test sets when using the LCTM$_{base}$ (i.e. the model that gives the highest strength value to all lexical chains, ignoring the mentioned parameters) instead of the LCTM. Furthermore, the percentage of the improvements over the baseline decrease by half.

Some translation examples using our method are illustrated in Figure 3. In the first example,

the ambiguous German noun *Politik* gets correctly translated into *politics*. *Politik* is connected to *politischer* ("political") in the lexical chain, and therefore *politics* is semantically more related to *political* than *policy*. Our method is also good at enforcing the translation of all words in the lexical chain, since an untranslated word will decrease the score of the translated lexical chain, and accordingly, the overall LCTM score (see Example 2). In the last example, the method produces a wrong translation of the German word *lohn* ("wage", "salary"), whereas the baseline translates it correctly. The word *lohn* is linked to *erhöht* ("increase") and *lohnerhöhungen* ("wage increases") in the lexical chain. Both words provide good context for the translation. However, our method incorrectly translates it into *pay*, whereas the baseline translates it correctly into *wage*.

In the third example, we observe that the method produces a different but equally good translation compared to the baseline. In the lexical chain, the German word *Rakete* is linked to another occurrence of the same word that is translated into *missile*. Since the highest similarity score is obtained when both translations are the same, our method encourages consistency, translating both into *missile* (Carpuat, 2009; Carpuat and Simard, 2012). Consistency is possible since we assume that there is only a unique sense per word in each document (Gale et al., 1992).

Figure 4 illustrates the benefits and issues of consistent translation. These are special cases, where the word in the lexical chain is linked only to other occurrences of the same word.

In the first example, we observe that the baseline translates the wrong sense of the word *wahl* (i.e. *choice*). Here, *wahl* is linked to another oc-

| | |
|---|---|
| Input | er entschloss ..., sich an der **wahl** vor der letzten hauptversammlung zu beteiligen |
| Ref. | he decided to participate in the ***elections*** before the last general meeting ... |
| Base. | he decided ..., the ***choice*** of the last hauptversammlung to participate |
| LC | he decided ..., the ***election*** of the last hauptversammlung to participate |

Linked to:

| | |
|---|---|
| Input | ... für die heutigen probleme mit der **wahl** die euphorie verantwortlich ist ... |
| Ref. | ... current problems with ***elections*** are caused by the euphoria there was ... |
| LC | ... for today's problems, with the ***election*** of the euphoria is responsible ... |

---

| | |
|---|---|
| Input | das **verhältnis** der länge der beiden erwähnten finger ... |
| Ref. | the ***ratio*** of the length of those two fingers ... |
| Base. | the ***ratio*** of the length of the two ... |
| LC | the ***relationship*** between the length of the two ... |

Linked to:

| | |
|---|---|
| Input | ... dennoch halte er das **verhältnis** zwischen der fingerlänge und dem krebsrisiko ... |
| Ref. | ... but in his opinion the ***relationship*** between the length of the fingers and the cancer ... |
| LC | ... but it the ***relationship*** between the fingerlänge and the risk of cancer ... |

Figure 4: These examples show how the presented method behaves when a word in the lexical chain is linked to the same word in the text. In the first example, the German word *wahl* is linked to another occurrence of *wahl* in the text. The later is correctly translated into *election*, and therefore the LCTM gets a higher score when the first sentence is translated into the same term. This produces an improvement over the baseline that wrongly translates it into *choice*. In the second example, both senses of the word *verhältnis* occur in the same document, forcing the first occurrence to be incorrectly translated.

currence of the same word in the lexical chain, which is translated into the other sense *election*. Since the method obtains the highest score when the translations are the same, it either encourages both occurrences to be translated into *election* or *choice*. The LCTM score competes with other models such as language and translation model. The overall score when using the translation *choice* is then lower than when using *election* due to the other models, since *choice* does not fit in the local context of the other sentence.

In the second example, however, the method translates the wrong sense of *verhältnis*. That is because the two senses of the word *verhältnis* ("ratio" and "relationship") are in the same document. This fact violates the one-sense-per-discourse hypothesis, and when the only context provided by the lexical chain is the word itself, the method cannot disambiguate the senses.

## 6  Summary and Conclusions

We present a method that utilises lexical chains to improve the quality of document-level SMT output, showing that the translation improves when discourse knowledge is considered. Specifically, the method improves the translation of the words in the chains, keeping the semantic similarity from the source to the translation. Each lexical chain captures a portion of the cohesive structure of a document. It is therefore essential to ensure that the words in the lexical chains are well translated.

The method is divided into two steps that consist of detecting the lexical chains in the source and preserving the semantic similarity among the words in their counterpart target lexical chains. We therefore implement an automatic detection of the lexical chains based on a manual approach proposed by Morris and Hirst (1991) and a feature function in the document-level decoder Docent (i.e the LCTM) that preserves the semantic similarity in the translated chains.

Our method uses word embeddings instead of external lexical resources to deal with word similarity. To detect the similarity between polysemic words, we need to disambiguate words in the training phase. We therefore apply the approach described by Thater et al. (2011), which relies on syntactic information to differentiate a word that appears in different contexts.

We assess the performance of the lexical chain detection on the translation task. The manual evaluation of the results show that the proposed method improves between 36% and 48% of the changes over a baseline that does consider lexical chains or any document-level knowledge. The results of the method are also evaluated against the method proposed by Galley and McKeown (2003), which uses a dictionary instead.

The method shows a bias for consistently translating the words in the chain. Since we assume the one-sense-per-discourse hypothesis (Gale et al., 1992), this is the preferred behaviour. Here, the method has the advantage that during decoding the LCTM competes with other feature functions. Therefore, the decoder favours the consistent translation of the repeated words in a chain that fits in all their contexts, avoiding consistently translating the wrong sense.

When the one-sense-per-discourse hypothesis does not hold, different senses of the same word may be linked in the same lexical chain. This poses a problem when each sense has a different translation in the target language. The method cannot distinguish between different senses and incorrectly translates them in the same way.

The lexical chains detected in the source differ from each other in length, density, and total of repetitions. To ensure that they have a different degree of impact on translation depending on their strength in the document, the LCTM takes that into account in the computation of the model score. To assess the importance of distinguishing between lexical chains, we implement a simplified version of the LCTM ($LCTM_{base}$) that gives the same strength value to all chains in the document. The experimental results show that the method that uses the $LCTM_{base}$ performs worse that LCTM in all test sets.

## Acknowledgments

The author would like to thank Don Tuggener and Annette Rios for the helpful discussions and the manual annotation. This research was supported by the Swiss National Science Foundation under the Sinergia MODERN project (grant n. 147653, see www.idiap.ch/project/modern/).

## References

Regina Barzilay and Michael Elhadad. 1997. Using Lexical Chains for Text Summarization. In *Proceedings of the Workshop on Intelligent Scalable Text Summarization*. Madrid, Spain, pages 10–17.

Marine Carpuat. 2009. One Translation Per Discourse. In *Proceedings of the Workshop on Semantic Evaluations: Recent Achievements and Future Directions*. Boulder, CO, USA, pages 19–27.

Marine Carpuat and Michel Simard. 2012. The Trouble with SMT Consistency. In *Proceedings of the $7^{th}$ Workshop on Statistical Machine Translation*. Montréal, Canada, pages 442–449.

Xinxiong Chen, Zhiyuan Liu, and Maosong Sun. 2014. A Unified Model for Word Sense Representation and Disambiguation. In *Proceedings of the $13^{th}$ Conference on Empirical Methods in Natural Language Processing*. Doha, Qatar, pages 1025–1035.

David Chiang. 2005. A Hierarchical Phrase-based Model for Statistical Machine Translation. In *Proceedings of the $43^{rd}$ Annual Meeting on Association for Computational Linguistics*. Stroudsburg, PA, USA, pages 263–270.

Jacob Cohen. 1960. A coefficient of agreement for nominal scale. *Educational and Psychological Measurement* 20:37–46.

Gertrud Faaß and Kerstin Eckart. 2013. SdeWaC – A Corpus of Parsable Sentences from the Web. In *Language Processing and Knowledge in the Web*, Springer Berlin Heidelberg, volume 8105, pages 61–68.

John R Firth. 1957. A Synopsis of Linguistic Theory, 1930-1955. Blackwell.

William A Gale, Kenneth W Church, and David Yarowsky. 1992. One Sense per Discourse. In *Proceedings of the Workshop on Speech and Natural Language*. Harriman, NY, USA, pages 233–237.

Michel Galley and Kathleen McKeown. 2003. Improving Word Sense Disambiguation in Lexical Chaining. In *Proceedings of the $18^{th}$ International Joint Conference on Artificial Intelligence*. San Francisco, CA, USA, pages 1486–1488.

Eva Martínez Garcia, Carles Creus, Cristina España i Bonet, and Lluís Màrquez. 2017. Using Word Embeddings to Enforce Document-Level Lexical Consistency in Machine Translation. DE GRUYTER OPEN, volume 108, pages 85–96.

Zhengxian Gong, Min Zhang, and Guodong Zhou. 2011. Cache-based Document-level Statistical Machine Translation. In *Proceedings of the $10^{th}$ Conference on Empirical Methods in Natural Language Processing*. Edinburgh, UK., pages 909–919.

Liane Guillou. 2013. Analysing Lexical Consistency in Translation. In *Proceedings of the Workshop on Discourse in Machine Translation*. Sofia, Bulgaria, pages 10–18.

Michael Alexander Kirkwood Halliday and Ruqaiya Hasan. 2014. *Cohesion in English*. Routledge.

Birgit Hamp and Helmut Feldweg. 1997. GermaNet - a Lexical-Semantic Net for German. In *Proceedings of the Workshop on Automatic Information Extraction and Building of Lexical Semantic Resources for NLP Applications*. Madrid, Spain, pages 9–15.

Patrick Hanks. 2000. Do word meanings exist? *Computers and the Humanities* 34(1):205–215.

Christian Hardmeier, Sara Stymne, Jörg Tiedemann, and Joakim Nivre. 2013. Docent: A Document-Level Decoder for Phrase-Based Statistical Machine Translation. In *Proceedings of the 51$^{st}$ Annual Meeting of the Association for Computational Linguistics*. Sofia, Bulgaria, pages 193–198.

Eva Hasler, Barry Haddow, and Philipp Koehn. 2014. Dynamic Topic Adaptation for SMT using Distributional Profiles. In *Proceedings of the 9$^{th}$ Workshop on Statistical Machine Translation*. Baltimore, MD, USA, pages 445–456.

Kenneth Heafield. 2011. KenLM: Faster and Smaller Language Model Queries. In *Proceedings of the 6$^{th}$ Workshop on Statistical Machine Translation*. Edinburgh, Scotland, pages 187–197.

Ignacio Iacobacci, Mohammad Taher Pilehvar, and Roberto Navigli. 2016. Embeddings for Word Sense Disambiguation: An Evaluation Study. In *Proceedings of the 54$^{th}$ Annual Meeting of the Association for Computational Linguistics*. Berlin, Germany, pages 897–907.

Adam Kilgarriff. 1997. I Don't Believe in Word Senses. *Computers and the Humanities* 31:91–113.

Adam Kilgarriff. 2006. *Word Senses*. Springer Netherlands, Dordrecht.

Philipp Koehn, Hieu Hoang, Alexandra Birch, Chris Callison-Burch, Marcello Federico, Nicola Bertoldi, Brooke Cowan, Wade Shen, Christine Moran, Richard Zens, et al. 2007. Moses: Open source toolkit for statistical machine translation. In *Proceedings of the 45$^{th}$ Annual Meeting on Association for Computational Linguistics*. pages 177–180.

Philipp Koehn, Franz Josef Och, and Daniel Marcu. 2003. Statistical Phrase-based Translation. In *Proceedings of the 4$^{th}$ Conference of the North American Chapter of the Association for Computational Linguistics on Human Language Technology*. Edmonton, Canada, pages 48–54.

Laura Mascarell, Mark Fishel, Natalia Korchagina, and Martin Volk. 2014. Enforcing Consistent Translation of German Compound Coreferences. In *Proceedings of the 12$^{th}$ Konvens Conference*. Hildesheim, Germany, pages 58–65.

Tomas Mikolov, Kai Chen, Greg Corrado, and Jeffrey Dean. 2013. Efficient Estimation of Word Representations in Vector Space. In *Proceedings of the Workshop at the International Conference on Learning Representations*. Scottsdale, AZ, USA.

George A Miller. 1995. WordNet: A Lexical Database for English. *Communications of the ACM* 38(11):39–41.

Jane Morris and Graeme Hirst. 1991. Lexical Cohesion Computed by Thesaural Relations as an Indicator of the Structure of Text. *Computational Linguistics* 17(1):21–48.

Franz Josef Och. 2003. Minimum Error Rate Training in Statistical Machine Translation. In *Proceedings of the 41$^{st}$ Annual Meeting on Association for Computational Linguistics*. Sapporo, Japan.

Franz Josef Och and Hermann Ney. 2003. A Systematic Comparison of Various Statistical Alignment Models. *Computational Linguistics* 29(1):19–51.

Kishore Papineni, Salim Roukos, Todd Ward, and Wei-Jing Zhu. 2002. BLEU: A Method for Automatic Evaluation of Machine Translation. In *Proceedings of 40$^{th}$ Annual Meeting of the Association for Computational Linguistics*. Philadelphia, PA, USA, pages 311–318.

Mohsen Pourvali and Mohammad Saniee Abadeh. 2012. Automated Text Summarization Base on Lexicales Chain and Graph using of WordNet and Wikipedia Knowledge Base (sic!). *Computing Research Repository* .

Xiao Pu, Laura Mascarell, and Andrei Popescu-Belis. 2017. Consistent Translation of Repeated Nouns using Syntactic and Semantic Cues. In *Proceedings of the 15$^{th}$ Conference of the European Chapter of the Association for Computational Linguistics*. Valencia, Spain, pages 948–957.

Xiao Pu, Laura Mascarell, Andrei Popescu-Belis, Mark Fishel, Ngoc-Quang Luong, and Martin Volk. 2015. Leveraging Compounds to Improve Noun Phrase Translation from Chinese and German. In *Proceedings of the ACL-IJCNLP Student Research Workshop*. Beijing, China, pages 8–15.

Antonio M. Rinaldi. 2009. An Ontology-Driven Approach for Semantic Information Retrieval on the Web. *ACM Transactions on Internet Technology* 9(3):10.

Sascha Rothe and Hinrich Schütze. 2015. AutoExtend: Extending Word Embeddings to Embeddings for Synsets and Lexemes. In *Proceedings of the 53$^{rd}$ Annual Meeting of the Association for Computational Linguistics and the 7$^{th}$ International Joint Conference on Natural Language Processing*. Beijing, China, pages 1793–1803.

Mark Stairmand. 1996. *A Computational Analysis of Lexical Cohesion with Applications in Information Retrieval*. Ph.D. thesis, University of Manchester.

Kaveh Taghipour and Hwee Tou Ng. 2015. Semi-Supervised Word Sense Disambiguation Using Word Embeddings in General and Specific Domains. In *Proceedings of the 14$^{th}$ Conference of the North American Chapter of the Association for Computational Linguistics*. Denver, Colorado, pages 314–323.

Stefan Thater, Hagen Fürstenau, and Manfred Pinkal. 2011. Word Meaning in Context: A Simple and Effective Vector Model. In *Proceedings of the 5$^{th}$ International Joint Conference on Natural Language Processing*. Chiang Mai, Thailand, pages 1134–1143.

Jörg Tiedemann. 2010. Context Adaptation in Statistical Machine Translation Using Models with Exponentially Decaying Cache. In *Proceedings of the Workshop on Domain Adaptation for Natural Language Processing*. Uppsala, Sweden, pages 8–15.

Tong Xiao, Jingbo Zhu, Shujie Yao, and Hao Zhang. 2011. Document-level Consistency Verification in Machine Translation. In *Proceedings of the 13$^{th}$ Machine Translation Summit*. Xiamen, China, pages 131–138.

Deyi Xiong, Yang Ding, Min Zhang, and Chew Lim Tan. 2013. Lexical Chain Based Cohesion Models for Document-Level Statistical Machine Translation. In *Proceedings of the 12$^{th}$ Conference on Empirical Methods in Natural Language Processing*. Seattle, WA, USA, pages 1563–1573.

Deyi Xiong and Min Zhang. 2013. A Topic-based Coherence Model for Statistical Machine Translation. In *Proceedings of the 27$^{th}$ AAAI Conference on Artificial Intelligence*. Bellevue, WA, USA.

Deyi Xiong and Min Zhang. 2014. A Sense-Based Translation Model for Statistical Machine Translation. In *Proceedings of the 52$^{nd}$ Annual Meeting of the Association for Computational Linguistics*. Baltimore, MD, USA, pages 1459–1469.

Zhi Zhong and Hwee Tou Ng. 2010. It Makes Sense: A Wide-Coverage Word Sense Disambiguation System for Free Text. In *Proceedings of the 48$^{th}$ Annual Meeting of the Association for Computational Linguistics. System Demonstrations*. Uppsala, Sweden, pages 78–83.

# On Integrating Discourse in Machine Translation


**Karin Sim Smith**

Department of Computer Science, University of Sheffield, UK
{kmsimsmith1}@sheffield.ac.uk



## Abstract

As the quality of Machine Translation (MT) improves, research on improving discourse in automatic translations becomes more viable. This has resulted in an increase in the amount of work on discourse in MT. However many of the existing models and metrics have yet to integrate these insights. Part of this is due to the evaluation methodology, based as it is largely on matching to a single reference. At a time when MT is increasingly being used in a pipeline for other tasks, the semantic element of the translation process needs to be properly integrated into the task. Moreover, in order to take MT to another level, it will need to judge output not based on a single reference translation, but based on notions of fluency and of adequacy – ideally with reference to the source text.


## 1 Introduction

Despite the fact that discourse has long been recognised as a crucial part of translation (Hatim and Mason, 1990), when it comes to Statistical Machine Translation (SMT), discourse information has been mostly neglected. Recently increasing amounts of effort have been going into addressing discourse explicitly in MT, with research covering lexical cohesion (Wong and Kit, 2012; Xiong et al., 2013b,a; Gong et al., 2015; Mascarell et al., 2015), discourse connectives (Cartoni et al., 2012, 2013; Meyer and Popescu-Belis, 2012; Meyer, 2011; Meyer et al., 2011; Steele, 2015; Steele and Specia, 2016), discourse relations (Guzmán et al., 2014), pronoun prediction (Guillou, 2012; Hardmeier et al., 2013b; Guillou,

2016) and negation (Fancellu and Webber, 2014; Wetzel and Bond, 2012).

Considerable progress was made in the field of SMT over the past two decades, culminating in models which give surprisingly good output given the limited amount of crosslingual information they have. Neural Machine Translation (NMT) models are now the most performant, to the extent that in the past year they have been the best performing at WMT (Bojar et al., 2016), and although deeper than the linguistically superficial SMT, to evaluate progress we need to be able to measure the extent to which these models successfully integrate discourse. Besides the difficulty of the task, one of the issues preventing progress is a lack of understanding regarding the problem: what is the purpose of translation. In order to fulfil its role, MT needs to capture and transfer the communicative message of the Source Text (ST) into the Target Text (TT). While MT cannot be expected to assess the pragmatics, in terms of the intended effect on the target audience of the Source Language (SL) and ensuring a corresponding effect on the target audience of the Target Language (TL), there is a basic communicative intent in terms of the semantics which has to surely be taken into account in evaluation, if we are to move beyond stringing together phrase matches.

Despite agreement on the shortcomings of BLEU (Papineni et al., 2002), for example (Smith et al., 2016), the standard metrics are still based on comparison to a single reference translation, which is inflexible (requiring a professional translation for every text automatically translated), and is also unrealistic as a text can be translated many ways, all of them valid. We would also argue that it does not incentivise the integration of deeper linguistic elements.

In the next section (Section 2) we give a brief survey of recent work on Discourse in MT. We

110


*Proceedings of the Third Workshop on Discourse in Machine Translation*, pages 110–121,
Copenhagen, Denmark, September 8, 2017. ©2017 Association for Computational Linguistics.

then describe the constraints of SMT architecture (Section 3), followed by a brief description of the translation process from the human translator's perspective (Section 4) and a review of the limitations of the current evaluation paradigm (Section 6).

## 2 Discourse in MT

While the survey by Hardmeier (2012) provides a good overview of Discourse in SMT at the time, his survey has been superceded by a flurry of work, much of it in association with the Workshop on DiscoMT (Webber et al., 2013, 2015). We give a brief survey of more recent research in the field of discourse, since his survey, specifically as it relates to discourse phenomena in the MT context.

**Reference resolution and pronoun prediction** Anaphora resolution, as reference resolution to something or someone previously mentioned, is a very challenging issue in MT which has been studied by several researchers over the past few years (Hardmeier, 2012). It is something that SMT currently handles poorly, again due to the lack of intersentential references. Anaphoric references are affected in several ways. The context of the preceding sentences is absent, meaning that the reference is undetermined. Even once it is correctly resolved (by additional pre-training or a second-pass), reference resolution is directly impacted by linguistic differences. For example, the target language may have multiple genders for nouns while the source only has one. The result is that references can be missing or wrong.

Novák and Žabokrtský (2014) developed a crosslingual coreference resolution between Czech and English, with mixed results, indicating the complexity of the problem. Subsequently Hardmeier et al. (2013b) have attempted a new approach to anaphora resolution by using neural networks which independently achieve comparable results to a standard anaphora resolutions system, but without the annotated data.

Luong and Popescu-Belis (2016) focus on improving the translation of pronouns from English to French by developing a target language model which determines the pronoun based on the preceding nouns of correct number and gender in the surrounding context. They integrate by means of reranking the translation hypotheses and improving over the baseline of the DiscoMT 2015 shared task.

Luong and Popescu-Belis (2017) develop a probabilistic anaphora resolution model which they integrate in a Spanish-English MT system, to improve the translation of Spanish personal and possessive pronouns into English using morphological and semantic features. They evaluate the Accuracy of Pronoun Translation (APT) using the translated pronouns of the reference translation and report an additional 41 correctly translated pronouns from a base line of 1055.

More recently, pronoun prediction in general has been the focus of increased attention, resulting in the creation of a specific WMT Shared Task on *Cross-lingual Pronoun Prediction* (Guillou et al., 2016), and to the development of resources such as test suites (Guillou and Hardmeier, 2016) for the automatic evaluation of pronoun translation. This has led to varied submissions on the subject, predicting third person subject pronouns translated from French into English; (Novák, 2016; Loáiciga, 2015; Wetzel et al., 2015). Most recently, we have seen an entire thesis on incorporating pronoun function into MT (Guillou, 2016), the main point being that pronouns should be handled according to their function– both in terms of handling within SMT and in terms of evaluation.

However, progress has been hard and Hardmeier (2014) suggests that besides evaluation problems, this is due to a failure to fully grasp the extent of the pronoun resolution problem in a crosslingual setting, and that anaphoric pronouns in the ST cannot categorically be mapped onto target pronouns. If these issues can be successfully addressed, it will mark significant progress for MT output in general.

In her thesis Loaiciga Sanchez (2017) focuses on pronominal anaphora and verbal tenses in the context of machine translation, on the basis that a pronoun and its antecedent (the token which gives meaning to it), or a verbal tense and its referent, can be in different sentences and result in errors in MT output, directly impacting cohesion. She reports direct improvements in terms of BLEU scores for both elements. Again one cannot help wondering whether the improvement in terms of quality of the text as a whole is actually much higher than reflected in the improvements over BLEU score.

**Verb tense** In specific work on verbs, (Loaiciga et al., 2014) researches improving alignment for non-contiguous components of verb phrases by

POS tags and heuristics. They then annotated Europarl and trained a tense predictor which they integrate in an MT system using factored translation models, predicting which English tense is appropriate translation for a particular French verb. This results in a better handling of tense, with the added benefit of an increased BLEU score.

Again on verbs, but this time with a focus on the problems that arise in MT from the verb-particle split constructions in English and German, Loáiciga and Gulordava (2016) construct test suites and compare how syntax and phrase-based SMT systems handle these constructs. They show that often there are alignment issues (with particles aligning to null) which lead to mistranslations, and that the syntax-based systems performed better in translating them.

**Lexical Cohesion**  There has been work in the area of lexical cohesion in MT assessing the linguistic elements which hold a text together, and how well these are rendered in MT.

Wong and Kit (2012) study lexical cohesion as a means of evaluating the quality of MT output at document level, but in their case the focus is on it as an evaluation metric. While human translators intuitively ensure cohesion, their research indicated that MT output is often represented as direct translations of ST items that may be inappropriate in the target context. They conclude that MT needs to learn to use lexical cohesion devices appropriately.

These findings are echoed by Beigman Klebanov and Flor (2013) in their research on word associations within a text, who consider pairs of words and define a metric for calculating the *lexical tightness* of MT versus Human Translation (HT). The fact that they had to first improve on the raw MT output before the experiment, indicates that it was of insufficient quality in the first place, however this is perhaps due to the age of data (dating to 2008 evaluation campaign), as MT has progressed considerably since then.

Xiong and Zhang (2013) attempt to improve lexical coherence via a topic-based model, using a Hidden Topic Markov Model (HTMM) to determine the topic in the source sentence. They extract a coherence chain for the source sentence, and project it onto the target sentence to make lexical choices during decoding more coherent. They report very marginal improvement with respect to a baseline system in terms of automatic evaluation.

This could indicate that current evaluation metrics are limited in their ability to account for improvements related to discourse.

Xiong et al. (2013a) focus on ensuring lexical cohesion by reinforcing the choice of lexical items during decoding. They subsequently compute lexical chains in the ST, project these onto the TT, and integrate these into the decoding process with different strategies. This is to try and ensure that the lexical cohesion, as represented through the choice of lexical items, is transferred from the ST to TT. Gong et al. (2015) attempt to integrate their lexical chain and topic based metrics into traditional BLEU and METEOR scores, showing greater correlation with human judgements on MT output.

In their work on comparative crosslingual discourse phenomena, Lapshinova-Koltunski (2015) find that use of various lexical cohesive devices can vary from language to language, and also depend on genre. In a different context, Mascarell et al. (2014) experiment with enforcing lexical consistency at document level for coreferencing compounds. They illustrate that for languages with heavy compounding such as German, translations of coreferencing constituents in subsequent sentences are sometimes incorrect, due to the lack of context in SMT systems. They experiment with two SMT phrase based systems, applying a compound splitter in one of them, caching constituents in both systems, and find that besides improving translations the latter also results in fewer out-of-vocabulary nouns.

Guillou (2013) investigates lexical cohesion across a variety of genres in HT, in an attempt to determine standard practice amoung professional translators, and compare it to output from SMT systems. She uses a metric (Herfindahl Hirschman Index (HHI)) to determine the terminological consistency of a single term in a single document, investigating consistency across words of different POS category. She finds that in SMT consistency occurs by chance, and that inconsistencies can be detrimental to the understanding of a document.

One of the problems with repetition is indeed automatically recognising where it results in consistency, and where it works to the detriment of lexical variation. Most recently, Martìnez Garcia et al. (2017) use word embeddings to promote lexical consistency at document level, by implementing a new feature for their document-level decoder. In particular, they try to encourage consistency for the same word to be translated in a similar manner throughout the document. They deploy a cosine similarity metric between word embeddings for the current translation hypothesis and the context to check if they are semantically similar. Despite the fact that a bilingual annotator judging at document level found the improved output to be better than the baseline 60% of the time, and equal 20% of the time (i.e. the improved output is better or the same for 80% of the documents), there was *no statistical significance* in the automatic evaluation scores (Martìnez Garcia et al., 2017).

**Word Sense Disambiguation** The very nature of languages is such that one word in a particular language has no one-to-one mapping in another; a particular word in the source could be semantically equivalent to several in the target, and there is a need to disambiguate.

In their work, Mascarell et al. (2015) use trigger words from the ST to try to disambiguate translations of ambiguous terms, where a word in the source language can have different meanings and should be rendered with a different lexical item in the TT depending on the context it occurs in.

Xiong and Zhang (2014)'s sense-based SMT model tries to integrate and reformulate the Word Sense Disambiguation (WSD) task in the translation context, predicting possible target translations. Zhang and Ittycheriah (2015) experiment with three types of document level features, using context to try and improve WSD. They use context on both target and source side, and establish whether the particular alignments had already occurred in the document, to help in disambiguating the current hypothesis. Experimenting with the Arabic-English language pair, they show an increased BLEU (Papineni et al., 2002) score and a decreased error rate.

**Discourse relations and discourse connectives** Discourse relations have long been recognised as crucial to the proper understanding of a text (Knott and Dale, 1993), as they provide the structure between units of discourse (Webber et al., 2012). Discourse relations can be implicit or explicit. If explicit, they are generally signalled by the discourse connectives.

While Marcu et al. (2000) and Mitkov (1993) previously investigated coherence relations as a means of improving translation output and en-

suring it was closer to the target language this was taken no further at the time. Taking inspiration from Rhetorical Structure Theory (RST), Tu et al. (2013) proposed an RST-based translation framework on basis of elementary discourse units (EDU)s, in an attempt to better segment the ST in a meaningful manner, and ensure a better ordering for the translation. This approach is more sensitive to discourse structure, and introduces more semantics into the SMT process. Their research is effected using a Chinese RST parser, and they aim to ensure a better ordering of EDUs, although the framework still has a limited sentence-based window.

There have been a few previous experiments specifically assessing discourse relations in an MT context. Guzmán et al. (2014) used discourse structures to evaluate MT output. They hypothesize that the discourse structure of good translations will have similar discourse relations. They parse both MT output and the reference translation for discourse relations and use tree kernels to compare HT and MT discourse tree structures. They improve current evaluation metrics by incorporating discourse structure on the basis that 'good translations should tend to preserve the discourse relations' (Guzmán et al., 2014).

Discourse connectives, also known as discourse markers, are cues which signal the existence of a particular discourse relation, and are vital for the correct understanding of discourse. Yet current MT systems often fail to properly handle discourse connectives for various reasons, such as incorrect word alignments, the presence of multiword expressions as discourse markers, and the prevalence of ambiguous discourse markers. These can be incorrect or missing (Meyer and Poláková, 2013; Steele, 2015; Yung et al., 2015).

In particular, where discourse connectives are ambiguous, e.g. some can be temporal or causal in nature, the MT system may choose the wrong connective translation, which distorts the meaning of the text. It is also possible that the discourse connective is implicit in the source, and thus needs to be inferred for the target. While a human translator can detect this, an MT system cannot.

In their work, Zufferey and Popescu-Belis (2017) automatically labelling the meaning of discourse connectives in parallel corpora to improve MT output. In separate work on discourse connectives, Li et al. (2014b) also find that some connectives are ambiguous in English, and in their research on the Chinese-English language pair subsequently report on a corpus study into discourse relations and an attempt to project these from one language which has a PDTB resource, to another which lacks it (Li et al., 2014a). They again mention that there are mismatches, between implicit and explicit discourse connectives. For the same language pair, Yung et al. (2015) research how discourse connectives which are implicit in one language (Chinese), may need to be made explicit in another (English). This is similar to work by Steele (2015) who use placeholder tokens for the implicit items in the source side of the training data, and trains a binary classifier to predict whether or not to insert a marker in the TT. This notion of *explicitation*, and the opposite *implicitation*, is the subject of research by Hoek et al. (2015), who find that implicitation and explicitation of discourse relations occurs frequently in human translations. There seems to be a degree to which the implicitation and explicitation of discourse relations depends on the discourse relation they signal, and the language pair in question.

**Negation**   Recently work has begun on negation in MT, decomposing the semantics of negation and with an error analysis on what MT systems get wrong with negation (Fancellu and Webber, 2015a). For the language pair which they considered (Chinese-English) the conclusion was that determining the scope of negation was the biggest problem, with reordering the most frequent cause. Subsequently, Fancellu and Webber (2015b) show that the translation model scoring is the cause of the errors in translating negation. In general, MT systems often miss the focus of the negation, which results in incorrectly transferred negations that affect coherence.

**Coherence**   Sim Smith et al. (2015) illustrate the type of discourse errors that often arise in MT, which affect coherence in particular. They then illustrate how assessing coherence in an MT context is very different from previous monolingual coherence tasks (Sim Smith et al., 2016), which are often performed on a summarized or shuffled version of a coherent document and where the task is to reorder the sentences correctly. In the latter, the sentences in question are themselves coherent, unlike in MT. They reimplement existing entity models, in addition to a syntax model, which is

extended to improve on the state-of-the-art for the shuffling task (Sim Smith et al., 2016).

**Trends**   While there has been much solid research on discourse in MT, the results that are reported are surprisingly limited. In considering why this is the case, we believe while the constraints in the SMT decoder have provided a ceiling on progress, we cannot help wondering whether the accepted current methods of evaluation are at fault, failing to recognise progress in discourse.

## 3   Constraints

The dominance of SMT a couple of decades ago was detrimental to the inclusion of many linguistic elements. As reported by Hardmeier (2015), "the development of new methods in SMT is usually driven by considerations of technical feasibility rather than linguistic theory". Most decoders work on a sentence by sentence basis, isolated from context, due to both modelling and computational complexity. This directly impacts the extent to which discourse can be integrated.

Docent (Hardmeier et al., 2013a) is a document level decoder, which has a representation of a complete TT translation, to which changes can be made to improve the translation. It uses a multi-pass decoding approach, where the output of a baseline decoder is modified by a small set of extensible operations (e.g. replacement of phrases), which can take into account document-wide information, while making the decoding process computationally feasible. To date, attempts to influence document level discourse in SMT in this manner have been limited. Stymne et al. (2013) attempted to incorporate readability constraints into Docent, in effect jointly achieving the translation and simplification. A similar document level framework was recently developed by Martìnez Garcia et al. (2017), who developed a new operation to ensure that changes could be made to the entire document in one step, making (see Section 2).

As Hardmeier (2015) points out, training on *domain* has traditionally been seen as a way of making the output more relevant. But this is insufficient– it may well capture translation probabilities appropriate to a specific kind of text at training time, but SMT does not capture the full context of the lexical items during decoding and hence sometimes fails to correctly disambiguate. So while Hardmeier (2015) suggests that the "crosslinguistic relation defined by word alignments is a sort of translational equivalence relation", we would claim that equivalence in a translation context traditionally includes an element of semantics which is totally absent in SMT, which is the paradigm he was referring to. While SMT is a complex and finely tuned system, which brought about considerable progress in the MT domain, it is linguistically impoverished, superficially concatenating phrases which have previously been found to align with those of another language when training, with no reference to the intended meaning in context. NMT has been proven to capture elements of context (syntactic and semantic), which are already helping to make NMT output better than that of SMT.

All of these constraints in SMT have restricted integration of linguistic elements and prevented progress to another level. With the success of NMT and the changed architecture it brings, embrace this opportunity to advance to a deeper level of translation. As illustrated by recent comparative research into output from Phrase Based Machine Translation (PBMT) and NMT systems (Popović, 2017; Burchardt et al., 2017), the latter is capable of producing output which is far more linguistically informed.

It would seem a good time to revisit the basics of translation theory, with a view to taking MT to a deeper level.

## 4 Translation as communication

The popularity of SMT in the past couple of decades has largely been to the exclusion of deeper linguistic elements (besides the linguistically-informed element of syntax-based systems). Performance of SMT systems surpassed previous rules-based systems, and progress was characterised by the famous quote by Frederick Jelinek :"Every time I fire a linguist, the performance of the speech recognizer goes up".

Translation theory has evolved over the years, from the functional and dynamic equivalence of Nida and Taber (1969), to Baker (1992)'s view of equivalence (word, grammatical, textual, pragmatic equivalence), Hatim and Mason (1990)'s view of the translator as a communicator and mediator and the Relevance theory of Sperber and Wilson (1986).[1] Essentially nowadays there is

broad agreement on the importance of discourse analysis: on the need to extract the communicative intent and transfer it to the target language- in an appropriate manner, taking account of the cultural context, and the genre.

While there is now a great need for translation, which cannot be met by humans (in terms of the cost or number of human translators), MT can be usefully deployed for gisting, and for some language pairs even as a good quality first draft. However, if it is to be more, for example to be used as part of a pipeline for a series of tasks, then it needs to embrace its role in terms of semantics. Used in pipelines such as voice translators, where Speech Acts are relevant, or as vital components of a multimodal framework, we cannot ignore the fact that semantics are currently not a core building block in MT.

As has been said by others previously (Becher, 2011), MT could benefit from mimicking the way a human translator works. Translators makes several passes on a text. They begin by reading the ST, and extracting the communicative intent– establishing what the author of the text is trying to say. They identify any cultural references, and any acronyms or terminology relevant to the domain. For the former, they need to be aware of the significance of the references and their connotations. They then attempt to transfer these *in an appropriate manner* to the TT, taking account of their TT audience. While MT is far from this it has to at least begin to grapple with semantics, if it is to perform a meaningful role.

## 5 Semantics

In terms of proposing how this might look for evaluation purposes, we would suggest that semantic parsing may offer one way forward. While this is not available in many languages, and may start off as a limited evaluation method, there are ways in which this can be done.

Progress in the field of semantics has been considerable recently, and in particular work based on Univeral Dependencies (UD)[2] would seem to offer new opportunities which MT evaluation could benefit from: UD are annotations of multilingual treebanks which have been built to ensure crosslingual compatibility. The latest version (2.0) covers 50 languages. Recent work by (Reddy et al., 2016)

---

[1]Cognitive Linguistics is a further development which is

beyond the scope of this paper

[2]http://universaldependencies.org/

to build on this and transform dependency parses into logical forms (for English) opens up opportunities for crosslingual semantic parsing. While still a field in development, it is one option to be explored if we want to evaluate the semantic transfer in MT. We could foresee that initially at least it could be achieved by developing text cases (see Section 6) on the back of annotations, ensuring that the basic semantics of a sentence in one language (the ST) match that of another (the TT). While ultimately this requires the MT to be of a good standard for parsing, for NMT with a good language pair this is now the case, and indeed has to be for any meaningful attempt to integrate discourse. In the short term, test cases can be devised that do not involve a parser, merely test the ability of a system to effect semantic transfer. In Reddy et al. (2017), they give a concrete example using their semantic interface based on UD for a multilingual question-answering experiment, where they generate ungrounded logical forms for several languages in parallel and map these to Freebase parses which they use for answering a set of standard questions (translated for the German and Spanish). They simplify to ensure crosslingual compatibility, but essentially illustrate how semantic parsing can work crosslingually. For an indepth explanation of the process, see Reddy et al. (2017).

Using these as a test bed and running against WMT systems as additional evaluation could be very useful, perhaps indicating which systems are more capable of capturing and translating the *meaning* of the source. In the long run, ideally the aim is to capture the meaning of the ST, and then based on that generate the TT (a kind of concept-to-text-generation). That would of course involve a shift in paradigm for MT.

## 6  Evaluation of MT output

**Current evaluation methods** Hardmeier (2012) already touches on the problem of current evaluation methods. In particular, he mentions the shortcomings of ngram-based metrics and the issue of sentence level evaluation, where much of discourse is document level: "However, it could be argued that the metric evaluation in the shared task itself was biased since the document-level human scores evaluated against were approximated by averaging human judgments of sentences seen out of context, so it is unclear to what extent the evaluation of a document-level score can be trusted." It has to be pointed out that that human evaluation is also not at document level. The problems with BLEU are well illustrated in research by (Smith et al., 2016), proving that optimizing by BLEU scores can actually lead to a drop in quality. However, another major problem is the fact that the evaluation of MT output is still largely based on comparison to a single reference or gold standard translation. A reference, or gold standard translation, is *one* version. A text can be translated in *many* ways, all of which will reflect the translator's interpretation of what the ST is saying. To constrain the measure of correctness to a single reference is only consulting *one* interpretation of the ST. There could be equally good (or better) examples of MT output which are not being scored as highly as they should, simply because they employ a different lexical choice.

Recently, there has also been a trend towards totally ignoring the ST during evaluation of WMT submissions, where 'human assessors are asked to rate a given translation by how adequately it expresses the meaning of the corresponding reference translation' (Bojar et al., 2016). So human assessors are asked to rate a given translation by how close it is to the *reference* translation, with no regard to the *source* text. The process is treated as a monolingual direct assessment of translation fluency and adequacy. We would argue that surely adequacy should be based on how well the meaning of the ST has been transferred to the TT, and that to ignore the ST (simply relying on the one rendering of it) is to lose that direct dependency. Whereas a proper measure of adequacy is whether the translation captures and transfers the semantics from ST to TT.

Moreover, the human assessment of the output has recently become 'researcher based judgments only'- which is also problematic, in that the researchers in question are not generally trained in translation, and some are monolingual. This means that they will not necessarily capture discourse information, such as the implicit discourse relations of the reference translation, for example, and know to look for them in the MT output. Not knowing the source language means that you cannot assess the correctness of the output if it alters from the reference.

**Moving forward** As mentioned by Guzmán et al. (2014), 'there is a consensus in the MT community that more discourse-aware metrics need to be proposed for this area to move forward'. In terms of evaluation in training, one novel idea is the use of post edits in evaluation (Popović et al., 2016)- this can be seen as more informative and reliable feedback, if done by a human translator, and can be directly used to improve the system. Post edits could also form the basis of test items.

Both Popović (2017); Burchardt et al. (2017) directly or indirectly touch on the issue of evaluation. As part of her analysis Popović (2017) attempts to classify the type of errors made by each system. A most constructive development, Burchardt et al. (2017) introduces a test suite which while it is common and invaluable in software engineering, is not widespread for this domain. With the suite of tests they aim to cover different phenomena, and how the systems handle them, saying they aim to focus on new insights not on how well the systems match the reference (Burchardt et al., 2017).

In the past there have been examples of unit testing for evaluation of MT quality, in particular (King and Falkedal, 1990) who developed theirs for evaluation of different MT systems before financial outlay. Nevertheless, a substantial amount of the logic is still valid: evaluating the strengths and weaknesses of output from various MT systems, with tests focussing on specific aspects (syntactic, lexical ambiguity etc) for particular language pairs.

In a more general vein, Lehmann et al. (1996) develop test suites for NLP in their Test Suites For Natural Language Processing work, for the general evaluation of NLP systems. Their test suites aimed to be reusable, focused on particular phenomena and consisted of a database which could identify test items covering specific phenomena. Similarly, the MT community could potentially develop relevant tests in github, with agreement on format and peer reviews.

This type of method could easily be adopted as a means of evaluation in the context of WMT tasks, and besides being much more informative, would help to pinpoint strengths and weaknesses, leading to more focussed progress. Existing test suites, such as the ones developed by Guillou and Hardmeier (2016) and Loáiciga and Gulordava (2016), could be integrated and added to, giving a more comprehensive and linguistically-based evaluation of system submissions. Unit tests can be added to by interested parties, with peer reviewing if appropriate. The resulting suite could eventually cover a whole host of discourse aspects, and an indication therefore of how different systems perform, and where there is work to be done. The concept is not new, and could build on previous initiatives and experience, such as (Hovy et al., 2002) to ensure it is adaptable yet robust, providing a baseline for progress in particular aspects of discourse.

## 7 Conclusions

As is clear from the amount of work in Section 2, there has recently been a wealth of research on discourse in MT, which now needs to be integrated, but the incentive to integrate much of it into an MT system is not there while evaluation remains reference-based.

The fact that Martìnez Garcia et al. (2017) found in their recent substantial and innovative research that automatic metrics "are mostly insensitive to the changes introduced by our document-based MT system", is a clear illustration that something is not working. MT is progressing, and evaluation needs to do the same.

There are numerous difficulties with evaluation of discourse phenomena, particularly if it is automatic. But the potential advantages of progressing beyond single reference-based evaluation are considerable– not least the ability to evaluate without first commissioning a reference translation each time. At a time when MT is being used in a pipeline where dialogue acts play an important role, it is vital that evaluation of MT be based on something more substantial than string matching to a single reference, or judgements made without regard for ST. Once MT begins to integrate an element of semantics, it no longer makes sense to evaluate on a single reference. While the translator's role as mediator will not easily be replaced by machines– as yet it cannot capture the pragmatics or recreate the contextual richness for the target audience– nevertheless we must ensure we assess MT output based on a measure of adequacy compared to the *source*, if it is to fulfil its purpose in terms of communication.

### Acknowledgments

Many thanks to the anonymous reviewers for their insightful comments and pointers to any omissions.

## References

Mona Baker. 1992. In Other Words: A Coursebook on Translation. Routledge.

Viktor Becher. 2011. When and why do Translators add connectives? A corpus-based study. *Target*, volume 23, pages 26–47.

Beata Beigman Klebanov and Michael Flor. 2013. Associative Texture is Lost in Translation. In *Proceedings of the Workshop on Discourse in Machine Translation*. Association for Computational Linguistics, Sofia, Bulgaria, pages 27–32. http://www.aclweb.org/anthology/W13-3304.

Ondřej Bojar, Rajen Chatterjee, Christian Federmann, Yvette Graham, Barry Haddow, Matthias Huck, Antonio Jimeno Yepes, Philipp Koehn, Varvara Logacheva, Christof Monz, Matteo Negri, Aurelie Neveol, Mariana Neves, Martin Popel, Matt Post, Raphael Rubino, Carolina Scarton, Lucia Specia, Marco Turchi, Karin Verspoor, and Marcos Zampieri. 2016. Findings of the 2016 Conference on Machine Translation. In *Proceedings of the First Conference on Machine Translation*. Association for Computational Linguistics, Berlin, Germany, pages 131–198. http://www.aclweb.org/anthology/W/W16/W16-2301.

Aljoscha Burchardt, Vivien Macketanz, Jon Dehdari, Georg Heigold, Jan-Thorsten Peter, and Philip Williams. 2017. A Linguistic Evaluation of Rule-Based, Phrase-Based, and Neural MT Engines. In *Proceedings of the 20th Annual Conference of the European Association for Machine Translation*. Charles University, Prague, Czech Republic.

Bruno Cartoni, Andrea Gesmundo, James Henderson, Cristina Grisot, Paola Merlo, Thomas Meyer, Jacques Moeschler, Andrei Popescu-Belis, and Sandrine Zufferey. 2012. Improving MT Coherence Through Text-Level Processing of Input Texts: the COMTIS Project. http://lodel.irevues.inist.fr/tralogy/index.php.

Bruno Cartoni, Sandrine Zufferey, and Thomas Meyer. 2013. Annotating the Meaning of Discourse Connectives by Looking at their Translation: The Translation Spotting Technique. *Dialogue & Discourse* 4(2):65–86.

Federico Fancellu and Bonnie Webber. 2015a. Translating Negation: A Manual Error Analysis. In *Proceedings of the Second Workshop on Extra-Propositional Aspects of Meaning in Computational Semantics (ExProM 2015)*. Association for Computational Linguistics, Denver, Colorado, pages 2–11. http://www.aclweb.org/anthology/W15-1301.

Federico Fancellu and Bonnie Webber. 2015b. Translating Negation: Induction, Search And Model Errors In *Syntax, Semantics and Structure in Statistical Translation*, pages 21–29.

Federico Fancellu and Bonnie Webber. 2014. Applying the semantics of negation to SMT through n-best list re-ranking. In *Proceedings of the 14th Conference of the European Chapter of the Association for Computational Linguistics*. Gothenburg, Sweden, EACL, pages 598–606. http://aclweb.org/anthology/E/E14/E14-1063.pdf.

Zhengxian Gong, Min Zhang, and Guodong Zhou. 2015. Document-Level Machine Translation Evaluation with Gist Consistency and Text Cohesion. In *Proceedings of the Second Workshop on Discourse in Machine Translation*. Association for Computational Linguistics, Lisbon, Portugal, pages 52–58. http://www.aclweb.org/anthology/W/W15/W15-2504.pdf.

Liane Guillou. 2012. Improving Pronoun Translation for Statistical Machine Translation. In *Proceedings of the Student Research Workshop at the 13th Conference of the European Chapter of the Association for Computational Linguistics*. Association for Computational Linguistics, Stroudsburg, PA, USA, EACL '12, pages 1–10. http://dl.acm.org/citation.cfm?id=2380943.2380944.

Liane Guillou. 2013. Analysing Lexical Consistency in Translation. In *Proceedings of the Workshop on Discourse in Machine Translation*. Association for Computational Linguistics, Sofia, Bulgaria, pages 10–18. http://www.aclweb.org/anthology/W13-3302.

Liane Guillou. 2016. Incorporating Pronoun Function into Statistical Machine Translation. Ph.D. thesis, University of Edinburgh.

Liane Guillou and Christian Hardmeier. 2016. PROTEST: A Test Suite for Evaluating Pronouns in Machine Translation. In Nicoletta Calzolari (Conference Chair), Khalid Choukri, Thierry Declerck, Sara Goggi, Marko Grobelnik, Bente Maegaard, Joseph Mariani, Helene Mazo, Asuncion Moreno, Jan Odijk, and Stelios Piperidis, editors, *Proceedings of the Tenth International Conference on Language Resources and Evaluation (LREC 2016)*. European Language Resources Association (ELRA), Paris, France.

Liane Guillou, Christian Hardmeier, Preslav Nakov, Sara Stymne, Jörg Tiedemann, Yannick Versley, Mauro Cettolo, Bonnie Webber, and Andrei Popescu-Belis. 2016. Findings of the 2016 WMT Shared Task on Cross-lingual Pronoun Prediction. In *Proceedings of the First Conference on Machine Translation (WMT16), Berlin, Germany. Association for Computational Linguistics*. Berlin, Germany.

Francisco Guzmán, Shafiq Joty, Lluís Màrquez, and Preslav Nakov. 2014. Using Discourse Structure Improves Machine Translation Evaluation. In *Proceedings of the 52nd Annual Meeting of the Association for Computational Linguistics, 2014, June 22-27, 2014, Baltimore, MD,*

*USA, Volume 1: Long Papers*. The Association for Computer Linguistics, pages 687–698. http://aclweb.org/anthology/P/P14/P14-1065.pdf.

Christian Hardmeier. 2012. Discourse in Statistical Machine Translation. *Discours 11-2012* (11).

Christian Hardmeier. 2014. Discourse in Statistical Machine Translation. Ph.D. thesis, Uppsala University, Department of Linguistics and Philology.

Christian Hardmeier. 2015. On Statistical Machine Translation and Translation Theory. In *Proceedings of the Second Workshop on Discourse in Machine Translation*. Association for Computational Linguistics, Lisbon, Portugal, pages 168–172. http://aclweb.org/anthology/W15-2522.

Christian Hardmeier, Sara Stymne, Jörg Tiedemann, and Joakim Nivre. 2013a. Docent: A Document-Level Decoder for Phrase-Based Statistical Machine Translation. In *51st Annual Meeting of the Association for Computational Linguistics, 2013, Proceedings of the Conference System Demonstrations, 4-9 August 2013, Sofia, Bulgaria*. pages 193–198. http://aclweb.org/anthology/P/P13/P13-4033.pdf.

Christian Hardmeier, Jörg Tiedemann, and Joakim Nivre. 2013b. Latent Anaphora Resolution for Cross-Lingual Pronoun Prediction. In *Proceedings of the 2013 Conference on Empirical Methods in Natural Language Processing*. Association for Computational Linguistics, Seattle, Washington, USA, pages 380–391. http://www.aclweb.org/anthology/D13-1037.

Basil Hatim and Ian Mason. 1990. *Discourse and the translator*. Longman.

Jet Hoek, Jacqueline Evers-Vermeul, and Ted J.M. Sanders. 2015. The Role of Expectedness in the Implicitation and Explicitation of Discourse Relations. In *Proceedings of the Second Workshop on Discourse in Machine Translation*. Association for Computational Linguistics, Lisbon, Portugal, pages 41–46. http://aclweb.org/anthology/W15-2505.

Eduard Hovy, Margaret King, and Andrei Popescu-Belis. 2002. Principles of Context-Based Machine Translation Evaluation. *Machine Translation* 17(1):43–75. http://www.jstor.org/stable/40008209.

Margaret King and Kirsten Falkedal. 1990. Using Test Suites in Evaluation of Machine Translation Systems. In *Proceedings of the 13th Conference on Computational Linguistics - Volume 2*. Association for Computational Linguistics, Stroudsburg, PA, USA, COLING '90, pages 211–216. https://doi.org/10.3115/997939.997976.

Alistair Knott and Robert Dale. 1993. Using Linguistic Phenomena to Motivate a Set of Rhetorical Relations.

Ekaterina Lapshinova-Koltunski. 2015. Exploration of Inter-and Intralingual Variation of Discourse Phenomena. In *Proceedings of the Second Workshop on Discourse in Machine Translation*. Association for Computational Linguistics, Lisbon, Portugal, pages 158–167. http://aclweb.org/anthology/W15-2521.

Sabine Lehmann, Stephan Oepen, Sylvie Regnier-Prost, Klaus Netter, Veronika Lux, Judith Klein, Kirsten Falkedal, Frederik Fouvry, Dominique Estival, Eva Dauphin, Hervè Compagnion, Judith Baur, Lorna Balkan, and Doug Arnold. 1996. TSNLP: Test Suites for Natural Language Processing. In *Proceedings of the 16th Conference on Computational Linguistics - Volume 2*. Association for Computational Linguistics, Stroudsburg, PA, USA, COLING '96, pages 711–716. https://doi.org/10.3115/993268.993292.

Jessy Junyi Li, Marine Carpuat, and Ani Nenkova. 2014a. Cross-lingual Discourse Relation Analysis: A corpus study and a semi-supervised classification system. In *Proceedings of COLING 2014, the 25th International Conference on Computational Linguistics: Technical Papers*. Dublin City University and Association for Computational Linguistics, pages 577–587. http://aclweb.org/anthology/C14-1055.

Junyi Jessy Li, Marine Carpuat, and Ani Nenkova. 2014b. Assessing the Discourse Factors that Influence the Quality of Machine Translation. In *Proceedings of the 52nd Annual Meeting of the Association for Computational Linguistics (Volume 2: Short Papers)*,pages 283–288. http://aclweb.org/anthology/P14-2047.

Sharid Loáiciga. 2015. Predicting Pronoun Translation Using Syntactic, Morphological and Contextual Features from Parallel Data. In *Proceedings of the Second Workshop on Discourse in Machine Translation*. Association for Computational Linguistics, Lisbon, Portugal, pages 78–85. http://aclweb.org/anthology/W15-2511.

Sharid Loáiciga and Kristina Gulordava. 2016. Discontinuous Verb Phrases in Parsing and Machine Translation of English and German. *Proceedings of the Tenth International Conference on Language Resources and Evaluation (LREC 2016)*

Sharid Loáiciga, Thomas Meyer, and Andrei Popescu-Belis. 2014. English-French Verb Phrase Alignment in Europarl for Tense Translation Modeling. In *The Ninth Language Resources and Evaluation Conference*. EPFL-CONF-198442.

Sharid Loaiciga Sanchez. 2017. *Pronominal Anaphora and Verbal Tenses in Machine Translation*. Ph.D. thesis, University of Geneva.

Ngoc-Quang Luong and Andrei Popescu-Belis. 2016. A Contextual Language Model to Improve Machine Translation of Pronouns by Re-ranking Translation Hypotheses. *Baltic Journal of Modern Computing* 4(2):292.

Ngoc-Quang Luong and Andrei Popescu-Belis. 2017. Machine Translation of Spanish Personal and Possessive Pronouns Using Anaphora Probabilities. In *Proceedings of the 15th Conference of the European Chapter of the Association for Computational Linguistics (EACL)*. Association for Computational Linguistics, EPFL-CONF-225949.

Daniel Marcu, Lynn Carlson, and Maki Watanabe. 2000. The Automatic Translation of Discourse Structures. In *Proceedings of the 1st North American Chapter of the Association for Computational Linguistics Conference*. Stroudsburg, PA, USA, NAACL 2000, pages 9–17. http://dl.acm.org/citation.cfm?id=974305.974307.

Eva Martìnez Garcia, Carles Creus, Cristina España Bonet, and Lluís Màrquez. 2017. Using Word Embeddings to Enforce Document-Level Lexical Consistency in Machine Translation. In *Proceedings of the 20th Annual Conference of the European Association for Machine Translation*. Charles University, Prague, Czech Republic.

Laura Mascarell, Mark Fishel, Natalia Korchagina, and Martin Volk. 2014. Enforcing Consistent Translation of German Compound Coreferences. In *KONVENS*. pages 58–65.

Laura Mascarell, Mark Fishel, and Martin Volk. 2015. Detecting Document-level Context Triggers to Resolve Translation Ambiguity. In *Proceedings of the Second Workshop on Discourse in Machine Translation*. Association for Computational Linguistics, Lisbon, Portugal, pages 47–51. http://aclweb.org/anthology/W15-2506.

Thomas Meyer. 2011. Disambiguating TemporalContrastive Discourse Connectives for Machine Translation. In *Proceedings of the ACL 2011 Student Session*. Association for Computational Linguistics, Stroudsburg, PA, USA, HLT-SS '11, pages 46–51. http://dl.acm.org/citation.cfm?id=2000976.2000985.

Thomas Meyer and Lucie Poláková. 2013. Machine Translation with Many Manually Labeled Discourse Connectives. In *Proceedings of the 1st DiscoMT Workshop at ACL 2013 (51st Annual Meeting of the Association for Computational Linguistics)*. Sofia, Bulgaria, page 8.

Thomas Meyer and Andrei Popescu-Belis. 2012. Using Sense-labeled Discourse Connectives for Statistical Machine Translation. In *Proceedings of the Joint Workshop on Exploiting Synergies Between Information Retrieval and Machine Translation (ESIRMT) and Hybrid Approaches to Machine Translation (HyTra)*. Association for Computational Linguistics, Stroudsburg, PA, USA, EACL 2012, pages 129–138.

Thomas Meyer, Andrei Popescu-Belis, Sandrine Zufferey, and Bruno Cartoni. 2011. Multilingual Annotation and Disambiguation of Discourse Connectives for Machine Translation. In *SIGDIAL Conference*. The Association for Computer Linguistics, pages 194–203.

Ruslan Mitkov. 1993. How Could Rhetorical Relations be used in Machine Translation. In *Proceedings of the ACL Workshop on Intentionality and Structure in Discourse Relations*.

Eugene A. Nida and C.R. Taber. 1969. *The Theory and Practice of Translation*. E. J. Brill, Leiden.

Michal Novák. 2016. Pronoun Prediction with Linguistic Features and Example Weighing. In *Proceedings of the First Conference on Machine Translation (WMT). Volume 2: Shared Task Papers*. Association for Computational Linguistics, Stroudsburg, PA, USA, pages 602–608.

Michal Novák and Zdeněk Žabokrtský. 2014. Cross-lingual Coreference Resolution of Pronouns. In *Proceedings of COLING 2014, the 25th International Conference on Computational Linguistics: Technical Papers*. Dublin City University and Association for Computational Linguistics, Dublin, Ireland, pages 14–24.

Kishore Papineni, Salim Roukos, Todd Ward, and Wei-Jing Zhu. 2002. BLEU: a Method for Automatic Evaluation of Machine Translation. In *Proceedings of the 40th Annual Meeting on Association for Computational Linguistics*. Stroudsburg, PA, USA, pages 311–318. https://doi.org/10.3115/1073083.1073135.

Maja Popović, Mihael Arčan, and Arle Lommel. 2016. Potential and Limits of Using Post-edits as Reference Translations for MT Evaluation. In *Proceedings of the 19th annual conference of the European Association for Machine Translation (EAMT)*. Riga, Latvia.

Maya Popović. 2017. Comparing Language Related Issues for NMT and PBMT between German and English. In *Proceedings of the 20th Annual Conference of the European Association for Machine Translation*. Charles University, Prague, Czech Republic.

Siva Reddy, Oscar Täckström, Michael Collins, Tom Kwiatkowski, Dipanjan Das, Mark Steedman, and Mirella Lapata. 2016. Transforming dependency structures to logical forms for semantic parsing. *Transactions of the Association for Computational Linguistics* 4.

Siva Reddy, Oscar Täckström, Slav Petrov, Mark Steedman, and Mirella Lapata. 2017. Universal Semantic Parsing. *arXiv preprint arXiv:1702.03196* .

Karin Sim Smith, Wilker Aziz, and Lucia Specia. 2015. A Proposal for a Coherence Corpus in Machine Translation. In *Proceedings of the Second Workshop on Discourse in Machine Translation*. Association for Computational Linguistics, Lisbon, Portugal, pages 52–58. https://aclweb.org/anthology/W/W15/W15-2507.pdf.

Karin Sim Smith, Wilker Aziz, and Lucia Specia. 2016. The Trouble with Machine Translation Coherence. In *Proceedings of the 19th annual conference of the European Association for Machine Translation (EAMT)*.

Aaron Smith, Christian Hardmeier, and Jörg Tiedemann. 2016. Climbing Mount BLEU: The Strange World of Reachable High-BLEU Translations. In *Proceedings of the 19th annual conference of the European Association for Machine Translation (EAMT)*.

Dan Sperber and Deirdre Wilson. 1986. *Relevance: Communication and Cognition*. Harvard University Press, Cambridge, MA, USA.

David Steele. 2015. Improving the Translation of Discourse Markers for Chinese into English. In *Proceedings of the Conference of the North American Chapter of the Association for Computational Linguistics*. Denver, Colorado, NAACL, pages 110–117. http://aclweb.org/anthology/N/N15/N15-2015.pdf.

David Steele and Lucia Specia. 2016. Predicting and Using Implicit Discourse Elements in Chinese-English Translation. In *Proceedings of the 19th annual conference of the European Association for Machine Translation (EAMT)*. Riga, Latvia, pages 305–317.

Sara Stymne, Jörg Tiedemann, Christian Hardmeier, and Joakim Nivre. 2013. Statistical Machine Translation with Readability Constraints. In *Proceedings of NODALIDA*. pages 375–386.

Mei Tu, Yu Zhou, and Chengqing Zong. 2013. A Novel Translation Framework Based on Rhetorical Structure Theory. In *The Association for Computer Linguistics*, pages 370–374.

Bonnie Webber, Marine Carpuat, Andrei Popescu-Belis, and Christian Hardmeier, editors. 2015. *Proceedings of the Second Workshop on Discourse in Machine Translation*. Association for Computational Linguistics, Lisbon, Portugal. http://aclweb.org/anthology/W15-25.

Bonnie Webber, Markus Egg, and Vali Kordoni. 2012. Discourse Structure and Language Technology. *Natural Language Engineering* 18(4):437–490.

Bonnie Webber, Andrei Popescu-Belis, Katja Markert, and Jorg Tiedemann. 2013. *Proceedings of the ACL Workshop on Discourse in Machine Translation (DiscoMT 2013)*. Association for Computational Linguistics. http://www.aclweb.org/anthology-new/W/W13/#3300.

Dominikus Wetzel and Francis Bond. 2012. Enriching Parallel Corpora for Statistical Machine Translation with Semantic Negation Rephrasing. In *Proceedings of the Sixth Workshop on Syntax, Semantics and Structure in Statistical Translation*. Jeju, Republic of Korea, SSST-6, pages 20–29. http://dl.acm.org/citation.cfm?id=2392936.2392940.

Dominikus Wetzel, Adam Lopez, and Bonnie Webber. 2015. *A Maximum Entropy Classifier for Cross-Lingual Pronoun Prediction*, Association for Computational Linguistics, pages 115–121.

Billy Tak-Ming Wong and Chunyu Kit. 2012. Extending Machine Translation Evaluation Metrics with Lexical Cohesion To Document Level. In *Proceedings of EMNLP-CoNLL*. pages 1060–1068.

Deyi Xiong, Guosheng Ben, Min Zhang, Yajuan Lv, and Qun Liu. 2013a. Modeling Lexical Cohesion for Document-Level Machine Translation. In *Proceedings of IJCAI*.

Deyi Xiong, Yang Ding, Min Zhang, and Chew Lim Tan. 2013b. Lexical Chain Based Cohesion Models for. Document-Level Statistical Machine Translation. In *Proceedings of EMNLP*. pages 1563–1573.

Deyi Xiong and Min Zhang. 2013. A Topic-Based Coherence Model for Statistical Machine Translation. In *Proceedings of AAAI*. pages 977–983.

Deyi Xiong and Min Zhang. 2014. A Sense-Based Translation Model for Statistical Machine Translation. In *Association for Computational Linguistics*. pages 1459–1469.

Frances Yung, Kevin Duh, and Yuji Matsumoto. 2015. Crosslingual Annotation and Analysis of Implicit Discourse Connectives for Machine Translation. In *Proceedings of the Second Workshop on Discourse in Machine Translation*. Association for Computational Linguistics, Lisbon, Portugal, pages 142–152. http://aclweb.org/anthology/W15-2519.

Rong Zhang and Abraham Ittycheriah. 2015. Novel Document Level Features for Statistical Machine Translation. In *Proceedings of the Second Workshop on Discourse in Machine Translation*. Association for Computational Linguistics, Lisbon, Portugal.

Sandrine Zufferey and Andrei Popescu-Belis. 2017. Discourse connectives: theoretical models and empirical validations in humans and computers. In *Formal Models in the Study of Language*, Springer International Publishing, pages 375–390.

# Author Index